"WHERE IS THE GOD OF JUSTICE?"

"Where is the God of Justice?"

The Old Testament and Suffering

Michael E. W. Thompson

☙PICKWICK *Publications* • Eugene, Oregon

"WHERE IS THE GOD OF JUSTICE?"
The Old Testament and Suffering

Copyright © 2011 Michael E. W. Thompson. All rights reserved. Except for brief quotations in critical publications or reviews, no part of this book may be reproduced in any manner without prior written permission from the publisher. Write: Permissions, Wipf and Stock Publishers, 199 W. 8th Ave., Suite 3, Eugene, OR 97401.

Pickwick Publications
An Imprint of Wipf and Stock Publishers
199 W. 8th Ave., Suite 3
Eugene, OR 97401

www.wipfandstock.com

The Scripture quotations contained herein are from The New Revised Standard Version of the Bible, copyright © 1989 by the Division of Christian Education of the National Council of the Churches of Christ in the United States of America, and are used by permission. All rights reserved.

ISBN 13: 978-1-61097-262-8

Cataloging-in-Publication data:

Thompson, Michael E. W.

"Where is the God of justice?" : the Old Testament and suffering / Michael E. W. Thompson.

xiv + 222 p. ; 23 cm. Includes bibliographical references and indexes.

ISBN 13: 978-1-61097-262-8

1. Suffering—Biblical teaching. 2. Theodicy—Biblical teaching. 3. Bible. O.T. Job—Criticism, interpretation, etc. I. Title.

BT161 T46 2011

Manufactured in the U.S.A.

For

Isabella

Euan

Jack

Finn

I am not at ease, nor am I quiet;
I have no rest; but trouble comes.

(Job 3:26)

Whom have I in heaven but you?
And there is nothing on earth that I desire other than you.
My flesh and my heart may fail,
but God is the strength of my heart and my portion forever.

(Psalm 73:25–26)

Contents

Preface • ix
Abbreviations • xii
Introduction • 1

1 **Suffering**: A "Deserved Calamity"? • 7

2 **"All is Vanity"**: The Book of Ecclesiastes • 22

Psalmic Interlude 1: "How long, O Lord" (Psalm 13) • 31

3 **Via Dolorosa for Jeremiah** • 35

Psalmic Interlude 2: "Do not fret because of the wicked" (Psalm 37) • 58

4 **Watching and Waiting**: Habakkuk and Joseph • 62

Psalmic Interlude 3: "Mortals cannot abide in their pomp" (Psalm 49) • 81

5 **New Light on Suffering**: Isaiah 53 • 85

Psalmic Interlude 4: "I saw the prosperity of the wicked" (Psalm 73) • 100

6 **The Great Debate**: The Book of Job • 105

7 **The Long View**: The Apocalyptic Hope • 157

8 **Retrospect and Reflection** • 174

Bibliography • 197

Index of Subjects • 207

Index of Authors • 210

Index of Biblical References • 214

Preface

This is the book I had in my mind for a number of years, having given talks and lectures to various church groups in sundry places on the subject of what the Old Testament has to contribute to questions about suffering. However, the writing of the book had to wait until "retirement," a phase of life that I had fondly and rather naively expected would give me all the "leisure" and time I needed. Now that I come to the end of the task, I am aware of my imperfect grasp of the Old Testament material and, in a particular way that fellow workers in the field will recognize, of what has been written *about* this material.

    The book is intended in the first place for those who come asking what there is in the Old Testament that will perhaps assist us in those age-old questions that we all have about the sufferings individuals and communities experience in their lives. These questions, needless to say, are particularly acute for those who believe in a God of love and power, and even more so when those whose sufferings they witness or hear about appear to be innocent sufferers. Does the Hebrew Bible have anything to say that might help such people, and does it have a word for those of us who seek to make a Christian proclamation in our particular age and culture? I believe that it does and I trust that something of that will be made clear in what follows. My hope is also that this modest work will both make some small contribution to questions about the place of the Old Testament in the life of the Christian church today, and will also be of service and help to those who study these writings in more academic ways.

    In general my biblical quotations are from the New Revised Standard Version, though sometimes I have quoted other recent translations, and at other times have offered my own. The chapter and verse enumerations quoted are those of the English versions, and where I have indicated a Hebrew word the form of transliteration is that of the *SBL Handbook of Style*, with some exceptions particularly when making reference to the volumes of *Theological Dictionary of the Old Testament*. Yet at the same time no knowledge of Hebrew is presupposed for the reading of the work. My citations of literature in the footnotes are all in shortened form, with full titles and details being given in the Bibliography.

It will be observed that already I have used the terms Old Testament and Hebrew Bible interchangeably, and this I continue to do in the rest of the work. Although I come from the Protestant Christian—to be more precise, Methodist—tradition, and in that setting find the title "Old Testament" suitably descriptive of the first part of the Christian Bible, equally I am aware of the fact that these same documents are *the* Scriptures for Jewish people and, in that regard, are also appropriately named Hebrew Bible. Thus I continue to use these two names in what follows. However to designate the eras I use BCE and CE rather than BC and AD.

I am most grateful to those who have encouraged me in this project, and especially those who have gone so far as saying they were looking forward to reading the finished result. I can only hope that they are not too disappointed with what is now offered. For library facilities I am most grateful for the provisions and the helpful staffs at the Hallward Library of the University of Nottingham and at St John's College Library, Nottingham. Here in Farnsfield the friendly staff at our public library are indefatigable in getting for me my inter-library loan requests and I do thank them. In my retirement I have been part-time lecturer in Old Testament with the ecumenical East Midlands Ministry Training Course, and am grateful for the challenge that the teaching, questioning, and discussing has brought to me and my studies. I am grateful now to Wipf & Stock publishers for accepting the work for publication under their Pickwick Publications imprint, and in particular to Robin Parry for his editorial expertise and help.

My thanks above all go to my wife, Hazel, for her encouragement, support and love, for her intellectual companionship on the "way," and also for her skills, and associated willingness to help, on those frequent occasions when ambition has outrun my computer skills. At the same time one cannot write a book such as this on the subject of suffering without thinking of grandchildren, and it is to them that I dedicate the work—along with the prayer that their feet may be guided into the way of peace.

Michael E. W. Thompson
On the Festival of Polycarp,
Bishop and Martyr
February 23, 2011

Abbreviations

ABD	*Anchor Bible Dictionary*. 6 vols. Edited by David Noel Freedman. New York: Doubleday, 1992
CBQMS	*Catholic Biblical Quarterly* Monograph Series
BZAW	Beihefte zur *Zeitschrift für die alttestamentliche Wissenschaft*
DCH	*The Dictionary of Classical Hebrew*. Edited by David J. A. Clines, Sheffield: Sheffield Academic Press/Sheffield Phoenix Press, 1993–
EDB	*Eerdmans Dictionary of the Bible*. Edited by David Noel Freedman, Grand Rapids: Eerdmans, 2000
EVV	English Versions
ExpT	*Expository Times*
IB	*The Interpreter's Bible*. 12 vols. Edited by George Arthur Buttrick et al. Nashville: Abingdon, 1952–57
IDB	*Interpreter's Dictionary of the Bible*. 4 vols. Edited by George A. Buttrick. Nashville: Abingdon, 1962
IDBSup	*Interpreter's Dictionary of the Bible. Supplementary Volume*. Edited by Keith Crim. Nashville: Abingdon, 1976
Int	*Interpretation*
JBL	*Journal of Biblical Literature*
JSOT	*Journal for the Study of the Old Testament*
JSOTSup	*Journal for the Study of the Old Testament* Supplement Series
KJV	King James Version of the Bible, 1611
LHBOTS	Library of Hebrew Bible/Old Testament Studies
LXX	Septuagint (Greek translation of the Old Testament)
MT	Masoretic Text (Hebrew Text)
NIB	*The New Interpreter's Bible*. 12 vols. Edited by Leander K. Kleck et al. Nashville: Abingdon, 1992–98
NRSV	New Revised Standard Version of the Bible, 1989

REB	Revised English Bible, 1989
RSV	Revised Standard Version of the Bible, 1952
TDOT	*Theological Dictionary of the Old Testament.* 15 vols. Edited by G. Johannes Botterweck, Helmer Ringgren, and Heinz-Josef Fabry. Translated by David E. Green et al. Grand Rapids: Eerdmans, 1974–2006
TynB	*Tyndale Bulletin*
VT	*Vetus Testamentum*
VTSup	Supplements to *Vetus Testamentum*
ZAW	*Zeitschrift für die alttestamentliche Wissenschaft*

Introduction

In Fyodor Dostoevsky's novel *The Brothers Karamazov* two of the brothers Karamazov, Ivan and Alyosha, are engaged in an extended and wide-ranging discussion about the Christian faith. Ivan claims that it is exceedingly difficult to believe in God in the light of the evil and terrible things that happen in the world. In contrast Alyosha is a more naturally religious person, yet at the same time aware that the sufferings of individuals in the world constitute a serious problem to belief in a loving God. Thus Ivan, having spoken at length, says that he wishes to give back his entrance ticket to the world, proclaiming, "and if I am an honest man I am bound to give it back as soon as possible. And that I am doing. It's not God that I don't accept, Alyosha, only I most respectfully return Him the ticket." "'That's rebellion,' murmured Alyosha, looking down." And the conversation continues,

> "Rebellion? I am sorry you call it that," said Ivan earnestly. "One can hardly live in rebellion, and I want to live. Tell me yourself, I challenge you—answer. Imagine that you are creating a fabric of human destiny with the object of making men happy in the end, giving them rest and peace at last, but that it was essential and inevitable to torture to death only one tiny creature—that little child beating its breast with its fist, for instance—and to found that edifice on its unavenged tears, would you consent to be the architect on those conditions? Tell me, and tell the truth."
>
> "No, I wouldn't consent," said Alyosha softly.[1]

---

1. Dostoevsky, *The Brothers Karamazov*, 226. In reading Dostoevsky in this regard I have been particularly helped by Jones, "Dostoevskii and Religion"; Williams, *Dostoevsky*.

Dostoevsky, through the words of his character Ivan Karamazov, is here putting his finger on one of the great ongoing and imponderable problems experienced by humanity, namely the reality of suffering in the world. This problem of suffering both spans the ages, and also embraces all sorts and conditions of people. Further, suffering poses an especially acute problem for religious people, in particular for those who believe themselves to be held in the strength and care of a loving God. And if faithful religious people have to endure much suffering, then sooner or later questions will be raised about the apparent justice of God in his dealings with his people. Sooner or later an agonized cry such as the one uttered by the people in the days of the prophet Malachi will be made, "Where is the God of justice?" (Mal 2:17).²

The word translated "justice" here comes from the Hebrew *mišpāṭ*, which can have a number of meanings, one among which being, "what is right, proper, righteousness."³ Thus Amos calls upon the people of Israel to "let justice [*mišpāṭ*] roll down like waters" (Amos 5:24), that is to bring about a national situation that is right and proper, in particular where those who have particular needs, namely the poor, find help and protection—and find it too in abundance. Amos also speaks of those who turn "justice to wormwood" and bring "righteousness to the ground" (Amos 5:7), that is about those who are guilty of turning the God-given standards of life for his covenant people upside down. Thus the people's cry recorded in Mal 2:17—"Where is the God of justice?"—is their expression of confusion about what they perceive is a serious lack of activity on the part of God for their deliverance from their situation of need and distress. In that particular case, the prophet is recorded as being able to assure them of forthcoming—perhaps in fact, surprisingly sudden—activity of God: "See, I am sending my messenger to prepare the way before me, and the Lord whom you seek will suddenly come to his temple. The messenger of the covenant in whom you delight—indeed, he is coming, says the Lord of hosts" (Mal 3:1).

2. See the opening words of Silberman, "'You Cannot See My Face' . . .", "Reading the daily newspaper, listening to a radio news report, watching a television screen cannot but raise ever and again for anyone who shares in the religious traditions of Western culture the unsettling question of divine justice . . . How often has one heard a distraught person cry out in uncomprehending anguish: 'why me?' 'why us?' Poets and philosophers, theologians and plain folk wonder if it is possible to hold on to justice and to God, and how."

3. For full details see Johnson "*mišpāṭ*," *TDOT* 9:86–98, esp. 92.

Alas, in the Old Testament such a positive assurance and expression of hope for the future is not always given to a suffering individual or group. Rather, within the pages of the Old Testament there are recorded for us many and varied cries of both individuals and communities, all coming from a range of situations and circumstances, which at least to some extent echo that cry of the people in the days of Malachi, "Where is the God of justice?" These varied cries from the sufferings of individuals and communities, and the equally varied responses and answers that the Old Testament is able to offer, constitute the subject of the following pages.

The word that was coined by the German philosopher and mathematician G. W. F. Leibniz (1646–1716) for the attempt to defend the justice of God, in spite of human suffering, was "theodicy," a word formed from the two Greek words, *theos* (God) and *dikē* (justice), "the justice of God."[4] John Hick says, "The word is thus a kind of technical shorthand for: the defence of the justice and righteousness of God in face of the fact of evil."[5] We should note that this word "theodicy" is commonly used in two senses, not only to indicate theodicy as a subject, but also in the sense of *a* theodicy, that is a particular attempt at answering/explaining the problem of evil. I shall be employing both of these usages in what follows in this work.

However, the issue of theodicy—though without the benefit of that name—had long been discussed. It is there in the Old Testament, most obviously in the book of Job, but also, as the following pages make clear, in other books too. It is there, further, in some of the writings in cultures contemporary with the Hebrew Bible, as for example in the so-called "Babylonian Theodicy," coming probably from between 1400 and 1000 BCE, "a debate which attempts to reconcile the concept of divine justice prevailing in the world with actual experience."[6] In the Christian era, the issue was raised for example by Boethius (c.480–c.524) with his, "If God is righteous, why evil?"[7] Then later, in the Europe of

---

4. Leibniz, *Theodicy*.

5. Hick, *Evil and the God of Love*, 6.

6. So W. G. Lambert in his introduction to the text of "The Babylonian Theodicy," 97, in Thomas, *Documents*, 97–103.

7. The answer that Boethius gave was: Either God wishes to prevent evil and cannot, in which case he is just but not omnipotent. Or he can prevent evil but does not want to, in which case he is omnipotent but not just.

the eighteenth century, there occurred a serious earthquake in Lisbon, and that raised questions about the harmony of the world and whether it was really ruled by a gracious and powerful God. In the twentieth century such issues were again raised as to the presence of God in the world as so many thousands of people perished in the horrors of the Holocaust (Shoah) in Auschwitz and elsewhere.[8]

Yet the whole issue of suffering and theodicy is before us not only in what we might call the great events such as the Lisbon earthquake and the Holocaust/Shoah, but also in the lives of individual people, in their setbacks and difficulties, in their dangers and disappointments. It is as James Strahan said finely in the beginning of his commentary on the book of Job,

> The problem of suffering is the great *enigma vitae*, the solution of which, for ever attempted, may for ever baffle the human mind. Why our planet has been invaded by physical and moral evil; why a God of infinite love and power has ordained and permitted the suffering of sentient beings; why his "whole creation groaneth and travaileth in pain together until now"; why, in particular, the operation of pain is apparently so indiscriminate that the innocent suffer with the guilty—these questions are asked in bewilderment to-day, and the facts which evoke them have troubled the spirit of man ever since it began to grope for a meaning and purpose in life.[9]

The Hebrew Bible engages with this theme,[10] this great enigma of life, and sets forth issues of suffering, and—to speak anachronistically, borrowing the later language of the philosophers—presents a number of theodices. In fact, it may be said that the issue of theodicy occupies a considerably "centre-stage" place in the Old Testament. John Barton

---

8. On this subject see Sweeney, *Hebrew Bible After the Shoah*, 5–17 for "Jewish Theological Discussion of the Shoah," and 17–22 for "Biblical Theology and the Shoah," See also Astell, "Reading the Bible"; Wiesel, *Night*; Boys, "Holocaust."

9. Strahan, *Job*, 1.

10. As has already been observed, treatment of this theme is not only found among the people of ancient Israel and in the Old Testament. See, for example, Bowker, *Problems of Suffering* (Judaism, Christianity, Islam, Marxism, Hinduism, Buddhism, Dualism, Duality and the Unification of Experience); Garrison, *Why are You Silent, Lord?* (Greek, Roman, and Biblical Traditions); Hebblethwaite, *Evil, Suffering and Religion* (major world religions); Laato and de Moor, *Theodicy* (Ancient Near East, Hebrew Bible, Early Jewish writings, New Testament, Rabbinic Judaism).

in his article "Introduction to the Old Testament" in *The Oxford Bible Commentary* speaks of there being what he refers to as "four interlocking themes" in the Old Testament, namely, Creation and Monotheism, Covenant and Redemption, Ethics, and Theodicy, observing further that the treatments of theodicy "bulk large" in the writings of the Old Testament.[11]

It is my aim and purpose in this work to present and discuss the main theodicies that are to be found in the Old Testament. These are indeed of a varied style and nature: some are presented calmly, others less calmly; some are presented in styles that may be felt to be moving towards the borderlands of rebellion against God (the worry expressed by Alyosha Karamazov against Ivan). Certainly there is in some of them a marked outspokenness on the part of the suffering individual, or community, to God, in which the accusation is along the lines of "Where is the God of justice?"—though that particular formulation may not be employed. Perhaps the most extreme outspokenness in the Old Testament in this regard must be in some of the extensive speeches of the suffering man Job, in particular where Job's address is to God. Bildad the Shuhite, one of the friends of Job, can declaim to Job in a calmness of manner—one intended maybe to express criticism of what he considers to be a certain intemperateness on the part of Job—and say,

> How long will you [Job] say these things,
> And the words of your mouth be a great wind?
> Does God pervert justice?
> Or does the Almighty pervert the right?
> (Job 8:2–3)

Yet before Job has said all that clearly he so deeply feels, he will have as good as doubted the justice of God, as in, for example, these words where he is pointing indignantly to the ongoing prosperity of the wicked. Thus Job says,

> They spend their days in prosperity,
>   and in peace they go down to Sheol.
> They say to God, "Leave us alone!
>   We do not desire to know your ways.
> What is the Almighty, that we should serve him?
>   And what profit do we get if we pray to him?"

---

11. Barton and Muddiman, *Oxford Bible Commentary*, 9–10.

> Is not their prosperity indeed their own achievement?
> The plans of the wicked are repugnant to me.
>
> (Job 21:13–16)

That is, the words of Job here raise the question, "Where is the God of justice?" and though we have reached as far as chapter 21 of the book that bears his name, no answer has been offered that will satisfy Job, though the friends will claim time after time that there is sufficient answer and explanation in the fact that Job must be a sinner, that it is his sinfulness that has brought him to his present parlous state.

However, the answer of the friends of Job to his expostulations about his sufferings—their theodicy—that he must be a sinner, is by no means an answer that they alone propound. Rather, this is the most dominant and commonly expressed theodicy in the whole of the Old Testament, and further, it should be added, in other religions too. Those parts of the Hebrew Bible that offer this particular approach to understanding and explaining the presence of suffering in individual lives, and also in the lives of whole communities, will make the subject of the next part of this work, and to this we now turn.

1

Suffering

A "Deserved Calamity"?

The novel of Albert Camus *The Plague* is about the crisis for the town and port of Oran in the north of Algeria when so many of its inhabitants were beset with plague, and desperate measures had to be taken to control and contain the crisis. Thus all travel in and out of the town was stopped, the hospital was needed for the care of those who had contracted the plague, the doctors—including Dr Rieux, one of the main characters in the story—and other medical workers were under great pressure. There were many deaths, and we are told that among other things taking place the ecclesiastical authorities "resolved to do battle against the plague with the weapons appropriate to them, and organised a Week of Prayer." This culminated on the Sunday with a High Mass, the sermon in the cathedral being preached by Father Paneloux, a Jesuit priest, we are told, "who had shown himself a stalwart champion of Christian doctrine at its most precise and purest". Father Paneloux began his sermon, "Calamity has come on you, my brethren, and, my brethren, you deserved it," and a little later he said, "Thus from the dawn of recorded history the scourge of God has humbled the proud of heart and laid low those who hardened themselves against Him. Ponder this well, my friends, and fall on your knees."[1]

---

1. Camus, *The Plague*, 78–80. Although at one level *The Plague*, first published in 1948, is a novel about the crisis of a plague, it seems that at a deeper level it is concerned

Now whatever we may feel about the appropriateness or otherwise of Father Paneloux's sermon from a caring and pastoral perspective, it has to be said that he was adopting a thoroughly biblical point of view. In fact, he was sharing with his fellow citizens *one* of the biblical understandings and interpretations of the meaning of suffering, namely that it is brought upon a person or a community though their sinfulness. Thus the priest's strong words about his people currently suffering a "deserved calamity."

This approach is prominently there, for example, in the book of Deuteronomy, a work presented to us in the form of a great sermon or speech by Moses that was addressed to the people of Israel on the eve of their crossing the River Jordan and going over into the promised land. The point is made that as long as these people walk in God's ways, and obey his commandments and ordinances, then all will go well for them.[2] Thus, for example (for this theme is oft-recurring in this book), we read, "You must therefore be careful to do as the Lord your God has commanded you; you shall not turn to the right or to the left. You must follow exactly the path that the Lord your God has commanded you, so that you may live, and that it may go well with you, and that you may live long in the land that you are to possess." (Deut 5:32–33)

The theme is also to be found in the so-called Deuteronomistic History,[3] in particular in the books of Kings.[4] In fact it is something of a *leitmotif*, a prevailing theme in these books, to the extent that the reign of each of the kings of Israel and Judah is assessed in terms of their faithfulness, or unfaithfulness as the case may be, to the commandments of the Lord, and it is on the basis of this that the successes and failures of their reigns are assessed. In fact, after the reigns of David and Solomon remarkably few kings are given positive approval and commendation, certainly none in the northern kingdom of Israel, and only

---

with the Nazi occupation of Algeria in the Second World War. At a further level the book is concerned to ask serious questions more generally about sufferings experienced by humanity.

2. See further, Houtman, "Theodicy in the Pentateuch."

3. What has come to be known as the Deuteronomistic History is that block of material in the Old Testament comprising the books of Josh, Judg, Sam and Kgs, and which displays much of the style, vocabulary and theological thought of the book of Deuteronomy. See, for example, Römer, *The So-called Deuteronomistic History*.

4. See further, Crenshaw, *Defending God*; Laato, "Theodicy in the Deuteronomistic History."

two in the southern kingdom, Hezekiah and Josiah. About Hezekiah the historian records, "He did what was right in the sight of the Lord just as his ancestor David had done" (2 Kgs 18:3). So this author warms to and elaborates on his theme and, pointing to all the successes of Hezekiah's reign, affirms that faithfulness to God leads to success in life.

> He trusted in the Lord the God of Israel; so that there was no one like him among all the kings of Judah after him, or among those who were before him. For he held fast to the Lord; he did not depart from following him but kept the commandments that the Lord commanded Moses. The Lord was with him; wherever he went, he prospered. He rebelled against the king of Assyria and would not serve him. He attacked the Philistines as far as Gaza and its territory, from watchtower to fortified city. (2 Kgs 18:5–8)

And then there was Josiah, king of Judah, good king Josiah, who came into his kingship when but a child, yet who did so many good things; in particular, according to the Deuteronomistic Historian, instituting a reform of the Jerusalem temple, throwing out liturgical artifacts that were to do with false, non-Israelite ways of worship, and setting about promulgating a book of the law that we are told had been found in the temple, having a Passover ceremony the celebration of which, according to the Historian, had for long years not taken place (2 Kgs 22–23). Thus the writer enthuses about Josiah,

> Moreover Josiah put away the mediums, wizards, teraphim, idols and all the abominations that were seen in the land of Judah and in Jerusalem, so that he established the words of the law that were written in the book that the priest Hilkiah had found in the house of the Lord. Before him there was no king like him, who turned to the Lord with all his heart, with all his soul, and with all his might, according to the law of Moses; nor did any arise after him. (2 Kgs 23:24–25)

On the other hand, Deuteronomy speaks of the fate of those who turned their backs on the ways of life laid down by God, as is made clear in the following passage (which gives the appearance of being a comment on the harsh experience of exile): "They turned and served other gods, worshiping them, gods whom they had not known and whom he had not allotted to them; so the anger of the Lord was kindled against that land, bringing on it every curse written in this book" (Deut

29:26–27). Or again, in 2 Kgs 17 we have an extended explanation on the part of the Deuteronomistic Historian why it was that the northern kingdom of Israel had in 722 BCE been defeated by the Assyrians with many of its citizens being taken into exile. "This occurred because the people of Israel had sinned against the Lord their God, who had brought them up out of the land of Egypt from under the hand of Pharaoh king of Egypt. They had worshiped other gods and walked in the customs of the nations whom the Lord drove out before the people of Israel, and in the customs that the kings of Israel had introduced. The people of Israel secretly did things that were not right against the Lord their God" (2 Kgs 17:7–9a) This sinfulness, so this writer affirms, would lead to exile, and thus he explains why it is that the kingdoms of both Israel and Judah experienced the harshness of life in exile. About Israel he says, "The people of Israel continued in all the sins that Jeroboam committed; they did not depart from them until the Lord removed Israel out of his sight, as he had foretold through all his servants the prophets. So Israel was exiled from their own land to Assyria until this day" (2 Kgs 17:22–23). And about Judah, concerning the nemesis that came upon that kingdom in 587 BCE, he says,

> Therefore thus says the Lord, the God of Israel, "I am bringing upon Jerusalem and Judah such evil that the ears of everyone who hears of it will tingle . . . I will cast off the remnant of my heritage, and give them into the hand of their enemies; they shall become a prey and a spoil to all their enemies, because they have done what is evil in my sight and have provoked me to anger, since the day their ancestors came out of Egypt, even to this day." (2 Kgs 21:12, 14–15)

Thus, Deuteronomy and the Deuteronomistic History set forth the principle that faithfulness to God leads to success, while on the other hand, sinfulness leads to disaster, and in particular—as these theologians understand the matter—the disaster of exile. And undoubtedly over the whole of the Deuteronomistic History there hover Israel and Judah's experiences of exile, that of the former, about which we know nothing beyond its having happened in the days of the Assyrian empire, and that of the latter, about which we do know something more, in the days of the Babylonian rule. Clearly, these were searing experiences for those who believed that they were the chosen people of the Lord God of Israel, and in a special way held in his care and protection. The

Deuteronomistic History has been called Israel's great corporate confession of sin, a sin that resulted in exile. However, it may be questioned how far it is correct to say that it is a *corporate* statement; perhaps rather it may be more correct to say that it expresses the *particular views* of the Deuteronomists (whoever they were; a group whose identity and possible composition remain as elusive as ever, but at least whose fruits of their literary and theological labors are well known to us). And it may be questioned too how appropriate it is to call the work a *confession*. It is perhaps more of a *theological explanation* for the destruction of lands, cities and temple(s), rather than "confession" to God for these things.[5] The issue that the completed Deuteronomistic History—and within that in particular the books of Kings—seems concerned to explain is the fact of the exiles of Israel and Judah, and this is done through the particular theodicy that understands that these calamities were brought about as a result of human sinfulness, a sinfulness on the parts both of the kings and other leaders, and also of the people.[6]

The horrendous nature, and the associated sense of catastrophe, of the Babylonian exile for the people of Judah and Jerusalem, with its loss of kingship, the deportation of many individuals within those populations, the destruction of the temple—and thereby the cessation of the sacrificial system and other parts of the cult—cannot but be felt as one reads the Old Testament book of Lamentations.[7]

This short book is made up of five lamentations that express extremes of sorrow over the desolation of the city of Jerusalem. What is surely being reflected here is an understandably deep feeling of divine abandonment. For where indeed is the God of justice when Jerusalem—the holy city!—has been destroyed by a foreign army? Further, this destruction and desolation of the holy city is understood as having come from God as a punishment for sins. Thus,

---

5. However, the aspect of confession is present in other, generally later, works that made their way into the Old Testament, as for example in the extended prayers of confession in Neh 9 and Dan 9.

6. See Laato and de Moor, *Theodicy in the World of the Bible*, 190–91, where Laato sets out what he understands as the five important theological themes in the Deuteronomistic History that "appear to be vehicles of theodicy" (ibid., 190). See also, Klein, *Israel in Exile*, 23–43, Klein, "The Secret Things and the Things Revealed: Reactions to the Exile in the Deuteronomistic History"; Sweeney, *King Josiah of Judah*, esp. 170–77.

7. On Lamentations see Salters, *Jonah and Lamentations*; Provan, *Lamentations*; Gottwald, *Lamentations*; Linafelt, *Surviving Lamentations*; O'Connor, *Lamentations and the Tears of the World*; Parry, *Lamentations*.

> Her [Jerusalem's] foes have become the masters,
> her enemies prosper,
> because the Lord has made her suffer
> for the multitude of her transgressions;
> her children have gone away, captives before the foe.
> . . .
> Jerusalem sinned grievously,
> so she has become a mockery;
> all who honored her despise her,
> for they have seen her nakedness;
> she herself groans,
> and turns her face away.
> (Lam 1:5, 8)[8]

It thus seems clear that within Lamentations there is this aspect of theodicy, and the particular theodicy here being set forth is, once again, that it is human sin that has brought about this dreadful suffering. Nevertheless in Lamentations there are other matters set forth: there are expressions of hope for the future (for example in 3:22–24, 55–66; 4:2).

However, the predominant tone in the book of Lamentations is that sense of distress about the present situation (see for example 3:1–20, 43–54), a sense of distress that is in marked contrast to what comes over to us as a sense of calmness, almost dispassionateness and distance, in which the theodicy material in the books of Kings is presented. Here in Lamentations, with its passion and senses of gloom and despair (Lam 2:11; 3:7–8; 5:22), with its complaint that prayer to God is not heard (Lam 3:44), we would appear to be moving in a direction that in the Old Testament we shall find in the so-called psalms of lament and in other material,[9] and which will culminate in some of those speeches of the man Job in the book that bears his name, such as for example, "Oh, that I knew where I might find him . . ." (Job 23:3) to which we shall come later in this study.[10]

---

8. There are further confessions of sin made in Lam 1:14, 18, 20, 22; 2:4; 3:39, 42; 4:6, 13, 22; 5:7, 16.

9. See below, 31–57.

10. See below, 133–35. It should also be admitted that in Lamentations there is the expression of a desired vengeance on Jerusalem's enemies for their cruelty and destruction. While this is understandable, at the same time it makes for difficulty in a Christian reading of the work. I shall return to this topic when I consider the so-called confessions of Jeremiah. See below, 35–57.

We now consider briefly the presentation in the books of Chronicles, a presentation that appears to have as background and backdrop once again those same terrible exilic experiences of the destruction of so much—buildings, artifacts, religious rites, security, ways of life, loss of freedom and self-rule in the chosen land, and so forth—but that does appear to have more of a forward look and a hope for the future than is in clear view in the Deuteronomistic History. While there is, for the Chronicler, the possibility of repentance, and thus some hope for the future, yet this presentation still seeks to present the crisis of the Babylonian exile as having been due to Israelite sinfulness. Frequently, this message of the Chronicler is put into the mouth of such a person as a prophet, one example of this being the word spoken by the prophet Azariah son of Oded (about whom we do not otherwise hear), who proclaimed to king Asa, "Hear me, Asa, and all Judah and Benjamin: The Lord is with you, while you are with him. If you seek him, he will be found by you, but if you abandon him, he will abandon you" (2 Chr 15:2).

For the Chronicler the sinfulness and failures of certain individuals, in particular the national leaders, are specially significant. Thus a good number of years ago von Rad's judgment was, "we must not fail to catch what it is the writer [the Chronicler] wants to hammer home to his readers in this critique, namely that each generation stands immediately before Jahweh, and stands or falls with its anointed [that is, king]."[11] That is, said von Rad, the sins and the failures of Israel's leaders were liable to lead to the judgment of God and the associated national suffering, and with this later scholarship has been in general agreement.[12]

This theme that devotion and faithfulness to God brings as its rewards good things for the human beings involved, while sinfulness inevitably brings in its train human disaster and suffering, is indeed widespread in the pages of the Old Testament, and makes its presence felt in parts not yet considered. Thus, further, it is firmly there in the book of Proverbs, as for example in 11:6,

> The righteousness of the upright saves them,
> but the treacherous are taken captive by their schemes.
> (Prov 11:6)

---

11. von Rad, *Theology*, vol. 1, 349.

12. See, for example, and for further details, Jones, *Chronicles*, 113–17; Johnstone, "Guilt and Atonement"; Williamson, *Chronicles*, 31–33; Japhet, "Theodicy in Ezra-Nehemiah and Chronicles," 445–69.

And again, in Prov 13:21,

> Misfortune pursues sinners,
> but prosperity rewards the righteous.

As Katharine Dell observes about this theme in the book of Proverbs:

> to the wicked, the fool, the sluggard or the evildoer punishment will come, but to the wise, the upright, the hard worker and the diligent rewards will be great. There is a just and individual accounting system in operation. It is a simple choice to be made by the one who wishes to learn—either that such people can take the path of wisdom that is smooth and straight and leads to all good things or they can take the path to folly which is full of pitfalls and covered with thorns. There are material rewards associated with these two paths: wealth is the result of wisdom, poverty comes to the unsuspecting fool ... The rewards are not only monetary ones; they include happiness, fulfillment and longevity.[13]

Further, we may add that the theme is also to be found in that piece of wisdom writing in the Apocrypha called the Wisdom of Jesus Ben Sirach, otherwise known in Christian circles as Ecclesiasticus. For example, in 2:10 we read,

> Consider the generations of old and see:
>   has anyone trusted in the Lord and been disappointed?
> Or has anyone persevered in the fear of the Lord and been
>   forsaken?
> Or has anyone called upon him and been neglected?
> (Sir 2:10)

This theme is also present in the Hebrew Bible's corpus of books of the prophets.[14] In all three main parts, for example, of the Isaiah book there is the notion, by now well-familiar to us, of understanding tragedy and suffering as being "deserved calamity"—to employ once again the language of Albert Camus's character Father Paneloux. It is prominently there in Isa 1–39, for example in the parable of the vineyard in 5:1–7. We are told of all the good husbandry that the vineyard owner (the Lord) bestowed on the vineyard (the house of Israel and the people of

---

13. Dell, "*Get Wisdom, Get Insight*," 18–19.
14. See further, Crenshaw, "Theodicy and Prophetic Literature."

Judah) (vv. 1–2). Yet, as the vineyard owner says, on discovering that no good grapes grew in it but only wild grapes (vv. 3–4), a dreadful judgment and destruction is to come upon that vineyard. Thus:

> And now I will tell you
> what I will do to my vineyard.
> I will remove its hedge,
> and it shall be devoured;
> I will break down its wall,
> and it shall be trampled down.
> I will make it a waste;
> it shall not be pruned or hoed,
> and it shall be overgrown with briers and thorns;
> I will also command the clouds
> that they rain no rain upon it.
> (Isa 5:5–6)

That is, situations of devastation and destruction are interpreted by the prophet Isaiah as having been caused by the sin of Israel, and it is *God*, so we are being told, who has intentionally brought about this destruction with the express purpose of effecting his judgment on his people for their sin. The point is made that it is the sin of the people of Israel that has caused the following terrible situation:

> Your country lies desolate,
> your cities are burned with fire;
> in your very presence
> aliens devour your land;
> it is desolate, as overthrown by foreigners.
> And daughter Zion is left
> like a booth in a vineyard,
> like a shelter in a cucumber field,
> like a besieged city.
> If the Lord of hosts
> had not left us a few survivors,
> we would have been like Sodom,
> and become like Gomorrah.
> (Isa 1:7–9)

Moreover, even in that most hopeful part of the Isaiah book, in those chapters redolent with their message of new life, hopes, and possibilities (Isa 40–55), *even there* the doctrine of the "deserved calamity" makes its appearance as the explanation for the calamity of the exile, that exile which here it is promised is soon to come to its end. Thus

> Comfort, O comfort my people, says your God.
> Speak tenderly to Jerusalem, and cry to her
> that she has served her term, that her penalty is paid,
> that she has received from the Lord's hand double for all her sins.
> (Isa 40:1–2)

And it is there in the third part of the Isaiah book (Isa 56–66), where even in those situations of apparent renewal and new life in the old homeland, human sin still abounds, yet again bringing about the associated divine judgment. This is to be seen, for example, in Isa 59:17–18.

This same theodicy is there in the prophecy of Jeremiah, for example as early as chapter 2 where what God has done over the years for his people is catalogued along with the attitudes and actions with which Israel has responded (Jer 2:1–35a). But now will come the judgment that will involve Israel in being shamed and rejected (2:35b–37). Further, in Ezekiel such matters are expressed in even stronger language, which is perhaps to be explained as having come out of this prophet's direct and personal experience of the exile itself. Thus Ezekiel sought passionately to inform his people how they might understand why it was that this disaster of such enormous dimensions had come upon them. So we read here of "Disaster after disaster! See, it comes" (Ezek 7:5), that the Lord is possessed of a great fury, and this because of his people's grave sinfulness (5:13). The prophet speaks of a terrible manifestation of divine wrath that will *one day* be experienced by them. In fact, it is more likely that this *has already happened* and that here in the prophecy of Ezekiel, it is being interpreted (see 5:2, 16–17). There can hardly be any stronger expression of the "deserved calamity" explanation for national suffering than what we find here in the oracles of the prophet Ezekiel.[15]

---

15. See further, Joyce, *Ezekiel*, 17–20, "Ezekiel's Theology of Judgement." It may be felt that the so-called "individual responsibility" spoken about in Ezek 18 modifies what earlier prophets preached. However, this may be due to an incorrect understanding of what Ezekiel was saying. In the talk about the parents and children in Ezek 18:3, the prophet seems to be saying that the "parents" make up the generation that lived in Judah and Jerusalem before the exile, and that they were the ones who sinned and who thereby *corporately* brought about the exile. The "children" are the exilic generation, and now they are called upon *corporately* to accept from the Lord "a new heart and a new spirit" (v. 31) and thus for the future to live and not die. On Ezekiel and suffering see also Tiemeyer, "To Read—Or Not to Read—Ezekiel as Christian Scripture."

Finally, we may also recall that this understanding of suffering is there in another prophetic piece as late as the days after the exile, when life was being re-established in Jerusalem. The prophet Haggai understands that the setbacks the people have been experiencing—such as poor harvests, scarcities of food and drink, lack of clothing and money—are all due to the fact that they have not been getting their priorities in life correctly sorted out, for they have not put first and foremost the rebuilding of the temple. See Hag 1:5–11, in particular vv. 9b–10, "Because my house lies in ruins, while all of you hurry off to your own houses. Therefore the heavens above you have withheld the dew, and the earth has withheld its produce." Further, it is the Lord who has caused this to happen, says the prophet: "And I have called for a drought on the land and the hills, on the grain, the new wine, the oil, on what the soil produces, on human beings and animals, and on all their labors" (Hag 1:11).

Here, in this understanding of destruction, suffering and calamity in certain places on earth, and in the lives of both communities and individuals, is the explanation given in various parts of the Old Testament as to its cause.[16] These calamities are due, so this particular Old Testament theodicy affirms, to the sin of some individual or other, or this or that group, with the result that the judgment of God is upon them. This is a major way in which the Old Testament seeks to justify the ways of God with his people, and thus in spite of those various apparently-negative things that are happening around them, the Lord is, and still is, the God of justice. Whether or not we ourselves are ready to be convinced by such explanations (even though they are to be found in the Bible) it is nevertheless by such argument and explanation that many parts of the Old Testament seek to "assert Eternal Providence, / And justifie the wayes of God to men."[17]

Yet it does have to be said that there are real problems with this explanation of the reality and experience of suffering in the world. It may be true to a certain rough-and-ready extent that what any of us sows we are generally liable to have to reap. Further, sometimes what we sow is

---

16. In addition to those texts already noted the following are among others that espouse the theological approach that sin leads to suffering, while righteousness leads to prosperity: Pss 1; 15; 106; Neh 9:6–37; Dan 9:4–19; Exod 34:6–7; Num 14:18; Ezra 9:6–15.

17. John Milton, *Paradise Lost*, Book I, lines 25–26. The quotation is taken from Milton, *Complete Poems*, 160.

liable to become the "harvest" reaped by members of a later generation. Yet, that having been said, the belief that sin leads to suffering while goodness and godliness lead to blessing is clearly no adequate single, catch-all answer to questions about the sufferings of people. In particular, it is no adequate explanation for *all* the sufferings experienced by devout religious people who believe themselves to be held in the care of a loving and caring God of strength. For manifestly, there are people who are apparently innocent and who yet suffer greatly, and as regards their lives and experiences we cannot in all honesty think in terms of—and much less speak of—them now experiencing their "deserved calamity." The clearly large number of exceptions to this theodicy render it an inadequate catchall understanding of suffering in the world that is believed to be held in the strength and love of God.

This problem with the "deserved calamity" theodicy would appear to make itself felt even within the Deuteronomistic History, for it would seem that with the death in battle at a comparatively early age of the good king Josiah of Judah (2 Kgs 23:28–30), a certain small cloud appeared on the horizon for this understanding that faithfulness to God leads to success and prosperity, while sin and failure equally surely lead to divine judgment and the resulting human disaster and suffering. For we read how in these days of Josiah, the Pharaoh Neco, king of Egypt, went up to the river Euphrates to the king of Assyria, and further that "King Josiah went to meet him" (v. 29). Now the text does not say explicitly which king, the Egyptian or the Assyrian, it was that Josiah of Judah went to meet, but what seems possible is that it was the Egyptian Pharaoh, Josiah understanding that an alliance with the Pharaoh might afford his country of Judah an opportunity to rebel against their overlord, the king of Assyria.[18] However, much more important and significant—and clearer—is that at the meeting at Meggido of Josiah and the Pharaoh, the Pharaoh killed Josiah, and that the servants of Josiah "carried him dead in a chariot from Megiddo, brought him to Jerusalem, and buried him in his own tomb" (v. 30a). And the account of the reign of king Josiah ends simply with the note, "The people of the land took Jehoahaz son of Josiah, anointed him, and made him king in place of his father" (v. 30b).

---

18. For details see e.g. Miller and Hayes, *History of Ancient Israel and Judah*, 391–402; Jagersma, *History of Israel to Bar Kochba*, Part 1, 167–72.

Now what is conspicuous by its absence here is some theological explanation as to why King Josiah, who we are told came to the throne when he was only eight years old and who reigned in Jerusalem for thirty-one years (2 Kgs 22:1), should have met his end in battle at the tender age of thirty-nine years. Now, to be sure, many a person dies in battle at that age, or much less, but what is surprising in this account is that the historian did not say anything about this fact or anything about *why* it had happened. For, as we have seen, one of the cardinal theological principles that informs this historian's writing is that those who walk in God's ways, and in particular kings who lead their people in God's ways, will enjoy life in the land. That is, what happened to Josiah went very much against the grain of the historian's understanding of history.

The fact is that this issue of why such a good king should die at a comparatively young age and his fine kingly services to his people be taken away so soon is not dealt with; it is not discussed; it is not explained; no attempt is made to explain it. Josiah might possibly have earned the censure of the Deuteronomistic Historian for becoming involved politically and militarily with Assyria, Babylonia, and Egypt, but at the same time he must have been regarded by them as a "good king" because of all that he had done to reform the cult, renew the temple and clamp down on unacceptable religious rites. It has been suggested that in the historian's account there is at this point "a conspiracy of silence."[19] Perhaps "conspiracy" is not quite the right word here, with its suggestion of a "cover-up;" maybe it was rather that the writer was "stuck for words" as we say. Sweeney speaks of the Historian here being "unable to account theologically for Josiah's death and simply passed over the matter without comment."[20] For perhaps indeed the historian had been put into a sense of "confusion" by this untimely death of good king Josiah and thus been unable to append one of his characteristic summary notices to conclude—his last word about Josiah. All, it would seem, that he could do was to append a "reason" to account for the coming disaster upon the kingdom—a disaster very much in the making *in spite of* all the good and positive things of Josiah's reign. Thus he adds, "Still the Lord did not turn from the fierceness of his great wrath, by which his anger was kindled against Judah, because of all the provocations with

---

19. See Frost, "The Death of Josiah."
20. Sweeney, *King Josiah of Judah*, 5.

which Manasseh had provoked him. The Lord said, 'I will remove Judah also out of my sight, as I have removed Israel; and I will reject this city that I have chosen, Jerusalem, and the house of which I said, My name shall be there'" (2 Kgs 23:26–27)

Of course, if only this historian could have said that for good people things in life do not *always* work out well, and further that for unrighteous people things in life sometimes *do* work well, then his mental and theological gymnastics with the reign of King Josiah of Judah would be been made a good deal easier. But then, that would have gone against the grain of his whole theological outlook and those governing theological principles of his presentation of the history of the kingdoms of Israel and Judah that informed his work.

For the facts of experience are surely that this rather simple schema of rewards for good living, and disaster for evil acts—or in Father Paneloux's formulation "Calamity has come upon you . . . and . . . you deserved it"—is no adequate explanation for *all* the ills and sufferings that humanity endures. Regarding this Deuteronomistic attempt thus to explain human suffering, James Crenshaw in a recent study says (and it is to be noted that he ends with a comment on the strange silence of the Deuteronomistic Historian on the death of Josiah), "Historical events, however, never as simple as biblical literature implies, frequently took perplexing turns that defied systematization. The Deuteronomistic understanding of strict reward and retribution activated by human choice was difficult to reconcile with the real-life experience of YHWH's people. Josiah's early death must have rendered speechless all who thought they had discovered a definitive historiography grounded in religious conviction. In the stark light of historical reality, how could the tradition be kept intact?"[21]

Finally, we may return to the novel of Albert Camus, *The Plague*, with which we began this chapter and so bring to a close our present consideration of this major theodicy that is to be found in the Old Testament (though we shall visit it again, especially as it is vigorously and consistently held and set forth by the friends of Job, though it should be added, it is equally vigorously and consistently rejected by the man who is actually experiencing the suffering, Job himself. We shall further visit it in Habakkuk and Ps 73[22]).

---

21. Crenshaw, *Defending God*, 76.

22. See below, 64–68, 100–104, 117–24, 153.

It is clear that in *The Plague* Camus is discussing the whole issue of suffering, and, as we have already seen, in Father Paneloux's cathedral sermon there is presented what I have been calling the "deserved calamity" theodicy. Later in the novel, we are told that the plague began to claim the lives of children, and we are given a harrowing description of the death of one of the children, and this in spite of Dr Rieux's best efforts to save the child. Father Paneloux is there with him, and the child having died, the doctor, "with such a strange look on his face" sought to leave the room. "Come, doctor," Paneloux began, to which Rieux responded angrily, "Ah! That child, anyhow, was innocent—and you know it as well as I do!" Later, they speak to one another, and the priest agrees, "That sort of thing is revolting because it passes our human understanding. But perhaps we should love what we cannot understand." Rieux, we are told, shook his head, and responded, "No, Father. I've a very different idea of love. And until my dying day I shall refuse to love a scheme of things in which children are put to torture."[23]

We are presumably to understand that the doctor's words "That child was innocent" were intended to refer back to the priest's sermon that the calamity of the plague was *deserved* by those who were living with it, and dying of it, and that, further, we are intended to understand that in the doctor's subsequent words we have Camus roundly rejecting such a way of understanding suffering. Later, Father Paneloux will speak with a different emphasis—in the words of, we might say, an alternative theodicy—but that will be best left until the last part of this study.[24]

---

23. Camus, *The Plague*, 177–78.
24. See below, 191–92.

2

"All is Vanity"

The Book of Ecclesiastes

If the passage in Eccl 3:1–8 which begins "For everything there is a season, and a time for every matter under heaven" (Eccl 3:1) has become the most well-known part of this Old Testament book, then the second must be the phrase with which the work opens,

> Vanity of vanities, says the Teacher,
> vanity of vanities! All is vanity.
> (Eccl 1:2)

That is the translation found in NRSV. REB, regarding the verse as being in prose, renders it, "Futility, utter futility, says the Speaker, everything is futile."

First, something needs to be said about "Teacher/Speaker," and then second about "vanity/futility." The very first words of this book are "The words of Qoheleth, the son of David, king in Jerusalem" (1:1). Now the name, or the title, Qoheleth, would appear to bear some relationship with assembling, an assembly, and thus these days is frequently translated "Teacher," as for example in NRSV, such a title fitting in well with the rather didactic nature of the work. Earlier English translations of the Bible tended to render Qoheleth "Preacher," this certainly not being inappropriate, for preachers expect, or like to have, an "assembly" to proclaim to, and because what follows in the book does indeed have a somewhat "preacherly" style about it. Further, the use of "Preacher" here does to some extent reflect the title of the book in the Latin Vulgate version of Jerome, *Liber Ecclesiastes*, "Church Book." Equally, and by much the same argument, REB's use of "Speaker" can be seen to be appropriate. In what follows I shall call the book Qoheleth, for so it is called in the Hebrew, and I shall refer to the one who speaks in it as Qoheleth, but for the sake of clarity references within this book will be to "Eccl."[1]

Then, second, the matter of the "vanity/futility" of 1:2, and further "vanity of vanities/futility, utter futility," and the accompanying "all is vanity/everything is futile". J. L. Crenshaw[2] has called 1:2–3 the "Motto and Thematic Statement" that in the remainder of the work will be unpacked, explained, illustrated, and expounded. Further, the Hebrew word for "vanity/futility" (*hebel* "vanity, worthlessness") recurs a large number of times in the rest of the work, this in fact being the greatest concentration of occurrences of the word in any book of the Hebrew Bible. Jerome in his translation rendered it "vanitas," and the "vanity of vanities" as "*vanitas vanitatum*." Further, the wording, "vanity of vanities," is in the Hebrew a way of expressing the superlative, that is, the writer wishes to speak of the *supreme* vanity—the vanity than which no greater vanity can be conceived. The word indicates what is ephemeral, transitory, futile, worthless, even absurd. Thus, as Crenshaw expresses it, for this writer "all human toil is wasted effort, completely devoid of profit,"[3] in a word, as REB translates it, "futile."

---

1. Although in 1:1 Qoheleth is referred to as "son of David" and "king in Jerusalem," pointing clearly to Solomon, it is widely felt that this is a literary fiction intended to add weight and authority to the work by the attachment of the name of one who was reputed to have manifested "wisdom" in the exercise of his high responsibilities (1 Kgs 3:9, 28). In all probability the book comes from a much later date than Solomon's; the Hebrew is "late"; it displays Aramaisms, and most likely comes from the period of transition from classical to Mishnaic Hebrew. However, in the book there are no clues that lead us to place it as late as the Hellenistic period, thus suggesting that some time in the third century BCE is likely. Further, because of a lack of total consistency of thought within the book, various suggestions have been made that certain parts of it do not come from Qoheleth. It may be, however, that what we are dealing with here is not a systematic and organised theological treatise, but something more in the nature of a looser collection of observations about life, and in particular about a number of its woes. Thus perhaps we would do well, and especially in the context of this particular study, to heed the words of Whybray that we should "take seriously the proposition that Ecclesiastes is substantially the work of one man, the man known as Qoheleth, and to attempt to interpret the complexities of its teaching on that basis" (Whybray, *Ecclesiastes*, 26).

2. Crenshaw, *Ecclesiastes*, 48, 57.

3. Ibid., 57. For a more detailed and nuanced consideration of the meaning of *hĕbĕl*, and its particular usage and meaning in Qoheleth see Seybold, "*hĕbĕl*."

Then this needs to be said: Qoheleth is not a Job. Qoheleth is not groaning under, being totally ground down by, a great weight of sufferings that causes him to cry out to God in anguished tones. In Whybray's words, "Job is an awesome figure, like King Lear overwhelming the reader with the intensity of his suffering."[4] Qoheleth, by contrast, as Whybray observed, displays neither heroic nor tragic dimensions in his life, but is one who raises some real questions about life in the world. This large contrast in the scale of the portrayed experiences and responses of Qoheleth and Job is the reason why this study begins with Qoheleth, and will come to Job only at a later stage. Thus, while Job may be asking great and deep questions about why he, a man who has sought to walk with God, should have to suffer so very grievously, Qoheleth by contrast asks a series of questions, or makes a number of observations, much more along the lines of "Why does life have to be like this?"; "What's the point of this sort of life?" There is indeed a sense in which Qoheleth is, "the one who unflinchingly 'tells it like it is,' a welcomed, yet dissonant, voice within the canonical chorus."[5]

Thus, Qoheleth having sounded his motto theme, "Vanity of vanities! All is vanity" (1:2), goes on to ask what it is that people gain from their earthly toil (1:3). Perhaps what follows in 1:4–8 is intended to serve as a series of examples of the sort of things and situations in the world that give rise to the above statement. Thus in v. 4 there is the comment about the transience of human life in a world that appears to be permanent. Further, there seems to be about life in the world a sameness of experience, the feeling that life goes on and on in its set ways, as if all is somehow going round in a repetitive series of circles. In the following verse we notice the—no doubt, deliberate—repeated use of a number of words, in particular noting the oft-occurring "goes round" of the wind, and at the end, as if to crown it all, the observation that it "returns"!

> The wind blows to the south,
>   and goes around to the north;
> round and round goes the wind,
>   and on its circuits the wind returns.
> (Eccl 1:6)

Thus the conclusion and summing-up of these observations goes,

---

4. Whybray, *Two Jewish Theologies*, 16.
5. From the Editorial, *Int* 55 (2001), 235.

> All things are wearisome;
> more than one can express;
> the eye is not satisfied with seeing,
> or the ear filled with hearing.
> What has been is what will be,
> and what has been done is what will be done;
> there is nothing new under the sun.
> (Eccl 1:8–9)

And before we lose sight of this imagery of the wind, we should perhaps take note of a further observation in the book as to the difficulty a person has—or at least one person has—in understanding these phenomena and other matters, in making sense of them.

> And I applied my mind to know wisdom and to know madness
> and folly. I perceived that this also is but a chasing after wind.
> For in much wisdom is much vexation,
> and those who increase knowledge increase sorrow.
> (Eccl 1:17–18)

Then in the first three verses of chapter 4, Qoheleth sets out another sad, even tragic, observation that he has made about life and death. He has come to the conclusion that the lot of certain people in life is grim and unsatisfying, so much so that really they would have been better off not having been born (4:1–3).

With Eccl 3:16 Qoheleth has already spoken of the matter of wickedness in the world, in particular in situations where justice and righteousness should have prevailed, and here he goes into more detail. His purpose is to point out that such unjust situations are all too prevalent in the world and that they have been caused by people who have "power." Qoheleth, unlike the Hebrew prophets who also had much to say about such happenings and goings-on, does not speak about any desirable, or needful, amendment of life on the part of these powerful people, but then that is not his purpose. He is not a prophet, but rather he is one who belongs to the wisdom tradition—he is one of the "wise" (ḥākām, see 12:9). That is, he is a thinker and perhaps taking action is not his *forte*. Further, nor does he suggest that God should do something directly about addressing this grievous situation, but rather Qoheleth's purpose is to draw attention to, to uncover as it were, this particular aspect of the way in which the world has been created and is governed by God. He appears to be registering his quiet protest about the way certain things are in the world, uncovering an aspect of apparent injustice on earth, having something to say about an aspect of human suffering.

Qoheleth returns to this theme of the contrast between righteous and unrighteous people in 7:15, here revealing a further uncomfortable fact of life, namely that in his own life he has observed a marked lack of correlation between righteousness and longevity in life, and between unrighteousness and perishing. Here, Qoheleth would seem to be challenging that major doctrine which, as we have seen in the preceding chapter, is set forth in a good deal of the Hebrew Bible, that the reward of righteousness is long life and prosperity, and conversely that unrighteousness leads to destruction and death. Thus Qoheleth says, "In my vain life I have seen everything; there are righteous people who perish in their righteousness, and there are wicked people who prolong their life in their evildoing" (Eccl 7:15).

Qoheleth observes that there are some strange aspects to life in the world, and these he attributes to God. That is, a crucial fact of life in the world is the very strangeness of God's ways. This theme is given a good airing in 6:1–2. "There is an evil that I have seen under the sun, and it lies heavy upon humankind: those to whom God gives wealth, possessions, and honor, so that they lack nothing of all that they desire, yet God does not enable them to enjoy these things, but a stranger enjoys them. This is vanity; it is a grievous ill" (Eccl 6:1–2). That is, in the creation there is this element of sheer inconsistency, in that life in the world carries with it a pronounced lack of consistency and dependability. According to Qoheleth this is because this is the way God has made things; this is how things have been set up for the human beings in their lives in the world. Thus in 7:13 Qoheleth invites those he addresses to consider this strange work of God, and asks, "who can make straight what he has made crooked?" When we come to the following verse perhaps Qoheleth is beginning to suggest that on the part of the creator there is an element of deliberate obfuscation about life in the world in that its twists and turns are inexplicable; as much as human beings try to understand the ways of God they are unable to do so. Thus Qoheleth advises, "In the day of prosperity be joyful, and in the day of adversity consider; God has made the one as well as the other, so that mortals may not find out anything that will come after them" (Eccl 7:14).

Robert Gordis called Eccl 7:13–14 "an admirable epitome of Koheleth's thought,"[6] and Crenshaw observes, "Before an all-powerful God, human beings must resign themselves to ignorance about the ebb and flow of events. They can enjoy the good and consider the nature of reality when misfortune strikes. Nothing can challenge God's sovereign power or secure human existence."[7]

But Qoheleth, as well as averring that God's ways in the world are inscrutable and beyond challenge, also opines on the reality of the deity's *distance* from the world and its people. In fact, what is affirmed in this book is that God is indeed transcendent, but further that he is *not* at the same time *immanent*. Qoheleth would seem to be making this point in Eccl 5:2b (Hebrew 5:1b) where there appears to be a deliberate variation on a verse of Deuteronomy.[8] This is surely instructive for us as regards Qoheleth's theological thought. In Deut 4:39 we read, "the Lord is God in heaven above and on the earth beneath," whereas in Eccl 5:2b we have, "for God is in heaven, and you upon earth." Now in comparing these two verses we notice (a) that whereas in Deut 4:39 there is the characteristic Deuteronomic formulation "the Lord God," or "the Lord is God," in contrast, in Eccl 5:2b the Hebrew YHWH (LORD) is omitted and there is just "God" (*'ĕlōhîm*). This is in accord with what we find throughout the book of Qoheleth, that the deity is consistently referred to as "God" (*'ĕlōhîm*). In this regard we may further note that there are no fewer than forty references to "God" in this book, which suggests that there is a very serious place given to God in the thinking of the person responsible for this work. That is, this is a book about God, but the issue is what sort of a God is it that is being spoken about?

That is really the second point to be noticed in this comparison of these two part verses, namely, (b) that Deuteronomy in the verse quoted (and this is characteristic of the portrayal of the Lord in Deuteronomy) speaks of God being present both in heaven *and also* on earth. That is, the Lord is both transcendent and immanent. In the hands of Qoheleth (for it does seem most likely that here Qoheleth is quoting and at the same time deliberately adapting the Deuteronomic thought) the point is made that the Lord is present in heaven, his place, and that mean-

---

6. Gordis, *Koheleth*, 274–75.
7. Crenshaw, *Ecclesiastes*, 139.
8. I am indebted to Schoors, "Theodicy in Qoheleth", 396–97, for this observation.

while the human beings are on the earth, in their place. Qoheleth here seems to be making the point that, as he understands the matter, God is somewhat conspicuous by his absence upon earth; in the language of theology, he is not immanent.

In fact, there is for Qoheleth, as we have seen, this sense of mysteriousness about the ways of God. For Qoheleth, God is a distant and mysterious Deity and it is this fact that motivates Qoheleth's particular theological approach, one in which life has a series of burdens that human beings have to bear, and in which they cannot easily find sense and meaning. Thus, he says, "then I saw all the work of God, that no one can find out what is happening under the sun. However much they may toil in seeking, they will not find it out; even though those who are wise claim to know, they cannot find it out" (Eccl 8:17). And elsewhere, "[I] . . . applied my mind to seek and to search out by wisdom all that is done under heaven; it is an unhappy business that God has given to human beings to be busy with" (Eccl 1:13).

Yet Qoheleth seems to have come to some accommodation, at least for himself, with these uncomfortable realities about the situation for human beings in the world. He acknowledges that all that there is in the world comes from the hand of God (2:25–26) and he advises those who will hear his words—or read them—that they should "fear God" (Hebrew *yr'*, perhaps meaning something akin to our "reverence God"; 3:14; 5:7; 7:18; 8:12; 12:13 and compare 8:13). Roland E. Murphy, in his commentary on Ecclesiastes, asks what might be the particular nuance of this "fear" of God spoken about by Qoheleth, and comes to the conclusion that it is to do with "the unchangeability, and ultimately the mystery (3:11), of divine activity, before which 'fear' is the appropriate response."[9] As we have seen, the understanding of God in Qoheleth is of one who is distant from humanity, inscrutable in his ways, certainly not near at hand to his people. Thus Murphy observes, and I believe correctly, "Qoheleth's understanding of what it means to fear God seems to flow from the mystery and incomprehensibility of God. If one cannot understand what God is doing (3:11; 8:17; 11:6), and if indeed one does not perceive either divine love or hatred (9:1), reverential fear is in order (cf. 3:14; 5:6)."[10]

---

9. Murphy, *Ecclesiastes*, lxv.
10. Ibid., lxvi.

Alongside this reverential fear of God, Qoheleth counsels the enjoyment of what we might call the ordinary things of life, food and drink, the satisfaction of work, for, as he says, "this is our lot" (5:18). This is the gift of God (5:19), and anyway, counsels our sage, the joys of life keep us sufficiently well occupied that we hardly have time to "brood" over things (5:20). So he commends the enjoyment of what can be enjoyed in life, in particular mentioning food and drink (8:15; 9:7). So indeed, enjoy the good things of life, make the most of them while you can, and what you can do in the world seek to do it well. Thus he enjoins, "Enjoy life with the wife whom you love, all the days of your vain life that are given you under the sun, because that is your portion in life and in your toil at which you toil under the sun. Whatever your hand finds to do, do with all your might; for there is no work or thought or knowledge or wisdom in Sheol, to which you are going" (Eccl 9:9–10).

It will readily be perceived that there is a duality of thought expressed in those last two verses quoted, and we may find ourselves asking whether Qoheleth really finds life good, or whether on the other hand he finds it negative, problematic and meaningless. In fact it has to be said that commentators on the book of Qoheleth have frequently found themselves asking whether overall this book is hopeful or whether its predominant theme is a darker one than that.

Something of a case can be made for there being hopeful aspects within the book. As we have seen above, it seems that Qoheleth has found his way to finding some satisfaction in life, even joy in certain aspects of it. Thus R. N. Whybray was able to write of "Qoheleth, Preacher of Joy,"[11] in which he pointed to a series of texts in which is recommended the whole-hearted pursuit of enjoyment, these being 2:24a; 3:12; 3:22a; 5:17; 8:15a; 9:7a, 8, 9a; 11:9a, 10a; 12:1a. Some of these texts have been cited above, and we have already come to conclusions similar to those to which Whybray, in this contribution, came. Thus we can agree with him that there are good things that God has given to us and that are intended for our enjoyment, and that in the giving of them he has shown his approval of our actions, and that to enjoy such things is actually to do the will of God.[12] However, to speak of Qoheleth as "preacher of joy," might be felt to be giving a somewhat exaggerated emphasis to those rather muted aspects of hope and joy in this biblical book.

11. Whybray, "Qoheleth, Preacher of Joy."
12. Ibid., 92.

Equally, it has to be said that in the thought of Qoheleth there is on the part of humanity a great ignorance of God's purposes, and the reason for the existence of evil in the world. There is further a rejection in this book of the equations of on the one hand suffering with sinful living, and on the other prosperity with righteousness. That is, there is a definite rejection of that particular theodicy, but at the same time Qoheleth is not able to come up with an alternative explanation of his own. It is almost as if Qoheleth withdraws himself to the parts of life where he can find satisfaction, some meaning, some enjoyment; withdrawing himself, that is, from those other aspects of life of which he is neither able to make sense nor find meaning.[13]

For in this book God is unfathomable mystery and thus even the employment of wisdom in seeking understanding is firmly limited. Further, what is portrayed in this book is a very tenuous relationship of a person with God. In this book there is no speaking to God—and there is certainly nothing about God speaking to Qoheleth or anyone else. Nothing here about God speaking out of the whirlwind such as he is portrayed as doing to Job, not even in a still small voice as with Elijah. As W. Lee Humphries points out, "a silence pervades the Book of Koheleth . . . About the deity Koheleth speaks, but *to* him, never."[14] So it is that for Qoheleth, as Crenshaw expresses it, "The most anyone can do is explore the world of sensory pleasure and enjoy the few benefits of existence, knowing that time and chance share a random dance, as do good and evil."[15] Such are the observations of Qoheleth about life in the world, and about God; but there is hardly a theodicy here.

---

13. See Gese, "The Crisis of Wisdom in Koheleth."

14. Humphries, *Tragic Vision*, 131, his italics.

15. Crenshaw, *Defending God*, 169. Schoors, "Theodicy in Qoheleth," 409, we may further note, ends, saying of this writer's understanding of God, "He is the maker of a problematic world, a *Deus absconditus*. He makes what is the way it is, but he is no factor in human knowledge about the world."

Psalmic Interlude 1

"How long, O Lord" (Psalm 13)

The opening two verses of this short psalm of just six verses are dominated by four questions that the psalmist puts to God, each of them beginning with the words "How long?" In v. 1 the questions are, "How long, O Lord? Will you forget me forever?" and "How long will you hide your face from me?," while in v. 2 they are, "How long must I bear pain in my soul, and have sorrow in my heart all day long?" and "How long shall my enemy be exalted over me?" Thus it was with good cause that C. A. and E. G. Briggs wrote, "Ps. 13 is a prayer expostulating with Yahweh for long continued neglect (vv. 2–3 [Hebrew vv.; in EVV vv. 1–2])."[1] Here then is a psalmist who remonstrates with God upon the matter of his present sufferings and the associated absence of the helping presence of God. For this psalmist the issue is indeed "Where is the God of justice?" (Mal 2:17).

The question "How long?" is a characteristic feature of a numerous group of biblical psalms designated by the German scholar Hermann Gunkel (1862–1932) *Individual Laments*.[2] In these psalms the psalmist laments the difficult situation in which that individual finds him- or herself. Among the types of the biblical psalms these individual laments are the most common, and they predominate particularly in the first part of the psalter, for example Pss 3–7; 9 and 10; 13; 17; 22; 25–28; 31; 35; 38–40; 42–43; 51–52; 54–57; 59; 61; 64; 69; 70 (= 40:13–17); 71; 77; 86;

---

1. Briggs and Briggs, *Psalms*, 99.
2. Day, *Psalms*, 19–32; Broyles, *Conflict of Faith and Experience*.

88; 94; 102; 109; 120; 130; 140–43. It should also be noted that another group of biblical psalms is made up of what have been called *Corporate Laments*. Here it is the whole community that is crying out to God and asking "how long" the present experience of suffering is to take place.[3]

Another common word found in the Individual Laments—and also in the Corporate Laments—is "Why?," again addressed to God, and calling for an answer from him as to why all this suffering has to be the experience of a person who is seeking to live a life of godliness and faithfulness. This urgent question is in addition to the one spoken of earlier: "How long?" must these conditions prevail. In these psalms there is a real outspokenness to God, and yet there is no apparent thought of abandoning trust and faith in God. It is as if the psalmist is determined to hang on to God in faith and trust, in spite of all the things that are going wrong in their life, but at the same time demands answers from God himself with regard to urgent questions that spring directly out of experiences of life—questions frequently centred around "Why?" and "How long?" Thus the theme of this individual lament psalm is theodicy, the psalmist questioning why it is that in the very living of faithful obedience to God there should be this suffering, this pain and sorrow, a sense of an enemy causing much grief.[4] In this psalm what is referred to as the "enemy" looks as if it is a personification of those forces and difficulties that the psalmist feels beset with.[5]

In Ps 13:3–4 the psalmist calls upon God to consider his plight and answer him, to give light to his eyes, "or I will sleep the sleep of death," and the enemy will say, "I have prevailed." Further, the psalmist's foes—and here it does sound as if a number of people are involved—"will rejoice because I [the psalmist] am shaken."

Then in vv. 5 and 6 comes another of the characteristic features of the individual lament psalms, namely the sudden change of mood, and the expression of a sense of peace on the part of the psalmist. Usually

---

3. On the Corporate Laments see Day, *Psalms*, 33–36; Broyles, *Conflict of Faith and Experience*, in particular 133–77.

4. On the biblical psalms and theodicy see, Lindström, "Theodicy in the Psalms"; and the very helpful contribution of Brueggemann, "The Costly Loss of Lament," where he speaks of our loss in the church when we do not take the lament psalms seriously, not least in regard to the issue of theodicy. Brueggemann says that with "the absence of lament is the *stifling of the question of theodicy*" (61; his italics). See also the remarks of Mursell, "Suffering," about these psalms.

5. See Croft, *The Identity of the Individual in the Psalms*, 41.

this change of mood comes at the end of these psalms, though just occasionally it may come earlier (see Pss 94:16–23; 142; 143), and just occasionally it is absent (see Pss 25; 38; 39; 88; 120; 141). However, it is never explained how it is that there occurs this dramatic change in mood, and perhaps the most likely possibility is that the psalmist, having entrusted the grievous and debilitating matter to God, comes to a sense of peace and assurance. This is what Heiler famously referred to in the following way: "the feeling of uncertainty and instability is replaced by the blissful consciousness of being cared for, hidden in the hand of a protecting higher Power."[6] In the particular psalm under consideration it could be said that this explanation is affirmed, for we read of the psalmist saying, now in very different tones from the ones employed earlier,

> But I trusted in your steadfast love;
> my heart shall rejoice in your salvation.
> I will sing to the Lord,
> because he has dealt bountifully with me.
> (Ps 13:5–6)

Something has happened for the psalmist through his trusting in what the psalmist calls the "steadfast love" (*ḥesed*) of the Lord. This has been described as "an unfailing love that is for all who trust in God and so provides a basis for confidence."[7] Further, it should be noted that the last verse speaks of a "completed action," "he has dealt bountifully with me": it is likely that in fact this is an expression of faith and trust in God that has been uttered while the psalmist is still beset with his problems (whatever they are), but such is his confidence in God that in the Hebrew the verbal form is that of a completed action. This is not uncommon, and is a confident expression that what it is believed God will at some future time do is therefore already as good as done.

What is lacking here is any intellectual statement or argument about why there were these grievous sufferings, and what precisely will happen so that the psalmist may arrive at the stage when he may joyfully sing his song of praise. Yet perhaps of more worth than an intellectual solution to his problem has been this one that springs from the sense of sure trust in the steadfast love of the Lord. Thus, the answer here to the

---

6. Heiler, *Prayer*, 60. For other explanations of the sudden change in mood in the lament psalms see Thompson, *I Have Heard Your Prayer*, 47–49; Villanueva, The "Uncertainty of a Hearing."

7. Curtis, *Psalms*, 27. See also Zobel, "*ḥesed*."

theodicy question lies in a deep and confident religious assurance about God and his love:

> I will sing to the Lord,
> because he has dealt bountifully with me.
> (Ps 13:6)

The ongoing significance of these psalms of lament is that they come out of a tradition of religious faith in which the suffering individual, or community, goes on both clinging to and also praying to God in the belief either that God will bring about a change in their situation or else that entrusting the matter to God is sufficient, and that thereby a sense of peace is found. There is no hint in these psalms that the suffering believer will cease trusting and believing in God. In the Hebrew Bible it is only "the fool" who does that (Ps 14:1). The wise ones continue to seek God (Ps 14:2), even when that finding process takes time, even apparently inordinate time.

There is undoubtedly here a particular way that some individuals, or communities, have found for dealing with sufferings from which they are unable to escape. They entrust themselves and their present sufferings in faith to God and thereby find peace and satisfaction. This cannot be called a theodicy, for it does not present an answer to the "why suffering?" question. What however it is, is a way of dealing religiously with the matter, adopting an adequate strategy. Sadly, it is a strategy that has become lost in parts of the Christian church, and it would surely be to our profit, help, and peace to rediscover it.[8] For here, clearly, is one way in which the Old Testament can speak "of movement from darkness to light, from pain wracked questions to joyous hope,"[9] that is, to persevere in the search for the *presence* of God in what at present may look very much like his *absence*.[10] Such is what some of the psalmists and others spoken about in the Hebrew Bible did. And such also is what the historical prophet Jeremiah is portrayed in the book that bears his name as having done, as I shall now set forth.

---

8. For a recent study of this see Morrow, *Protest Against God*.
9. Davidson, *The Courage to Doubt*, 9.
10. For this formulation I am indebted to Terrien, *The Elusive Presence*, 320.

3

Via Dolorosa for Jeremiah

> Then the Lord put out his hand and touched my mouth; and the Lord said to me,
> > "Now I have put my words in your mouth.
> > See, today I appoint you over nations and over kingdoms,
> > to pluck up and to pull down,
> > to destroy and to overthrow,
> > to build and to plant."
>
> (Jer 1:9–10)

Thus it is that right at the very beginning of the book of Jeremiah there is sounded this sombre note about the expected course of the prophet Jeremiah's ministry. This is to be a ministry that will involve plucking up and pulling down, destroying, and overthrowing. Such can hardly have been a recipe for any quiet and peaceful ministry.

We do indeed find in the book of Jeremiah a series of passages that is without parallel in the Old Testament's prophetic books. In these passages the prophet cries out to God in an agonized way about the sufferings and distresses that his being a prophet of the Lord has pitched him into. Scholarship has called these the "Confessions" of Jeremiah, but it is frequently claimed that the word "confessions" is not adequately descriptive of them, for they are neither confessions of sin nor are they really confessions of faith, in the way that Saint Augustine's *Confessions* are. Rather, they are much more akin to what we call the psalms of individual lament, that have already been considered,[1] in which the psalmist demands of God answers as to why it is that suffering and strife should be the lot of one who is seeking to live a life of faithfulness to the Lord.

Kathleen M. O'Connor has made the point that the word "confession" *does* have an appropriateness when applied to these passages in the book of Jeremiah, because they are statements of where in the matter of faith the person uttering them "is" at some particular point in his or her life. She says about these passages, "I think they are confessions of faith because, in the midst of profound suffering, they cling fiercely to God, even though they do so accusingly, and even though they verge towards despair."[2] At any rate I use the word "confessions" here for the "laments" of Jeremiah, and I shall be making reference to those individual laments that we find in the book of psalms which do appear to provide the form and pattern of expression for what we find in parts of the book of Jeremiah.

As has already been observed, there do occur in the individual lament psalms the words of the suffering one, "Why?" and "How long?," both being addressed to God with a real sense of urgency—and not always, it has to be said, in the most politely expressed language. While there is no expressed thought of turning away from God, there is the clinging onto God by the one experiencing the suffering, and demanding some answers to agonized questions that come out of experiences of life in the world. Kathleen O'Connor goes on to say, "That is what lament prayers do. They complain, whine, and berate God even as they keep relationship alive."[3] So it is also with these passages in Jeremiah, the so-called confessions, they too "complain, whine, and berate God even as they keep relationship alive." The confessions of Jeremiah occur at 11:18–23; 12:1–6; 15:15–21; 17:14–18; 18:19–23; 20:7–18, and to the contents of these we now turn.

The First Confession

> 18 It was the Lord who made it known to me, and I knew, then you showed me their evil deeds.

---

1. See above, 31–34.
2. O'Connor, "Lamenting Back to Life."
3. Ibid., 36.

> 19 But I was like a gentle lamb
> led to the slaughter.
> And I did not know it was against me
> that they devised schemes, saying,
> "Let us destroy the tree with its fruit,
> let us cut him off from the land of the living,
> so that his name will no longer be remembered!"
> 20 But you, O Lord of hosts, who judge righteously,
> who try the heart and the mind,
> let me see your retribution upon them,
> for to you I have committed my cause.
>
> 21 Therefore thus says the Lord concerning the people of Anathoth, who seek your life, and say, "You shall not prophesy in the name of the Lord, or you will die by our hand"—22 therefore thus says the Lord of hosts: I am going to punish them; the young men shall die by the sword; their sons and their daughters shall die by famine; 23 and not even a remnant shall be left of them. For I will bring disaster upon the people of Anathoth, the year of their punishment.
>
> (Jer 11:18–23)

But who is the speaker in this passage? Many years ago the Old Testament scholar John Skinner referred to the passage as being "of extraordinary biographical interest,"[4] but since then the status of such passages as biographical has been questioned. In particular, Robert P. Carroll was generally sceptical, especially in his commentary on the book of Jeremiah, saying that, "there is nothing inherent in the poetry to identify who the speaker might be."[5] While not as extreme in his views as Carroll, William McKane questioned how many of the situations and scenes represented by the text of the book can confidently be assigned to specific historical situations, yet felt that most of the poetry in the book does come from the prophet Jeremiah.[6] Meanwhile William

---

4. Skinner, *Prophecy and Religion*, 109.

5. Carroll, *Jeremiah*, 47, where he also says, "We have no *reason* [his italics] to believe the poems of [chs] 1–25 to be other than anonymous utterances from a variety of sources. The editors of the book have put them into the mouth of Jeremiah and we read them as his utterances."

6. McKane, *Jeremiah*, lxxxviii–xcii.

Holladay felt able to place most parts of the book of Jeremiah into those historical events in which we read of the prophet's involvement.[7]

Fortunately, for our present purposes, we do not need to adopt any one theory about the relationship of the historical Jeremiah with what we read about him in the book bearing his name.[8] We are concerned only with the confessions and these certainly do seem to exhibit signs of very personal suffering and anguish, such that they give the impression of coming out of personal experiences of suffering. To put the matter another way, my own view is that if they do *not* record the dangers and difficulties Jeremiah faced, then it has to be said that whoever was responsible for them was at some pains to present a very negative picture of the working out of a prophetic ministry.[9] I intend to proceed on the assumption that the confessions of Jeremiah do represent something of the turmoil and distress that Jeremiah experienced in his life as he sought to be faithful in the exercise of his divine call to be a prophet.

---

7. Holladay, *Jeremiah*. For something of a mediating position on this issue of whose words we are reading in the poetic parts of the book of Jeremiah, see Brueggemann, *Jeremiah*, 27–35; Job, *Jeremiah's Kings*, 1–14, 183–88. See also now Allen, *Jeremiah*, esp. 142–50.

8. Nor do we need, in this context, to deal with, and come to some working conclusions about, the two other main critical problems that are encountered in the study of Jeremiah, the first of these being the fact that the Greek text we have of Jeremiah is some 3,000 words shorter than the Hebrew, it puts the Oracles Against the Nations in a different place, and it gives more stress to the role of Baruch than does the Hebrew. The second concerns the three different types of material that occur in the Jeremiah book, namely the poetry, the prose, and what reads like Deuteronomistic matter. Fortunately for our present study the Confessions are all in chs 1–25 of the book, and are mostly in poetry. For a recent statement and consideration of these matters see the works of Holladay, Carroll, McKane, and Brueggemann cited above.

9. Even so we should be aware of the arguments that Carroll deploys about the Confessions. Concerning the first of them he says, "The autobiographical approach . . . is too anachronistic to be correct. Writing biographies and autobiographies is not a feature of ancient Semitic cultures" (Carroll, *Jeremiah*, 277–78). Such statements invite responses. We may point to such biographical and autobiographical writings, or at least to writings that are couched in such styles, in the Hebrew prophetical books as Hos 1–3; Isa 5:1–7(?); 6:1–13; 8:1–22; 40:6; 49:1–6; 50:4–9; 61:1–4; Jer 1:4–19; Ezek 1:1–7, 27(?); Amos 7:1—9:4; Hab 1:2–4; 2:1–5; 3:1–19 etc. Carroll, along with others, understands the Confessions as being "communal laments" in which the prophet acts as spokesman for the people. (H. G. Reventlow is another scholar who has this approach. See his, *Liturgie und prophetisches Ich*.) There are indeed in the book of Jeremiah communal laments, but these occur *as well as* the Confessions, and it is neither necessary nor satisfactory to compress them both into one *genre* of writing. For comments upon the work of Reventlow see McKane, *Jeremiah*, xcii–xcv.

McKane gives to the first of the confessions the title "A Lamb led to the Slaughter,"[10] and he makes the point that the words rendered in NRSV "gentle lamb" (Hebrew *keveś ʾalûp*) indicate rather a "pet lamb," a lamb that is very "trusting," in fact one portrayed here as rather naively trusting people. And Jeremiah acknowledges that he has been naive in his serving the Lord. Things have been going on behind Jeremiah's back (revealed to him by the Lord—v. 18), there have been evil deeds done against him (v. 18), schemes devised to curtail his activities and make sure he was forgotten (v. 19). Yet speaking, as it were, in defence of Jeremiah it may be argued that he was not being unreasonably naive in his relationship with these people, for the reason that he had been called by none other than God himself to go to them, and to speak the word of the Lord to them.

It emerges in v. 21 that those who are speaking and plotting against Jeremiah are the people of Anathoth, that is, the people of the prophet's own village. There is scholarly disagreement over whether or not vv. 21–23 did originally belong to and follow on from vv. 18–20, the former being in prose, the latter appearing to be in poetry (as set out in NRSV). But in the form in which the prophecy of Jeremiah has come down to us they are attached together, and we may consider them as making up one unit. Of course, the issue will emerge that what is so galling for the people of Anathoth is that their prophetic "son" appears now to have no good word for them, but has become the willing accomplice and mouthpiece of the Lord who pronounces his divine judgment upon them.

The reaction of Jeremiah, no doubt as he sought to move on from his earlier naive approach to his fellow townsfolk, is one of harsh vengeance (v. 20); he asks that he may see the retribution of the Lord of hosts upon them. Of course, this does seem frighteningly and inexcusably vindictive to us and such words, and no few others of a similar tone in the rest of the Old Testament, constitute a real problem for Christians as they appropriate the Old Testament as a part of their own Scriptures. However, Jeremiah is in deep anguish and is making his appeal to the Lord of hosts, whom he credits with judging righteously (v. 20). As D. R. Jones puts it, "It is quite simply the satisfaction of strict justice (v.

---

10. McKane, *Jeremiah*, 253.

20a) such as the Lord alone knows."[11] Two comments may be made at this point.

The first is that, as we shall come to see in what follows, this call for justice from the Lord for a person who is suffering is common in the individual psalms of lament, in which an individual cries out to God. This type of psalm, as we have observed, makes up a very significant part of the whole Psalter[12] and commonly within these psalms we have a suffering person's call to the Lord to do something to redress the situation that they find themselves in. Thus it is, as has been argued, that one of the closest parallels we have in the Hebrew Bible to the so-called confessions of Jeremiah is these individual psalms of lament; and indeed for what some call Jeremiah's confessions others feel a more appropriate description is "lament." Further, again as has already been observed, we may regard the psalmic laments as the "model" for the Jeremianic confessions.

Second, there is this to be said. What we are encountering here, once again, is a real outspokenness on the part of the suffering one, who is crying out to God, determined both to have a hearing from God, and also to gain some answer to their agonized questions of the moment. The sufferer is clinging on to God—in no way abandoning the Lord in this situation, as if he has irretrievably failed this worshipper. Rather, the one who is suffering continues to believe that their help, strength, comfort, and consolation all do reside in God, and there is no talk of looking elsewhere for help.

And yet, perhaps the sufferer is asking questions about whether God is truly and properly aware of the depths of despair that this loyal and faithful worshipper is at present enduring. Thus the language used towards God in such prayers and outbursts is not always "polite," and in the terms and *mores* of some cultures will perhaps appear to be verging upon the blasphemous. We should take note of the fact that in this confession although there is a reply from the Lord concerning what will happen to the people of Anathoth, there is no personal word of either encouragement or support for Jeremiah as the prophet who is suffering in all this, and at that, as the servant of the Lord. But there are some developments to be observed in the second of the confessions, and to that we now turn.

---

11. Jones, *Jeremiah*, 188–89.
12. See above, 31–34.

The Second Confession

> 1 You will be in the right, O Lord,
> when I lay charges against you;
> but let me put my case to you.
> Why does the way of the guilty prosper?
> Why do all who are treacherous thrive?
>
> 2 You plant them, and they take root;
> they grow and bring forth fruit;
> you are near in their mouths
> yet far from their hearts.
>
> 3 But you, O Lord, know me;
> You see me and test me—my heart is with you.
> Pull them out like sheep for the slaughter,
> and set them apart for the day of slaughter.
>
> 4 How long will the land mourn,
> and the grass of every field wither?
> For the wickedness of those who live in it
> the animals and the birds are swept away,
> and because people said, "He is blind to our ways."
>
> 5 If you have raced with foot-runners and they have wearied you,
> how will you compete with horses?
> And if in a safe land you fall down,
> how will you fare in the thickets of the Jordan?
>
> 6 For even your kinsfolk and your own family,
> even they have dealt treacherously with you;
> they are in full cry after you;
> do not believe them,
> though they speak friendly words to you.
>
> (Jer 12:1–6)

Now the prophet lays a specific charge against the Lord. McKane makes the point that the vocabulary of v. 1 is legal and that Jeremiah addresses God as a judge.[13] And the main issue that the prophet puts to his "Judge," set out in the second part of the verse, is that of theodicy. It is this: How can the prosperity of the wicked be reconciled with God's righteousness?[14] The prophet accepts that the Lord is righteous—"You will be in the right" (so NRSV). This may be read as indicating that

---

13. McKane, *Jeremiah*, 261.
14. So the Jewish scholar Kimchi, says McKane, *Jeremiah*, 261.

Jeremiah is both encouraged but also perplexed; encouraged because he perhaps feels himself able to put his trust in God but at the same time perplexed by having to observe the prosperity of the wicked.[15]

Something of this sense of confusion about the apparent ways of God in the world is reflected in the poem of Gerard Manley Hopkins that came out of a time of deep darkness for him, in fact from the last year of his life. Its "text" is Jer 12:1, for Hopkins in the Latin, Vulgate, "Justus quidem tu es, Domine."[16]

> Thou art indeed just, Lord, if I contend
> With thee; but, sir, so what I plead is just.
> Why do sinners' ways prosper? And why must
> Disappointment all I endeavour end?[17]

We should take note of three further statements or questions that Jeremiah puts to the Lord, the divine reply in these matters comprising just one major statement. Jeremiah in the first place protests his own loyalty and commitment to God—"You see me and test me—my heart is with you" (v. 3). That is, God being God must know for sure that his servant is still his servant, and the unexpected things that have been happening for Jeremiah have not deflected him in his commitment.

This perhaps helps us to understand and appreciate, in the second place, the words that then follow from Jeremiah about divine preparation for the slaughter of his (Jeremiah's) enemies. Such would, the prophet argues, demonstrate to him the Lord's acceptance of his faithfulness, and further, the Lord's judgment upon Jeremiah's enemies. Yet while that may help us understand and appreciate Jeremiah's harsh words, it does

---

15. Crenshaw ("Theodicy and prophetic Literature," 245–46) expresses it thus, "Torn between an intense desire to give YHWH the benefit of the doubt, Jeremiah feels the equal force of brutal reality, events that challenge his worldview. Violent people succeed without the anticipated punishment from above, thus encouraging popular questioning of the principle of reward and retribution undergirding religion itself." See also Crenshaw, *A Whirlpool of Tormen*, 31–56; Mills, *Alterity, Pain and Suffering*, 110–34.

16. See White, *Hopkins*, 444–47, especially where he says (ibid., 446–47), "How can a chosen prophet argue with his God? It is this problem that brings the minds of Hopkins and Jeremiah together. Jeremiah had found a literary method of articulating the division between his sense of duty and his human nature. Hopkin's poem is a dramatic articulation of his division, though it takes the form of a contention between servant and master."

17. Phillips, *Gerard Manley Hopkins*, 165.

not lessen their harshness or make them any the more acceptable to us. Their usage within the Christian church's canon of Scripture continues to be a problem.

In the third place, and briefly, we may take note of the fact that the prophet plies God with the question "how long?," that is, how long is this dreadful situation going to prevail for the prophet? In the Hebrew Bible material that speaks of the sufferings of individuals and communities, the question "how long?" commonly occurs—and it is a question that is usually urgently expressed to the Lord.

The Lord's response to Jeremiah in his sufferings is not perhaps of the sort that he was desirous of hearing. One imagines that he was hoping for something more than this.[18] Nevertheless, what the Lord has to say to his suffering prophet is expressed in two different ways, but they amount to much the same thing. That is, the Lord says to Jeremiah that at the moment his difficulties are of a certain magnitude, but in later times they are going to be far greater (v. 5), and if he cannot deal with things as they are at the moment, how will he be, and indeed will he survive, when they become greater and more intense? This response appears to carry within it the assumption on the part of the Lord that Jeremiah *will* remain faithful to him and, at the same time, constitutes the warning that the prophet's difficulties and burdens are set to become greater. Further, Jeremiah is warned that he will have to be careful about taking human counsel—perhaps to be aware particularly of those who "speak friendly words" to him (v. 6).

The Third Confession

> 15 O Lord, you know;
> remember me and visit me,
> and bring down retribution for me on my persecutors.
> In your forbearance do not take me away;
> know that on your account I suffer insult.
>
> 16 Your words were found, and I ate them,
> and your words became to me a joy
> and the delight of my heart;
> for I am called by your name,
> O Lord, God of hosts.

---

18. "God's method of comforting people is sometimes not at all what they were hoping for." McKeating, *Jeremiah*, 85.

> 17 I did not sit in the company of merrymakers,
> nor did I rejoice;
> under the weight of your hand I sat alone,
> for you had filled me with indignation.
>
> 18 Why is my pain unceasing,
> my wound incurable,
> refusing to be healed?
> Truly, you are to me like a deceitful brook,
> like waters that fail.
>
> 19 Therefore, thus says the Lord:
> If you turn back, I will take you back,
> and you shall stand before me.
> If you utter what is precious, and not what is worthless,
> you shall serve as my mouth.
> It is they who will turn to you,
> not you who will turn to them.
>
> 20 And I will make you to this people
> a fortified wall of bronze;
> they will fight against you,
> but they shall not prevail over you,
> for I am with you
> to save you and deliver you, says the Lord.
>
> 21 I will deliver you out of the hand of the wicked,
> and redeem you from the grasp of the ruthless.
>
> (Jer 15:15–21)

The prophetic reproach directed against God continues, here taking on a new intensity. This third confession opens with a renewal of the prophet's request that the Lord will effect his judgment upon Jeremiah's persecutors (v. 15). Then the prophet makes the statement that the great joy of his life was to have been entrusted with something of the word of God for his generation—of the prophet finding God's words, eating them with joy and delight, and yet, because of their content and burden, thereby becoming separated to a certain extent from those who were enjoying life (vv. 16–17). Then comes the question to God—a further variation on the theme of the ongoing prophetic questioning of God. The "why?" question now concerns his pain which is like an unhealing wound (v. 18). Presumably this particular pain is that of loneliness and the sense of separation from others in life. The merrymaking of others is denied to Jeremiah because he is burdened with the knowledge of what is going on in the counsels of the Lord, and this knowledge the prophet has because he has ingested the word of the Lord.

Thus it is that Jeremiah accuses the Lord of being to him like a deceitful brook (v. 18). Presumably what the prophet has in mind is a stream that at one time in the year will be a raging torrent causing much destruction, at another time a good and ready source of water, and at another a dried-up watercourse, empty and no source of water. That is, Jeremiah accuses the Lord of being erratic in his care of him, and therefore unreliable, undependable as a source of help and support. Certainly the imagery is bold, and the language is nothing if not boldly outspoken.[19] Thus it is that Jeremiah not only speaks harshly to the Lord about his fellow citizens, but also with a like harshness to the Lord about the way that the Lord is treating his suffering prophet! For not only does the prophet have to endure the pain of his being the Lord's servant, he must also experience what he refers to as an incurable wound causing continued distress and resistance to healing, and he also has to manage without the Lord as his strength and stay.

It is in this moment of abject darkness for the prophet that he is answered by the Lord (vv. 19–21). It is a message of hope for Jeremiah, assuring him that as long as he remains faithful to the Lord, the Lord will be with him and will give him strength to withstand all that he receives from those around him. The divine word in no way suggests that the forces against him will lessen, nor that he will have some new presence of God with him, yet he is afforded strong assurance of being strengthened for his task, and that he will be saved and delivered out of the hand of the wicked, that he will be redeemed from the grasp of the ruthless (v. 21).

The Fourth Confession

> 14 Heal me, O Lord, and I shall be healed;
> save me, and I shall be saved;
> for you are my praise.
> 15 See how they say to me,
> "Where is the word of the Lord?
> Let it come!"

---

19. Note the complaint using much the same language and imagery about perceived unreliability in Job 6:14–20, but then that is from Job, but only about his friends.

> 16 But I have not run away from being a shepherd in your service,
> nor have I desired the fatal day.
> You know what came from my lips;
> it was before your face.
>
> 17 Do not become a terror to me;
> you are my refuge on the day of disaster;
>
> 18 Let my persecutors be shamed,
> but do not let me be shamed;
> let them be dismayed,
> but do not let me be dismayed;
> bring on them the day of disaster;
> destroy them with double destruction!
>
> (Jer 17:14–18)

This confession is less coherent than are the earlier ones; it appears to comprise a number of random thoughts here collected together. Some regard it as beginning with v. 12, but it seems clear that the lament style begins with v. 14.[20] It opens with the prophet imploring God to heal him, save him (v. 14), pleas which are not uncommon in the psalms of individual lament (see for example Pss 6:2; 41:4). The plea, though, is portrayed as being uttered in a spirit of confidence and sure hope that the Lord will heal him, save him.

The words in v. 15 addressed to Jeremiah by the "they" (presumably we are to understand by this the people to whom Jeremiah proclaimed his message, and in particular the people of Anathoth)—"Where is the word of the Lord? Let it come!"—have occasioned a good deal of discussion. The most likely meaning would seem to be that what we have here is a mocking response, suggesting that there is no divine action to be seen although the one who claims to be the Lord's prophet has been so forceful in warning people of its coming upon them. That is, "they" demand some immediate proof that this disagreeable prophet has got things right—rather along the lines of the words of the unheeding ones of Isa 5:19, "Let him make haste, let him speed his work that we may see it; let the plan of the Holy One of Israel hasten to fulfillment, that we may know it!"

The word that NRSV, among other translations, renders "shepherd" in v. 16 is somewhat problematic—as indeed NRSV flags up in its

---

20. See Baumgartner, *Jeremiah's Poems of Lament*, 52–53.

marginal note "Meaning of Heb[rew] uncertain."[21] The fact is that apart from a grammatical problem with this word, there is also the consideration that elsewhere in the book of Jeremiah the word "shepherd" is used of political leaders (2:8; 6:3; 10:21; 12:10), and never of prophets. The LXX has "I have not tired of following after you," but perhaps more likely is the one that involves a small change in the Hebrew yielding, "I have not pressed you to send evil." The prophet goes on to say that it is not he, Jeremiah, who desired the day of disaster (NRSV "fatal day"), meaning, it would seem, that all this aggravation the prophet is experiencing (and that has sparked off his confessions) has not been of his making or desiring, but rather (understood) that this has come from the Lord. It is the Lord who has landed Jeremiah in all these troubles!

Thus (v. 17) the prophet implores the Lord that he (the Lord) should not become a terror to him (Jeremiah), and will the Lord affirm that when the day of disaster does actually come for the people, then in that moment of terror Jeremiah will have him as his "refuge." The prophet is saying that it is to the Lord that he looks expectantly for his security. Meanwhile, the depth of Jeremiah's distress and anguish into which he has descended stands starkly revealed in v. 18 as he asks the Lord that his persecutors may be shamed, dismayed, even destroyed, and that he may not be so dealt with. No doubt there are more excellent ways that have been shown to us, even laid upon us (see Matt 5:10–11), but these harsh words demonstrate the depths of suffering to which Jeremiah has been brought through what has been nothing less than his faithfulness to the Lord's call to him to be his prophet.

The Fifth Confession

> 19 Give heed to me, O Lord,
> and listen to what my adversaries say!
> 20 Is evil a recompense for good?
> yet they have dug a pit for my life.
> Remember how I stood before you
> to speak good for them,
> to turn away your wrath from them.
> 21 Therefore give their children over to famine;
> hurl them out to the power of the sword,

---

21. See the commentaries for full details. McKeating, *Jeremiah*, 103, observes, "how obscure the opening of v. 16 is in the Hebrew."

> let their wives become childless and widowed.
> May their men meet death by pestilence,
> their youths be slain by the sword in battle.
> 22 May a cry be heard from their houses,
> when you bring the marauder suddenly upon them!
> For they have dug a pit to catch me,
> and laid snares for my feet.
> 23 Yet you, O Lord, know
> all their plotting to kill me.
> Do not forgive their iniquity,
> do not blot out their sin from your sight.
> Let them be tripped up before you;
> deal with them while you are angry.
>
> (Jer 18:19–23)

Many commentators regard this confession as beginning with v. 18, but it seems best to regard that verse as separate. It may give some background information to what follows, but the confession proper begins with v. 19. Verse 18 speaks about the God-appointed ministries of the priests, the wise, and the prophets. Perhaps the thought is that it is only from Jeremiah, just one among all the other divinely-called guides, that the people are having such harsh and judgmental words, that they may feel justified in following the majority who speak to them in much more comforting and positive ways. And anyway, if they, so to speak, knock Jeremiah out of the equation, there are still various others to give them divine guidance.

The prophet begins his confession by calling the Lord to attend to him, in particular to take note of what his enemies are saying about him (v. 19). Jeremiah (v. 20) has done what he understood was the Lord's will, but his "good" work has been rewarded by the people with "evil," and—as it was with Joseph (Gen 37:24–28)—those people have "dug a pit for my life," no doubt to be understood metaphorically; they would like to see him disposed of. At this point (v. 20), Jeremiah reminded the Lord how he had sought—like Moses of old (Exod 32:11–14, 30–34)—to pray for his people, under judgment as they were for their sins. Such intercessions of prophets for their people are spoken of in the Hebrew Bible.[22] Here Jeremiah appears to be saying to God that he has tried

---

22. On these intercessions in the Old Testament see Thompson, *I Have Heard Your Prayer*, 89–118.

to do his best for his people. As well as informing them of their sins he has also prayed for them in their sinfulness and sought the divine forgiveness. And what acknowledgement and thanks has he received from those sinful people, poised as they are in such a precarious position in their relationship with God? All that he has received has been aggravation and threats and words of the harshest kind.

In vv. 21–3 Jeremiah utters exceedingly harsh words about his people, asking the Lord that dreadful things may happen to them. Further, it is as if the expected doom for these people—which earlier the prophet through his intercessions had sought to avert—is now being requested in a deeply intense outpouring of emotion. May it take place so that Jeremiah may know a sense of vindication for all the grief he has suffered! Thus where once there had been the prayers of intercession for the sinful nation, now comes the prayer of petition for the personal vindication of the prophet. And, in the very last part of v. 23 the parting shot of Jeremiah to the Lord is to the effect that let not God tarry in this task of judgment, lest he should change his mind. Let not procrastination be the thief of anger! Once again, there is the problem of reading these words, filled as they are with such violent thoughts, and totally lacking in any sense of forgiveness. Again, they demonstrate the depths of despair to which one servant of the Lord was driven—and no doubt not the last to be driven to such a sense of abandonment.

The Sixth Confession

> 7 O Lord, you have enticed me,
> and I was enticed;
> you have overpowered me,
> and you have prevailed.
> I have become a laughingstock all day long;
> everyone mocks me.
> 8 For whenever I speak, I must cry out,
> I must shout, "Violence and destruction!"
> For the word of the Lord has become for me
> a reproach and derision all day long.
> 9 If I say, "I will not mention him,
> or speak any more in his name,"
> then within me there is something like a burning fire
> shut up in my bones;

I am weary with holding it in,
and I cannot.
10 For I hear many whispering:
"Terror is all around!
Denounce him! Let us denounce him!"
All my close friends
are watching for me to stumble.
"Perhaps he can be enticed,
and we can prevail against him,
and take our revenge on him."
11 But the Lord is with me like a dread warrior;
therefore my persecutors will stumble,
and they will not prevail.
They will be greatly shamed,
for they will not succeed.
Their eternal dishonor
will never be forgotten.
12 O Lord of hosts, you test the righteous,
you see the heart and the mind;
let me see your retribution upon them,
for to you I have committed my cause.

13 Sing to the Lord;
praise the Lord!
For he has delivered the life of the needy
from the hands of evildoers.

14 Cursed be the day
on which I was born!
The day when my mother bore me,
let it not be blessed!
15 Cursed be the man
who brought the news to my father, saying,
"A child is born to you, a son,"
making him very glad.
16 Let that man be like the cities
that the Lord overthrew without pity;
let him hear a cry in the morning
and an alarm at noon,
17 because he did not kill me in the womb;
so that my mother would have been my grave,
and her womb forever great.

> 18 Why did I come forth from the womb
> to see toil and sorrow,
> and spend my days in shame?
>
> (Jer 20:7–18)

This is the last of the confessions of Jeremiah, and with it the prophet's laments reach their apotheosis, being at their most outspoken in condemnation of the Lord and of all that he has brought upon his prophet. For this prophet was, after all, bent only upon fulfilling what he believed to be the divine will.

The confession opens on a startling note with the expression of the prophet's feeling that the Lord has "deceived" him (*p-t-h*),[23] and that he has been "deceived, overpowered" (*ḥ-z-q*). The fact is that he is the subject of the people's mocking, that he has become a "laughing stock, a subject of mirth" all the time, permanently (v. 7). The reason for this is that the message the prophet has been given to proclaim is one that has at its heart a dagger—"Violence and destruction!" This violence and destruction has its roots and origin in God and will be effected by him as a judgment for sinfulness. Thus has the "word of the Lord" become for this prophet a "reproach and derision" *all day long*—a phrase found both in the preceding verse and also in the present one (v. 8).

The thought moves on in v. 9 to speak of further difficulty—even tragedy—for the prophet, his situation being that the only way he can free himself of being a "laughingstock," and his words being the source of his "reproach and derision," is to say nothing more of these matters. But he finds that he cannot, and must accept that that course of action is just not open to him. For if he tries to cease speaking of these matters then there is something within him "like a burning fire shut up in my bones," that wearies him with holding it in—and he cannot (v. 9). This is surely a strongly affirmative statement that the prophet is not in any way doubting that the message he is proclaiming *is* the true message of God in regard to his people at some particular time. That is, Jeremiah is not doubting the veracity of his proclamation, rather his complaint is that it had to be *his* particular lot to be compelled to proclaim it. Why should this have fallen upon him? For the fact of the matter is that the

---

23. This is a strong word and the usage is bold. In Exod 22:15 it is used of "seducing" a virgin, while in 1 Kgs 22:20–22 of the deception caused by a lying spirit. For more details about the language here see Carroll, *Jeremiah*, 399.

whisperings go on around him; there is for him a perpetual sense of terror, and ever those—whom he had in earlier days regarded as "close friends!"—watching and waiting for him to stumble, and so give them the opportunity to take their revenge (v. 10).

With vv. 11–12 there is at last some expression of confidence on the part of the prophet—he is sure of the Lord's presence with him, "like a dread warrior," that is to say he is sure that there is strength—and at that, divine strength—on his side.[24] This "dread warrior"-strength comforts Jeremiah in that it will, he is sure, issue in shame, lack of success and abiding dishonor for his persecutors (v. 11). Thus he can go on in hope that he may see the divine retribution at work among these people (v. 12). One might wish that Jeremiah had asked for an understanding on the part of his enemies as to their situation vis-à-vis the Lord, or that he had called upon God to heal the rift between the people and himself,[25] but alas we have to accept that what is spoken of here is divine strength let loose to effect retribution for the benefit, standing and satisfaction of his chosen prophet. No doubt we experience a similar reaction within ourselves as we read the equally severe words of Ps 137, in particular its "Happy shall they be who take your [the Babylonians'] little ones / and dash them against the rock!" (Ps 137:9).[26]

With v. 13 we come to an expression of the praise of God, praise uttered in the assurance either that the life of the needy (presumably the prophet) *has been* rescued from the clutches ("hands") of the evildoers, or that such *will* assuredly take place.[27] However, its presence here does

---

24. On the subject of the Old Testament's rendering of the Lord as a warrior see, e.g., Brueggemann, *Theology of the Old Testament*, 241–44.

25. On the Lord as "Healer" in the Old Testament, see Brueggemann, *Theology of the Old Testament*, 252–55.

26. About these words Curtis, *Psalms*, 251, says, "Perhaps the best that can be said is that in such instances the words of the psalmists show us real people responding to their real situations and feeling able to share their real emotions with their real God." Such a comment is surely applicable mutatis mutandis to what Jeremiah is recorded as saying in Jer 20:12. See also the remarks of Salters, *Jonah and Lamentations*, 118–19, concerning such cries for vengeance.

27. The Hebrew usage of the "perfect" (as distinct from the "imperfect") of a verb indicates a completed action. However, this may include action that is regarded as being *as good as completed*, because the speaker is confident that God will do this particular thing, cause it to take place. Thus it has to be said that in Jer 20:13 we cannot be sure whether the expression of praise is for what *has already taken place*, or whether for what can confidently *be expected to take place* at some time in the future.

raise a number of critical questions about this confession, in particular as to whether we are dealing here with what should be regarded as one lament or two.

Frequently the psalms of lament have within them, as we have observed, an expression of confidence that the psalmist will be delivered from the troubles and difficulties that have occasioned that lament. However, an expression of confidence is not always present, but when it is, it is usually at the end of the lament. Further, the transition from lament to expression of confidence is sudden, even dramatic, and generally no explanation is given as to how and why the psalmist can move so quickly, and confidently, from lament to declaration of confidence in God. What seems to many of us to be the most likely reason is that the psalmist having committed the troublesome matter to God in prayer (and frequently these particular prayers are bold and outspoken), that person finds peace of mind and a new sense of trust and calmness.[28]

Now if this change of mood in the confession in Jer 20:7–18 came at the end of the piece, then we could readily understand it as one unit that has been expressed in the form and style of the psalmic individual laments. As it is, the expression of confidence comes earlier than at the end, at v. 13. Thereafter the lament material continues from v. 14 until it terminates at v. 18, but in this latter part there is no expression of confidence—a phenomenon that is not unknown among the psalms of individual lament (see for example Pss 25; 38; 39; 88; 120). This may suggest that we are dealing, then, with two Confessions in Jer 20, both being expressed in the style and language of the psalmic laments, the first in vv. 7–13 having the common expression of confidence, the second in vv. 14–18 being without an expression of confidence.

However, there are some psalms of lament where there is an expression of confidence to be found within the body of the psalm, *as well as* at the end (see Pss 5:7, 11–12; 7:10, 11(?), 17; 55:19b–21(?), 22–23; 57:5, 7–11; 59:10, 16–17; 61:5, 12; 86:12–13, 15–17; 102:12–22, 25–28; 109:20–21, 30–31). There is further a rather different arrangement of the lamenting/hopeful material in Pss 142 and 143: in both of these the lamenting/hopeful materials are rather intermixed in the course of each psalm, each of these psalms having within it underlying expressions of hope in, and reliance upon, God.

---

28. On this dramatic change of mood in these psalms, see Thompson, *I Have Heard Your Prayer*, 47–49; Villanueva, *The "Uncertainty of a Hearing."*

All this is to say that we should perhaps think of the style of the psalmic laments as being rather more flexible and variable than we had earlier assumed. This further allows us perhaps to accept that with Jer 20:7–18 we do have one confession expressed in the language and style of the psalms of lament, in this case the expression of confidence coming within the body of the composition. Nevertheless, in this case the whole composition does end on a note of the prophet still asking his questions as to the matter of God's calling him to the divine service.[29]

In fact, in the last verses of what I am arguing should be regarded as one lament we find a remarkably outspoken apostrophe to God; here the prophet curses not only the day of his birth (v. 14) but he also curses that person who brought what he thought in his innocence was good news to his father, that a son had been born to him (v. 15). Let that man remain under judgment for not ending Jeremiah's life there and then (vv. 16–17)! And thus the confession, and indeed this whole cycle of the confessions of Jeremiah, ends on the plaintive note of the prophet,

> Why did I come forth from the womb
> to see toil and sorrow,
> and to spend my days in shame?
> (Jer 20:18)

Before we leave this remarkable passage we should take note of the fact that there is a quite distinct relationship between it and the first statement of Job about his sufferings. In both there is the cursing the day of the speaker's birth, as well as the comment about the unfortunate ministry of the person who informed the father of his son's birth. Jeremiah 20:14–18 portrays the prophet in the last extremities of all that he can find both within and also outwith himself in order to sustain him, and this bears a marked similarity to what Job has to say about his most tenuous situation vis-à-vis his relationship with God and his worldly fortunes,

> I am not at ease, nor am I quiet;
> I have no rest; but trouble comes.
> (Job 3:26)

---

29. We should also take note of the fact that v. 13 is a very generalized expression of confidence. This could indicate that it has perhaps been drawn from the common stock of lament vocabulary, either by the composer of the rest of the composition, or by another.

We shall return to this matter later in this work, but for the time being it is surely not unreasonable to suggest the strong possibility that the author of the book of Job was at this point in his work dependent on the last of the so-called confessions of Jeremiah.[30]

We need now to return to the earlier-discussed matter of who the speaker is here. Is it the prophet Jeremiah or alternatively are we dealing with words that have been attributed to Jeremiah by a scribe, Baruch or another, or perhaps by an editor? Certainly, a case can be made for it having been the prophet himself, for the sort of experience that is set forth so starkly in the confessions is all of a piece with what else we are told happened to Jeremiah in the course of his ministry—his time in the stocks (Jer 20:2–3), his being put in prison (37:15–16), his breakdown in relationships with the people of his home town of Anathoth because of the harshness, as far as they were concerned, of what he had been called to proclaim (11:21–23), and—in a rather different way—his use of the "lament" form of speech which, apart from any routine knowledge of it he may have had, would surely have been known from his family background of being among "the priests who were in Anathoth in the land of Benjamin" (1:1). Of course, it could be argued that this consistency is attributable to careful editorial work, but if so then it was indeed *very careful* editorial work.

But perhaps at the end of the day, and in particular for the purposes of this present study, it does not matter greatly whether in the confessions we are dealing with the very words of Jeremiah himself, his *ipsissima verba*, or whether we are reading what another, or even some others, recorded of his rather dire experiences of being a prophet, about one who sought to remain faithful to the will of his Lord. If it be the latter, then it gives us the impression of being a remarkably faithful picture of a prophet who found his call such a grievous burden. For those who took upon themselves to edit the books of the prophets must have been possessed of a deep sense of care to pass on to others the importance of what had been said and the associated tragedy and sinfulness that had called forth such words. There must have been, for such editors, the temptation to airbrush out the failures of the prophets. As it is, and if the confessions are the work of one, or some, other than Jeremiah himself,

---

30. On the relationship between the books of Jeremiah and Job see Brueggemann, *Jeremiah*, 167–71.

we appear to have recorded for us the sufferings that for this prophet were brought about in his faithfulness to the Lord, reading about an understanding of this prophet's deep feeling of inadequacy and weakness in the face of the combination of hostility and strength of his opponents. Yet more than this, for the confessions of Jeremiah convey a deep sense of the prophet's feeling of having been betrayed by the Lord, for it appeared to him that the Lord has not adequately protected and helped his servant, keeping him free of enemy attacks of various kinds.

What, then, the book of Jeremiah witnesses to is this fact: that faithful service to the Lord may bring in its train many and various sufferings. In the course of these lament passages, the confessions, we see the prophet being granted shafts of light for his darkness, from time to time being assured that the Lord is with him to strengthen him and support him (15:20–21; 20:11–13). Yet the suffering goes on, the word from the Lord being about his strengthening presence with Jeremiah, but in no way the assurance that enough is enough of such sufferings for one person. Rather, this servant of God is called to shun the ways of the happy merrymaking of his compatriots and to sit in silence bearing sorrows that rightly should have been shared by all the people. And further, this prophet who was called to this particularly difficult and demanding road was no paragon of virtue, no constant utterer of pious and saintly words. Rather, this was a person of like passions as ourselves (Acts 14:15; Jas 5:17), who at times uttered fearsome imprecations against those he perceived to be his enemies (Jer 12:3b; 15:15; 17:18; 18:21–23).

What, then, do these texts have to contribute to our study of the experience of suffering in the Old Testament? At least two things, and to these we may append an observation. In the first place it is to be observed that here in portrayed situations of enormous difficulties and sufferings encountered by the faithful servant of the Lord is the placing of yet another question mark over that theological approach which seeks to explain suffering as being due to human sinfulness. Jeremiah's suffering came out of faithful service in the name of the Lord—surely this was not a "deserved calamity!" Once again the "deserved calamity" theory of Deuteronomy, the Deuteronomistic History, and other parts of the Old Testament is clearly shown to be inadequate as a general catchall explanation for sufferings in the world.

In the second place, the prophet is portrayed as lamenting before God as to his sufferings, and in the manner of the lament tradition thereby finds a sufficient sense of peace that enables him to continue his prophetic ministry. Thus, once again we are told about a person who in entrusting to God his sufferings finds the strength and courage to go on in the divine service. The prophet is in no way encouraged to believe that the suffering he is experiencing will decrease, but then he is assured that the Lord is with him. Such appears to be the experience of this one who "offered up prayers and supplications, with loud cries and tears" (Heb 5:7) and thereby found courage, strength, and peace. Robert Davidson in his *The Courage to Doubt* in speaking of what he refers to as the "Vocational Crisis" of Jeremiah has a helpful illustration of what is portrayed as his experience.

> Bishop Berggrav of Oslo, one of the leaders of the Norwegian church struggle against the Nazi-occupying forces, wrote to an English friend: "during such periods as that of 1942, half of your soul was in a hell of anxieties, doubt and fear; the other half of your soul is in heaven, carried on the wings of the faith which God bestows on you." This corresponds to Jeremiah's experience. He was caught somewhere between heaven and hell in that struggle for faith which cannot eliminate the darkness, yet discerns in the darkness a flickering light which the darkness is never able completely to extinguish.[31]

Thus it was that in the midst of all, yet perhaps only at certain moments, the affirmation of faith could be made, "Sing to the Lord; / Praise the Lord! / For he has delivered the life of the needy / From the hands of evildoers" (Jer 20:13).

All this may indicate the finding of a strategy to deal with the reality of suffering, but it cannot be called a theodicy. It does indeed point up, once again, the inadequacy of the "deserved calamity" theodicy, but it does not present its own theological explanation.

---

31. Davidson, *The Courage to Doubt*, 138. Davidson's quotation came from *Manchester Guardian Weekly*, February 12, 1959.

Psalmic Interlude 2

"Do not fret because of the wicked" (Psalm 37)

The issue in this psalm concerns the apparent prosperity of wicked people, and the threat therein of a feeling of envy on the part of those who put their trust in God—and who by implication are not doing nearly so well in the prosperity stakes. Three times the point is made: "Do not fret because of the wicked" (v. 1); "do not fret over those who prosper in their way" (v. 7); "Do not fret—it leads only to evil" (v. 8). It may be that the verb here, in the form that it is found in the Hebrew, should be understood as expressing a stronger emotion than "fret," rather "fly into a passion,"[1] or "be resentful."[2]

Let us take note of two points about this psalm. First, that it is arranged in an acrostic form—that is, it is composed with (generally) each pair of verses beginning with a succeeding letter of the Hebrew alphabet. Second, and more important, it is generally agreed that it should be regarded as a wisdom psalm, which is to say that it displays a certain kinship with the Old Testament wisdom literature, in particular as that is found in the books of Proverbs, Job, and Ecclesiastes. These books, says Katharine Dell, "represent the teaching of the wise men of ancient Israel: their maxims distilled from the experiences of many generations, their advice to the young seeking to understand and grow in maturity,

---

1. So Freedman and Lundbom, "ḥārâ," 172.

2. Thus Eaton, *Psalms*, 162, 165, translates the opening words of the psalm, "Do not be resentful at the evildoers," and saying about them, "The opening counsel is against a bitter rage, a hot resentment arising when unscrupulous villains seem to fare better than oneself."

their example tales and warnings."[3] While different scholars argue for different lists of what they think should be included in the wisdom psalms category, most would agree to the inclusion of Ps 37—and also the two psalms that will be studied in the Psalmic Interludes that follow in this work, namely Pss 49 and 73.[4] These psalms ask questions as to the apparent justice of God, and in particular ways they pose questions as to how it can be that wicked people seem to prosper while the righteous have to endure suffering.

What, then, we may ask is the psalmist of Ps 37 able to contribute to this debate,[5] and what reassurance and comfort is he able to offer to those who may be tempted "to fret" or "to be resentful"—even if they are perhaps not quite going as far as "to fly into a passion"? The psalmist has four things to say.

1. In vv. 1–11 the psalmist stresses the importance of trusting in God, advising against "fretting" (vv. 1, 7, and 8). Rather, let the believer trust in the Lord (vv. 3, 5), delight in the Lord (v. 4), commit their way to him (v. 5), remaining quiet before him and waiting patiently (v. 7). Such attitudes, the psalmist avers, will yield good fruits such as receiving "the desires of your heart" (v. 4), making "your vindication shine like the light," and revealing "the justice of your cause like the noonday" (v. 6). And there is, further, this: "so you will live in the land and enjoy security" (v. 3). It would seem that what is intended is that there is a real sense of satisfaction and security to be experienced by a person who lives in the Lord's Promised Land under his divine guidance and protection. By extension of the thought we may understand it as speaking of the blessings that are available for the godly person who lives in any land on the earth, for "the earth is the Lord's and all that is in it" (Ps 24:1). There are similar thoughts expressed in vv. 3, 9, and 11. In comparison how insecure and ephemeral are the lives of the wicked (see vv. 9–10).

---

3. Dell, "Get Wisdom, Get Insight," 1.

4. For introduction to the wisdom psalms see Day, *Psalms*, 54–56; Dell, "Get Wisdom, Get Insight," 64–76.

5. For Ps 37 and theodicy questions see Lindström, "Theodicy in the Psalms," 296–97; Brueggemann, "Psalm 37."

2. The wicked and their future make up the main subject in vv. 12–20, where it is stressed that the Lord will not allow their wicked ways to prevail (vv. 13–15), for their apparent strength is not as great as they imagine or may appear to others (vv. 16–17). Better surely is the lot of the humble, righteous person (vv. 14–15). And anyway, their malicious plans may well rebound on themselves and bring them grief (v. 15)! How contrastingly placed, as regards their care in the hands of God, are those who are righteous and those who are wicked (vv. 18–20).

3. In vv. 21–31 the psalmist returns to the theme of the blessings of God for the righteous, the psalmist here speaking out of his experience of life:

> I have been young, and now am old,
>> yet I have not seen the righteous forsaken
>> or their children begging bread.
>
> (Ps 37:25)

And,

> The law of their God is in their hearts;
>> their steps do not slip.
>
> (Ps 37:31)

4. Finally in vv. 32–40 the contrasting futures of the wicked and the righteous are set out, as, for example, in v. 34:

> Wait for the Lord, and keep to his way,
> and he will exalt you to inherit the land;
> you will look on the destruction of the wicked.

This means that the psalmist can end his composition with the confident assertion about the salvation of the righteous:

> The salvation of the righteous is from the Lord;
> he is their refuge in the time of trouble.
> The Lord helps them and rescues them;
> he rescues them from the wicked, and saves them,
> because they take refuge in him.
>
> (Ps 37:39–40)

It may be felt, and not unreasonably, that no very great steps have been made in this psalm as regards explaining the mystery and theological problem of the sufferings of the righteous. Further, the psalmist here still appears to believe in rewards for the righteous and ultimate downfall for the wicked, yet while there may be an element of truth in this approach, as we have seen, it is certainly not an adequate explanation for all experiences of suffering.[6] Would the prophet Jeremiah have been convinced and satisfied? That is unlikely and, as we shall come to see, the man named Job of the book of Job was certainly not convinced nor satisfied by this approach. That is, this psalmist does not come up with any radically new insights into these matters. Nevertheless, it is as if he has accepted that there does indeed remain a problem for his people with the traditional ways of answering questions concerning the sufferings of righteous people and, although he may not be able to offer an alternative solution, he has at least opened up the subject for some consideration and he does have some advice to offer for the benefit of those who are suffering. The psalmist of Ps 37 *has* moved beyond that silence which appears to have been all that the Deuteronomistic Historian could offer when he spoke of the death in battle of the young and good King Josiah of Judah (2 Kgs 23:28–30).[7]

Nevertheless this psalm does give some small practical guidance to help people deal with the obvious disparities in life between the fortunes of the righteous and the wicked, this guidance hinging around the notion of time. While in the short term the wicked may seem to have the better part, when viewed in longer and larger perspective the real blessings and abiding satisfactions in life are revealed by living in relationship with the Lord. Such a life is seen and understood here as being the way appointed and willed by God for his people. It is the meek that will inherit, or possess, the land, as is stressed in this psalm in verse after verse (vv. 3, 9, 11, 18, 22, 29, 34)—and as has been affirmed also for Christians in the Sermon on the Mount (Matt 5:5). Luther made reference to Ps 37 as presenting "A garment for the godly, with the inscription, 'Here is the patience of the saints,'"[8] which—serendipitously—prepares us for what follows, namely the issue of suffering as that is handled in the prophecy of Habakkuk and in the story of Joseph, in both of which there is emphasized patience, the taking of the long view.

---

6. Davidson, *The Courage to Doubt*, 26, says "The realism of Psalm 37 must be severely qualified. The psalmist is aware that life does not quite follow the religious script he has been handed; but instead of being prepared to rewrite the script he decides merely to add a few explanatory footnotes."

7. See above, 18–20.

8. Quoted by Kirkpatrick, *Psalms I–XLV*, 187.

4

Watching and Waiting

Habakkuk and Joseph

All too often there is in the human experience of suffering the associated experience of having to wait for some sort of resolution to the problem, a necessary time lapse in which to find some sense in what a person, or a group, even a nation, might be going through. Here, again, is needed "the patience of the saints" that, as we have seen, Luther spoke of in regard to Ps 37.[1]

Both the prophecy of Habakkuk and also the story of Joseph (Gen 37–50), although coming from different parts of the Old Testament (the former from the Prophets and the latter from Torah/Pentateuch), though different in their contents and styles, are yet united in that they are both touching, in one way or another, upon issues of suffering. As far as Habakkuk is concerned, it would be widely agreed that here is a composition intended to set forth a theological problem concerning the sufferings of a group of people. In contrast the story of Joseph is not specifically devoted to the matter of suffering and yet it touches on this theme a number of times as it progresses towards its resolution, for it tells of suffering set loose through family favoritism, in family violence and guilt, all being played out against the backdrop of the greater tragedies of famine and starvation. Yet in the fullness of time there is

---

1. See above, 61.

resolution and even a beneficial outcome of these various experiences of suffering. What both the book of Habakkuk and the story of Joseph have in common is what might be called the extended pause between the times of most intense sufferings and some sort of peaceful resolution and understanding of the suffering that had earlier been experienced. These works will now be considered in turn.

The Prophecy of Habakkuk

Part of the historical setting of the Old Testament books of the prophets is generally the overshadowing presence of other nations, sometimes those smaller and more local ones to the people of Israel—nations such as Syria, Edom and others—but also, and much more seriously, those larger, greater and more powerful nations, in turn Assyria, Babylonia, Egypt, Persia, and Greece. At times such nations are portrayed as representing a considerable threat to Israel; at other times one of them can be spoken of as enabling Israel to progress; at other times—in a most religiously positive way—of coming to worship the Lord God of Israel; and at others of being in the nature of an uncomfortable and threatening-large foreign nation on the doorstep. Sometimes the talk of such nations occurs in short passages, at other times the material has been gathered into larger collections which scholars have labeled, "Oracles Against the Nations."

Not infrequently in the Hebrew Bible the foreign nations feature in parts that are concerned with the issues of theodicy, where questions are being asked as to why various apparently negative and difficult things are happening to Israelite people. More often than not the nations feature in the prophets' thoughts concerning theodicy in so far as such and such a nation is being used by the Lord to effect his judgment upon his people for their sins. Thus when the question is asked as to how and why it is that the people of God find themselves under attack, even though they may suppose themselves to be under the guiding, protecting and sustaining hand of God, the answer may be given that it is because of their sins. Thus does Isaiah account for the warlike antics of the Assyrians (Isa 10:5–11), and so also both Jeremiah and Ezekiel for the advances of the Babylonians upon Judah and Jerusalem (for example, Jer 4:11–18; Ezek 17:1–21). Thus indeed there is a good deal in the books of the prophets about the issue of theodicy.[2]

---

2. See Crenshaw, "Theodicy in the Book of the Twelve."

The prophet Habakkuk, however, somewhat breaking ranks with his prophetic predecessors in this regard, proclaims himself as having a problem in accepting this particular understanding of the warlike incursions of a foreign nation acting as the agent of divine judgment upon the people of Israel. The foreign nation spoken of in Habakkuk is Assyria, the Assyrians being called here "Chaldeans,"[3] but these people who are in the process of effecting divine judgment are in fact bringing upon the people of Judah and Jerusalem greater evils and sufferings than those that had given rise to their having been called to this task! Thus Habakkuk has, or at least Habakkuk is portrayed as having, an ongoing problem with the issue of the justice of God, going at least some way towards questioning that common Old Testament explanation of evil and suffering as being due to human sinfulness. The book of Habakkuk is thus made up of something in the nature of a dialogue between the prophet and his God, which in its most basic form may be said to fall into three parts, thus:

1. The Dialogue between Habakkuk and the Lord (1:1—2:5)
2. A series of woe oracles (2:6–20)
3. The prayer of Habakkuk (3:1–19)

There are four players, characters—four personae—in this book, and in order to make it clear what is being said by whom, and to whom, the contents of it may be set out in the following way, fleshing out the above somewhat skeleton arrangement. Thus:

Title of the book	1:1
The prophet's first prayer to the Lord	1:2–4
The Lord's first response—to Habakkuk	1:5–11
The prophet's second prayer to the Lord	1:12–17
The prophet waits for the Lord's response	2:1
The Lord's second response, comprising,	2:2–20

---

3. The usage of this name "Chaldeans" for the Assyrians is also to be found in Isaiah (seven times), Jeremiah (forty times), Ezekiel (four times), Daniel (twelve times). We should take note of the fact that "Chaldeans" is a slightly slippery title, being used in the Old Testament for a number of Mesopotamian people. Just who were the intended "Chaldeans" in Habakkuk will depend on when we date the book. In the context of this particular study we can leave this matter on one side, as our concern is more with the theological approach in this Old Testament book than with historical matters. However, on "Chaldeans" in Habakkuk see, e.g., Roberts, *Nahum, Habakkuk, Zephaniah*, 95–96; Andersen, *Habakkuk*, 145–48.

His word to Habakkuk (2:2–5)
His word to the Chaldeans (2:6–20)
The prophet's third prayer to the Lord, comprising, 3:1–19a
Title and Rubric (3:1)
Vision (3:2–15)
The prophet waits prayerfully (3:16)
The prophet's confident hope (3:17–19a)
Rubric   3:19b

Each part of this prophecy, which displays the signs of having been carefully composed, calls for comment.[4]

The Title (1:1) is "The oracle that the prophet Habakkuk saw." The word here translated "oracle" (*maśśā'*) is rendered elsewhere "burden," and may in the first place refer to any particular burden that a person may have to carry, such as the "burden" under which a donkey lies (Exod 23:5) or what is not to be borne on the Sabbath (Jer 17:21, 27). A more specialized usage of the word is to do with prophetical "oracles" where it is more often than not in connection with foreign nations, frequently in passages where disaster is to take place.[5] What is the significance of the usage of "oracle" in Hab 1:1? It can be argued that what is to follow concerns a foreign nation (the Chaldeans, 1:5–17) and that there is the threat of disaster coming upon it (2:6–20). Could this mean that the prophet's theodicy question might be resolved, at least to some extent?[6]

In Hab 1:2–4 we have the first prayer of Habakkuk to the Lord, this being an agonized crying out to God that the prophet is having to look out onto "violence" (vv. 2, 3), "wrongdoing" (v. 3), and "destruction" (v. 3). The result of this violence, wrongdoing and destruction is the "strife and contention" (v. 3) that the prophet witnesses. Meanwhile, the

---

4. These comments are only those needed and apposite in the context of this particular study. The short prophecy of Habakkuk has generated a very large body of literature, from which the following may be mentioned: Roberts, *Nahum, Habakkuk, Zephaniah*; Andersen, *Habakkuk*; Smith, *Micah-Malachi*; Achtemeier, *Nahum-Malachi*.

5. Thus: Isa 13:1; 14:28; 15:1; 17:1; 19:1; 21:1, 11, 13; 22:1, 25; 23:1; 30:6; Nah1:1; Zech 9:1(?); 12:1(?); Mal 1:1(?).

6. The other element in Hab 1:1 that has drawn forth much discussion has been "the prophet," but we hardly have the evidence to argue either for or against the view that Habakkuk (of whom we hear nothing else in the Old Testament, and the references in Bel and the Dragon 14:3, 34, 35, 37, 39 and 2 Esdras 1:40 are hardly germane) was an official functionary as a prophet, perhaps even a "cultic prophet."

Lord appears not to be listening to the prophet's entreaties and to be deploying masterly inactivity (v. 2).

We may well ask who is it that is causing all this commotion? Is it coming from the Judean community, or is it rather coming from an external source? If the latter, are the Chaldeans, about whom we shall soon hear, the culprits? All the language of v. 4 seems to suggest that we should understand the troubles, this commotion, as being internal matters of Judean corruption and the breakdown of social life—such would seem to be clear from the talk about "law," "justice," and "judgment comes forth perverted." And who is it who suffers here, is it the people of Judah and Jerusalem in general? or is it perhaps Habakkuk himself, which the first personal pronouns in vv. 2–3 might suggest—"I cry for help," "make me see wrongdoing," "destruction and violence are before me"? Is it not something of both of these—of Habakkuk crying out to God in distress both at what he himself sees, and maybe suffers, and also about what some of his people are suffering so grievously? Surely, it is for both personal and vicarious reasons that the prophet cries out to God in the language of the prayers of laments, "why?" and "how long?"[7]

Thus we come to Hab 1:5–11, the Lord's first response, which certainly reads as if it is presenting Yahweh's response to the cries of his prophet, in particular to what I have referred to as "The prophet's first prayer to the Lord" (Hab 1:2–4). It conveys the startling news that the Lord is doing something; that he is not inactive in the situation of suffering that Habakkuk has cried out about. Yet it is a strange work indeed:

> Look at the nations, and see!
>   Be astonished! Be astounded!
> For a work is being done in your days
>   that you would not believe if you were told.
> (Hab 1:5)

The passage goes on to speak of the Lord rousing the Chaldeans, "that fierce and impetuous nation" (v. 6), who "all come for violence . . . Then they sweep on like the wind . . . their own might is their god!" (vv. 9, 11). This appears to be saying that the activity of the Lord that is about to take place will have a real strangeness about it, almost, perhaps one may say, a sense of incomprehensibility about it. And that at one level is no doubt an understanding of the ways of God that does need

7. See above 31–32.

to be taken with some seriousness in a study of what the Hebrew Bible has to say about God's government of the world and the fact of suffering that certain individuals and communities have to endure. At another level we are reminded of the words of Isa 28:21,

> For the Lord will rise up as on Mount Perazim,
> he will rage as in the valley of Gibeon
> to do his deed—strange is his deed!—
> and to work his work—alien is his work!

This comes as the climax of a section (or it may be later comment) about the judgment of the Lord upon Jerusalem, which will involve what is described as an "overwhelming scourge" passing through all and everything, not excluding those who are sure of their own wisdom and security (Isa 28:15, 18), and about his laying in Zion a foundation stone which will indeed be "a sure foundation: 'One who trusts will not panic'" (Isa 28:14–22, see v. 16). That is, the way to the future city of Zion will involve violence and suffering in the short term for the enduring of which the only appropriate attitude must be what is portrayed as having been inscribed on the new foundation stone of the whole building, "One who trusts will not panic" (v. 16). Thus it would appear that the word of the Lord to Habakkuk is of a divine intervention in the world of a similarly destructive kind, in this case to be effected by the Chaldeans.

The terrible nature of this divine judgment draws forth from Habakkuk what we may call his second prayer to the Lord (Hab 1:12–17), a prayer no calmer than the previous one (1:2–4), but another agonized outpouring from the Lord's prophet concerning what he is having to witness in the world with his people suffering grievously. It is another prayer of the lament genre, which, after some opening doxological expressions, makes the point that an unnamed one has been appointed for judgment—presumably the Chaldean spoken of in vv. 5–11—but just observe what havoc this agent of judgment is wreaking in the land, all being carried out with religious-like fervor complete with the making of sacrifice and offering to his fishing tackle, no less (v. 16)! Thus Habakkuk addresses God:

> Your eyes are too pure to behold evil,
> and you cannot look on wrongdoing;
> why do you look on the treacherous,
> and are silent when the wicked swallow
> those more righteous than they?

> You have made people like the fish of the sea,
> like crawling things that have no ruler.
> The enemy brings all of them up with a hook;
> he drags them out with his net,
> he gathers them in his seine,
> so he rejoices and exults.
> Therefore he sacrifices to his net
> and makes offerings to his seine;
> for by them his portion is lavish,
> and his food is rich.
> Is he then to keep on emptying his net,
> and destroying nations without mercy?
> (Hab 1:13–17)

Thus is that theodicy questioned which would account for the warmongering of foreign nations on the Israelite soil by understanding them as the human agents whereby God effects his judgment on his sinful people. But Habakkuk protests that surely the barbarity that the Chaldean manifests in this activity of judgment is totally out of proportion to the original sin that occasioned their call! How can the Lord tolerate this state of affairs? On this issue the prophet urgently and firmly addresses himself to the Lord, asking "why do you look on the treacherous, and are silent when the wicked swallow those more righteous than they?" (v. 13b). This in the first place is surely protest about such goings-on in the world that the prophet finds himself witnessing, but it is also, in the second place, protest about that theological explanation of such happenings as divine judgment on human sinfulness and worldly evil.

What now does the prophet do? He waits, and perhaps that is all that he can do. He needs to have some acceptable explanation for what he sees is going on around him in the life of his people, sinful though they may be. But he is ready to wait for any divine response to his urgent questioning. Thus we read,

> I will stand at my watchpost,
> and station myself on the rampart;
> I will keep watch to see what he will say to me,
> and what he will answer concerning my complaint.
> (Hab 2:1)

The imagery employed here is that of a person on watch duty, and while we do not need to understand this literally, yet the matter of "seeing" presumably does have some significance both here and in what follows. The expression "I will keep watch to see what he will say to me" may appear strange in its mixing of the verbs "see" and "say," but others of the prophets are spoken about as "seeing" the "word" (of the Lord)—thus, Isa 2:1; Amos 1:1; Mic 1:1; and also Hab 1:1. In particular Habakkuk is anxious for some answers from the Lord concerning his "complaint," that is, all that complaint in 1:2–4 and 1:12–17.

The Lord's (second) response (2:2–20) is given in two parts, both of which directly concern the prophet and his people. The first part (2:2–5) sets out the attitude and inner qualities that should be embraced by the people of God, and is addressed to the prophet. The second part (2:6–20) concerns the Chaldeans, warning them of their dreadful fate. We consider each of these in turn, though because of problems of translation and interpretation we shall have to give some extended discussion to the first. The Lord's word to Habakkuk (2:2–5) may be rendered as follows, and it will be observed that there are some changes here to what we find in NRSV.

> 2 Then the Lord answered me and said:
> Write the vision;
> make it plain on tablets,
> so he may run who reads it.
> 3 For there is still a vision for the appointed time;
> it speaks of the end, and does not lie.
> If it seems to tarry, wait for it;
> it will surely come, it will not delay.
> 4 Look at the proud!
> Their spirit is not right in them,
> but the righteous shall live by their (lit. "his") faithfulness.
> 5 Moreover, wealth is treacherous;
> the arrogant do not endure.
> They open their throats wide as Sheol;
> like Death they never have enough.
> They gather all nations for themselves,
> and collect all peoples as their own.
>
> (Hab 2:2–5)

Things are beginning to look hopeful: there *is* to be a vision, that is the prophet, as a prophet, is to be granted some insight into the things of

God,[8] and this revelation is to be made clear and plain. That is, presumably, it is not esoteric information but it is intended to be for general consumption. Further, this vision is to be preserved on tablets—the same word being used here as is employed in Exod 31:18 and Deut 9:9 to indicate the "tablets" upon which were inscribed the commandments that Moses brought down from the mountain. The vision to be given to Habakkuk could, then, be either brief or not so brief.[9]

What about the last line of v. 2, where it will be observed that the translation above deviates from that of NRSV? This is translated in NRSV "so that a runner may read it" and REB "so that it may be read at a glance." Now the Hebrew is indeed capable of being construed in this way, but more likely is the translation "so that [lit.] 'the reading one' [participle] may run," "run" being understood either as physical running or else in the sense of running in the way of life that God intended. Thus my translation above, which was also found in the earlier RSV translation.[10]

Once again in v. 3 the matter of waiting is emphasized, each of the four lines here stressing that patience and perseverance must be maintained. Among the contributions of the book of Habakkuk to the theodicy issue, the aspect of patient and expectant waiting has its place, the warning that caution should be exercised in coming to hasty, ill-considered judgments about God's ways in the world.

It could well be that we come to the heart of the matter in v. 4: what we have in this verse may-be makes up the vision spoken of in v. 2 that Habakkuk was to write clearly upon tablets. We cannot be sure about this, and it is certainly arguable that the "vision" comprises 2:4–5 plus 2:6–20. Fortunately it is not necessary to come to a decision about this: clearly if the "vision" comprises the larger of these options, even so the heart of the matter may be said to be expressed in 2:4.

---

8. The word for "vision" (*hāzôn*) is related to the word translated "seer" (*hōzeh*), one of the Hebrew Bible's words for "prophet." This appears to be one of the tasks to which the Israelite prophet was called, that is, to "see" into things and thus be enabled to come before people with a "revelatory word." Thus, Isa 1:1, "The vision [same word as in Hab 2:4] which Isaiah . . . saw concerning . . ."

9. It is widely felt that originally the Ten Commandments were most likely brief statements.

10. So also, e.g., Andersen, *Habakkuk*, 198, 204–5; Roberts, *Nahum, Habakkuk, Zephaniah*, 105, 108–10; Gowan, "Habakkuk," 602. On this and other translational and exegetical matters see Thompson, "Prayer, Oracle and Theophany," esp. 38.

Habakkuk 2:4 contrasts two different ways of life, two different approaches of individuals in the world. In the first place there is the one who is "proud."[11] In the case of this proud person, their spirit (*nepeš*, soul, life, heart, mind) is not right, upright within them. In contrast and in the second place is the righteous one, the one who will live by their (lit. "his") faithfulness.[12] This difficult verse sets in contrast those proud ones who have a most ephemeral, temporal, and tenuous hold on life and those who have a real grasp on things, who indeed will live by, and also in, their faithfulness to God.

Verse 5 makes it clear—if clarity is really needed—that the gains of the proud are ill gotten gains having no abiding worth. Moreover this wealth[13] is treacherous, presumably because not only is its pleasure transitory but also it is strangely and dangerously beguiling. Let those who feel they are having little of what life in the world has to offer take heart, and let them appreciate that there are better ways of life than those epitomized by the greedy conquests and insatiable desires of the Chaldeans!

In Hab 2:6–20 we have the second part of the divine response to Habakkuk's second complaint, the part concerning the Chaldeans. Fortunately it is rather more straightforward to deal with than what precedes. It is the word the prophet addresses to the Chaldean, and is portrayed as being an uncomfortable message, for it comprises a series of "woes" (translated in NRSV as 'Alas') concerning his fate. Each of these "woes" begins with the Hebrew *hôy* ("Woe!, Alas"), and it is generally thought that in the Old Testament such "woes" were something akin to

---

11. The Hebrew word here (*ʿupplāh*) is perhaps the most difficult word in the book of Habakkuk to understand and translate, and a wide range of proposals and possibilities have been offered. *ʿupplāh* would appear to come from the verb *ʿpl* (swell), and to be a third person feminine singular *puʿal* form, "she/it was puffed up" which does not seem quite right, but in a general way is understandable. In view of the difficulties with other possibilities and the lack of agreement, I accept it as it is but translate it (as does NRSV but compare REB's "the reckless") "the proud."

12. "Faithfulness" is the more likely translation than "faith," though of course the latter is how Paul uses the word in his quotation of Hab 2:4 in Rom 4:9. Note that NRSV accepts "faith" here, but perhaps REB with its somewhat free rendering, "while the righteous will live by being faithful," is rather more true to the spirit of the text.

13. It is widely agreed that the Hebrew word found here, *yayin*, "wine," should with a small emendation be read as *hôn*, "wealth." So NRSV.

an announcement of sentence of death, one that bore the uncomfortable message that those being addressed were already as good as dead.

It is not stated unequivocally who is the intended recipient of these "woes," but it does seem clear that it is the Chaldean who is at the heart of this message of "Woe." It seems clear that the one who should beware is the Chaldean, as most of the "woes" correspond to crimes perpetuated by the Chaldean and spoken of earlier in the prophecy. Thus the first "woe" (2:6–8) concerns plundering, a matter spoken of in 1:6 as being an activity engaged in by the Chaldean. The second (2:9–11) is about evil gains intended to make their home secure, with which we may compare 1:6. The third (2:12–14) concerns building a city through injustice, an issue articulated in 1:7 with its "their justice and dignity proceed from themselves"; the fourth (2:15–17) is about the crime of getting people drunk so as to take advantage of them; the fifth (2:19)[14] concerns consulting idols, with which we may compare 1:11 "their own might is their god!" This may be set out thus:

Subject	Crime Noted	Woe Stated
1. Plundering	1:6	2:6–8
2. Evil gains	1:6	2:9–11
3. Building a city through injustice	1:7	2:12–14
4. Causing drunkenness	–	2:15–17
5. Consulting idols	1:11	2:19

All this is to say that what we have in Hab 2:6–19 looks very much like an outright condemnation of the Chaldeans and what they have been doing among the people of Judah and Jerusalem. These have already been apostrophized in 2:4 as being proud, and in particular, "Their spirit is not right in them."

There is yet more to come, and Hab 2:20 comprises a solemn word of preparation for this future event. Thus,

> But the Lord is in his holy temple;
> let all the earth keep silence before him!

---

14. Verse 18 does not fit in with this arrangement of a series of "woes" and is generally thought to have been added, presumably to give added force to the theme of the following one, namely trusting in idols.

What follows is in ch. 3 of the prophecy. It is what I have called the prophet's third prayer to the Lord (see Hab 3:1), and is expressed in psalmic form. This composition invites a number of observations.

1. Much of Hab 3 is in the style of a biblical psalm, its title announcing it as a prayer (*tĕpillāh*), a usage found elsewhere in psalm titles in Pss 17, 86, 90, 102, and 142. It also bears the expression "according to Shigionoth," also found only in the title of Ps 7. The concluding expressions in v. 19 are to be found commonly among the biblical psalms—"To the leader/choirmaster" (?) in 55 of them, "with stringed instruments" in Pss 4, 6, 54, 55, 61, 67, 76 and also in Isa 38:20.

2. This chapter is very different from everything else in the book of Habakkuk, and it has been well noted that in the commentary on Habakkuk found at Qumran the chapter is missing. However, in the text of this book found at the neighboring Murabbaʿat this chapter *is* present, as it is also in the Greek scroll found at Qumran in 1952,[15] which clearly seems to indicate that the Qumran community knew of our three-chapter book of Habakkuk. However, if we take out the psalmic superscription in Hab 3:1, and also for good measure the concluding formula in 3:19b, then 3:2–19a follows on naturally from 2:20, and the "awe" on the part of the prophet spoken about in 2:20 is more than adequately set forth and emphasized in 3:2–15.

3. In actual content, however, Hab 3:2–15 is hardly typical of the biblical psalms, the only exception being Ps 107:23–32, where the great powers of the deep seas are overcome by the even greater powers of the Lord, in that case the purpose being for the saving of the lives of the sailors. In Hab 3:2–15 the great display of divine power is both to effect judgment on the Chaldeans, and also for the salvation of those people who were besieged by the (Chaldean) tyrant. Thus,

> You came forth to save your people,
> to save your anointed.
> You crushed the head of the wicked house,
> laying it bare from foundation to roof.
> (Hab 3:13)

15. For these and further details, see Roberts, *Nahum, Habakkuk, Zephaniah*, 148.

4. Yet there is a certain commonality between the psalm of Hab 3 and the biblical psalms of lament, with their oft-occurring change of mood most frequently making its appearance towards the end of the psalm.[16] Whereas the earlier part of the psalms of lament, both individual and corporate, are characteristically taken up with the troubles being experienced, the change of mood registers a spirit of praise and thanksgiving that the trouble appears to be over and that now the pray-er has moved into much more peaceful times. With Hab 3 we do not have the lamenting, complaining aspect, but in its place we do have the talk of the mighty appearance of the Lord, with its culminating words,

> I hear, and I tremble within;
> my lips quiver at the sound.
> Rottenness enters into my bones,
> and my steps tremble beneath me.
> I wait quietly for the day of calamity
> to come upon the people who attack us.
> (Hab 3:16)

Yet straight-way comes an expression of great confidence for the present and the future, expressed through the imagery of even greater suffering and deprivation.

> Though the fig tree does not blossom,
> and no fruit is on the vines;
> though the produce of the olive fails,
> and the fields yield no food;
> though the flock is cut off from the fold,
> and there is no herd in the stalls,
> yet I will rejoice in the Lord;
> I will exult in the God of my salvation.
> God, the Lord, is my strength;
> he makes my feet like the feet of a deer,
> and makes me tread upon the heights.
> (Hab 3:17–19a)

Thus does the book of Habakkuk end on a note of quiet and hopeful confidence in God, and with a real sense of hope and confidence for those negative, difficult, suffering-filled situations in life that may in the future be experienced.

---

16. See above, 31–34.

5. There is, however, another way in which we may think of Hab 3, another parallel that in Old Testament terms we may apply to it, and that is in relation to the two extensive speeches of the Lord in the book of Job. After all the various people in the book of Job have spoken and given expression to either their beliefs about, or else their experiences of, suffering, then—as if in response to what becomes Job's increasingly urgent importuning that he wishes to speak directly to God—there are two mighty speeches by God (Job 38:1—40:2; 40:6—41:34), both of these being announced as the Lord answering Job "out of the whirlwind" (Job 38:1; 40:6). Now the word "whirlwind" (sĕʿārāh) does not appear in Hab 3, though it certainly makes its appearance in Ps 107:25 and 29, a part of a psalm we have already taken note of above, yet the portrayal of the mighty, all-powerful and all-knowing Lord set forth in these speeches of Job does display similarities with what is said of him in Hab 3. The points being made in the two Job speeches and the Habakkuk psalm are rather different—in the former it is about God's greatness and otherness that cannot be grasped by mere human beings; in the latter it is about the Lord's power to bring total defeat upon the enemy. Nevertheless, in both the Job and the Habakkuk settings the issue is to do with the sufferings being experienced on earth and human perceptions of the divine rule on earth and God's care for his people.

The psalm of Habakkuk does not easily yield up its secrets to the reader,[17] but perhaps sufficient has been said already in chs. 1–2 of the prophecy before the reader comes to ch. 3. The agonized questioning directed to God that come from the prophet burdened with his sinful people's suffering receives answer in the divine word given to him: the true and authentic way of life is in living in faithfulness to God. This is the way in which life is to be lived, in which it is to be "run" (2:2). Thus,

> Look at the proud!
> Their spirit is not right in them,
> but the righteous shall live by their faithfulness.
> (Hab 2:4)

17. Nothing has been said here about the great textual problems the exegete encounters in Hab 3, which even in the relatively modest commentary of J. J. M. Roberts on the triad of prophets Nahum, Habakkuk, and Zephaniah amounts to no fewer than ninety-eight comments!

Further, the prophet has been warned that he must be prepared to wait for the fulfilling of these things, and that in his patient waiting he must not fail to go on trusting in God (2:3). At the same time he has been assured of the forthcoming doom of the oppressive enemy (2:6–19). Perhaps then, Hab 3 is intended to confirm this message and to speak about the power of the Lord in the face of human barbarity and cruelty, to speak about the fate of the oppressor, and to express the sense of peace and confidence that a devout and faithful person will come to.[18] This is the response set forth in the prophecy of Habakkuk to the issue of "why this suffering?" It cannot be called a "theodicy," but it is what we might call a religious strategy to be embraced in a time of suffering and the witnessing of the sufferings of others.

The Story of Joseph

Fortunately, the story of Joseph is rather easier to understand and interpret than is the book of Habakkuk. While Habakkuk is a brief prophetic book of just three chapters, but has, as we have seen, within its short compass many textual and interpretational problems, in contrast the story of Joseph is of considerable length, yet the prose of its story-style approach is straightforward both to follow and to understand.

The story of Joseph runs from Gen 37 to 50 (with Gen 38 and some parts of Gen 48–50 apparently being interpolations) and is in marked contrast to what has gone before in the stories of the Patriarchs—Abraham, Isaac, and Jacob—where the writing is episodic and the stories are brief.[19]

The Joseph story is a connected account that begins with the time when Joseph, his brothers, and their father Jacob were resident together in the land of Canaan, and it ends with them all reunited after many

---

18. As far as Hab 3 is concerned perhaps all that we can say is that here is a composition in the style of psalms, though with a rather different message from most of the biblical psalms, that either Habakkuk—or an editor?—had "to hand," or else composed himself. As I argued some years ago, Habakkuk was indeed something of an eclectic, ready to borrow from here and there! See Thompson, "Prayer, Oracle and Theophany," 45–50.

19. For literature on the Joseph story see, amongst others, von Rad, *Genesis*, 342–434; Houtman, "Theodicy in the Pentateuch," esp. 167; Westermann, *Genesis 37–50*; Coats, *From Canaan to Egypt*; Soggin, "Notes on the Joseph Story"; Amos, *The Book of Genesis*, 230–83; Wenham, *Genesis 16–50*, 343–93.

vicissitudes and various comings and goings in Egypt, with Joseph in a position of great responsibility there, and well able to provide food in days of famine for his family. Thus, not only are the descendants of Abraham in Egypt, from which in a future historical moment they will be liberated and delivered through what will be portrayed as mighty divine acts, but they have been enabled to survive a time of famine and thus can the purposes of God go on. For in Gen 12:1–3 Abraham was appointed as the new person through whom God would continue his work and purposes in the world, but with dreadful famine stalking the land of Canaan in the days of his grandson Jacob, those divine purposes looked imperiled indeed. The Joseph story tells how those purposes went on.

Genesis 37 records how Jacob and his family were settled in the land of Canaan, and it puts particular emphasis on the fact that Jacob (here sometimes called Israel) "loved Joseph more than any other of his children, because he was the son of his old age; and he had made him a long robe with sleeves." (Gen 37:3). Not altogether unpredictably, Joseph's brothers "hated him [Joseph], and could not speak peaceably to him" (37:4). Now add to what is portrayed here as being a potentially combustible situation the further fact that Joseph had dreams of his future grandeur and importance, and even more that he would insist on relaying the details of these to his brothers (37:5–9). Thus we are not totally taken aback when we read of the plottings of the brothers against Joseph (37:18–22), of their stripping him of his long robe with sleeves, throwing him into a pit (37:23–24), and selling him to a group of passing traders, either Ishmaelites (37:25–27) or Midianites (37:28, 36), who took Joseph to Egypt (37:28).

In Canaan, back at the family home, Joseph's father, Jacob, was overcome with grief at the loss of his son, the presentation of Joseph's bloodied coat having suggested to him that he had been consumed by a wild animal (37:29–36). Meanwhile, in Egypt Joseph had been sold to an officer of the Pharaoh, one Potiphar whom Joseph served well (39:1–6a) and by whom he was trusted. That is, until Joseph was falsely accused of a crime and thrown into prison (39:6b–23). Here Joseph came into contact with particular servants of the Pharaoh, and demonstrated his skills in understanding dreams (40:1–23), and eventually had the opportunity to interpret two troubling dreams of Pharaoh himself. Joseph was able to interpret these as concerning forthcoming and severe famine in Egypt, the upshot of which was that Joseph was appointed by

Pharaoh to be responsible for food and provisions for the people, to grow, harvest, and preserve food in the years of abundant harvests, and oversee their distribution in the later years of famine (41:1–57).

Thus it was that in their own search for food in what is portrayed as a general time of famine the brothers of Joseph came to stand before Joseph asking for food, which they received from him. Nevertheless, by a ruse owing to Joseph the brothers had to return to Egypt and stand before him the second time, and on this occasion their brother, who at the first meeting had recognized them, declared to them who he was (43:1—45:3). Thus come the words at the climax of the story of Joseph and his brothers, "Then Joseph said to his brothers, 'Come closer to me.' And they came closer. He said, 'I am your brother, Joseph, whom you sold into Egypt. And now do not be distressed, or angry with yourselves, because you sold me here; for God sent me before you to preserve life'" (Gen 45:4–5). And a few verses later: "So it was not you who sent me here, but God; he has made me a father to Pharaoh, and Lord of all his house and ruler over all the land of Egypt" (Gen 45:8). Yet again, this time at the end of the whole story of Joseph, the point is made, as if to make sure that it has been fully understood, Joseph being portrayed as saying, "Even though you intended to do harm to me, God intended it for good, in order to preserve a numerous people, as he is doing today" (Gen 50:20).

Now, to be sure, there is no element of protest to God for any, either real or apparent, injustices in the world that people are suffering, and there is hardly a hint of any crying out to God in agony and demanding answers to the questions "why?" and "how long?" the troublesome situation may prevail. In fact, this whole story is told in what appears to be the calmest way possible, although any sensitive reading of it will make the reader conscious of a series of tribulations through which the various characters in the story must be passing. There is the father Jacob/Israel who in his old age must be bereaved of his youngest and favorite son—and who, we are told, does indeed experience the depths of grief, refusing to be comforted, "No, I shall go down to Sheol to my son, mourning" (Gen 37:35). There is the burden of sinfulness that the brothers of Joseph presumably must have experienced for their dastardly deed in seeking to rid themselves of their (somewhat obnoxious) young brother who would insist on trumpeting to them the details of his dreams of future grandeur and importance.

There are, further, all the various sufferings that Joseph himself is portrayed as going through. In fact, Joseph is portrayed as having a life made up of a series of ups and downs, it is a somewhat seesaw existence he experiences, going from being his father's favorite in special clothing, to being put into a pit and sold to travelling merchants; from having a trusted place and responsibility in a well-to-do household to languishing in prison; and only thus to eventual status and responsibility again, but this time much greater responsibility than before. And hanging over the whole story is the great issue of how the purposes of God will go on when famine stalks the land of Canaan, and those in whose lives so much has been entrusted being imperiled by the possibility of starvation.

All this is to say that the suffering and theodicy issues are here embedded as parts of the very fabric of this finely narrated story. Yet although the talk of the sufferings may be somewhat muted, without them there would hardly be a worthwhile story of Joseph. Further, through the mouth of Joseph a serious theodicy is presented, one that insists that it is perhaps only in the long term that sense can be made of a person's life, and even that some sense, and even purpose, can be seen in the less-than-good deeds of other people. There is, however, within this story no attempt at explaining how God could have done these things, bringing out of them his own good purposes.[20] The human beings involved are portrayed "warts and all," and live their less-than-perfect lives, being subject to human foibles and failings. Yet through all these typical human attitudes and actions, in the mysterious purposes of God evil does not have the last word, but good comes out of it; suffering there is indeed, but before the end there is purpose to be perceived; the sense that what is understood as ongoing (in the days of the narrator?) is owing in no small measure to the mysterious workings of the Lord through both the good and the bad in human thoughts and deeds.[21] As Joseph says, "Even though you intended to do

---

20. Calvin, *Genesis*, 378, says of those who in the story of Joseph act perversely, "But God works wonderfully through their means, in order that, from their impurity, he may bring forth his perfect righteousness. This method of acting is secret, and far above our understanding."

21. Houtman, "Theodicy in the Pentateuch," 167, says of Joseph, "He himself . . . taking a retrospective view of what happened to him, appears to be in the position to discover sense in it. In his opinion his suffering had a very important function. Speaking to his brothers he reveals the meaning of his vicissitudes (Gen. 45:5b, 7, 8a; 50:20)."

harm to me, God intended it for good, in order to preserve a numerous people, as he is doing today" (Gen 50:20). Yet, as with the prophet Habakkuk, that is an insight that can only come as a result of having time to watch and wait.

Psalmic Interlude 3

"Mortals cannot abide in their pomp" (Psalm 49)

With this psalm we seem to be hearing only one side of a conversation or discussion but, fortunately, it is the replies that we are given. Thus, here are no expostulations about "why?" it is that the wealthy prosper, and "how long?" they are likely to go on being in that state, but it does seem clear from what we have before us in this psalm that that is the particular issue troubling the psalmist. The great concern here is about the perceived iniquity of the psalmist's persecutors (v. 5), "those who trust in their wealth / and boast of the abundance of their riches" (v. 6), those for whom "the wealth of their houses increases" (v. 16).[1]

This appears to be the issue, the "riddle" (v. 4) that is agitating this psalmist. Verses 1–4 provide the introduction to the psalm in which the psalmist calls upon his audience, which is no less than all the inhabitants of the world (v. 1), and, surely significantly, "both low and high, / rich and poor together" (v. 2). Presumably the psalmist intends to address both of these groups, to give some encouragement to the "low" and "poor," and some cautionary advice to the "high" and "rich." At any rate the psalmist believes that he has some words of wisdom to impart, some understanding from his "heart"—here perhaps being understood as the seat of wisdom.[2] Verse 4 gives the impression that the psalmist's response is in the nature of a "sung response," "I will solve my riddle

---

1. On this psalm as a contribution to the issue of theodicy see Lindström, "Theodicy in the Psalms," esp 297–99; Davidson, *The Courage to Doubt*, 31–32.

2. For the heart as the seat of wisdom in the Old Testament wisdom literature, see Fabry, "lēḇ," in *TDOT* 7: esp 422.

to the music of the harp." This response is in two interrelated parts, vv. 5–12 and 13–20.

The burden of verses 5–12 concerns the transitoriness of life (see especially v. 9), the uncomfortable fact that any wealth a person may gain in their lifetime has on their death to be left to others (v. 10). For the truth of the matter is that all must die—"fool and dolt perish together" (v. 10). Thus, as Mays observes, "Trust in riches as an immortality strategy doesn't work."[3] This part of the psalm is brought to a conclusion with the words, as rendered in NRSV "Mortals cannot abide in their pomp" (v. 12). The Hebrew literally is "Man [*ādām*, that is, "a man" or "a mortal"] cannot abide in [his/their] pomp [preciousness, honor]." And the second line is, as in NRSV's translation, "they are like the animals that perish." I understand this verse (12) as intended to summarize this first part of the psalmist's response to the riddle of the differing fortunes of those who are "low and poor" and "high and rich" in the life of the world, namely that there can be nothing "long term" about the earthly gains of wealth and fortune—much less permanence.

The burden of the second part of the psalmist's response in vv. 13–20 concerns the relationship the psalmist has with God, and associated with that the relationship the wealthy have with their possessions. Thus about those wealthy ones, it is said, "Such is the fate of the foolhardy, / the end of those who are pleased with their lot" (v. 13). Presumably these are the mortals that were spoken of in the preceding verse, "Mortals cannot abide in their pomp; / they are like the animals that perish" (v. 12).

Meanwhile, the psalmist's understanding of his relationship with God is expressed in v. 15,

> But God will ransom my soul [or "life"] from the power of Sheol,
> for he will receive [or "take"] me.
> (Ps 49.15)

What is the intended meaning of this verse? The Old Testament is notoriously quiet about what happens to human beings at death, apart from their going to Sheol.

More often than not the Old Testament speaks of Sheol as offering a person a restricted life, one for the most part cut off even from God

---

3. Mays, *Psalms*, 192.

(see Pss 18:5; 30:3; 31:17; 55:15; etc.). However, here in Ps 49:15 something more than this appears to be envisaged about a life beyond that shadowy one of Sheol. The psalmist speaks of God "receiving" him.

Now we should note that the Hebrew verb translated "receive," which is also used for "take" (*l-q-ḥ*), is also used in Gen 5:24, "Enoch walked with God; then he was no more because God took (*l-q-ḥ*) him." This may perhaps suggest that the psalmist was thinking of some sort of life beyond Sheol, though no details are given about what that life may be like. Nor in the Enoch story (Gen 5:24) are any details offered as to what form such a life might have been thought to take. If we consider other occurrences of such expressions of hope in the Hebrew Bible, then the question of the possible date of this psalm comes to the fore, a question that unfortunately is very difficult to answer. In fact, perhaps we have to say that we must wait for the time of the book of Daniel for a clear and confident expression of belief in the Old Testament of a life after death (Dan 12:1–3). However, until that time, that is around 165 BCE, we have a series of rather rudimentary expressions of belief concerning the possibility of life beyond death, expressions that are neither developed nor given in any detail. One of these is to be found here in Ps 49:15, but there are others, as we have already seen in Gen 5:24, but there also in Ps 73:24; 2 Kgs 2:9–11; Isa 53:10–12.[4]

After these somewhat enigmatic words of verse 15, the psalmist returns to his earlier point about the relationship between the wealthy and their wealth. Thus are the pious to take heart:

> Do not become afraid when some become rich,
> when the wealth of their houses increases.
> For when they die they will carry nothing away;
> their wealth will not go down after them.
> (Ps 49:16–17)

Thus we come to the final words of the psalm (v. 20) which, *pace* NRSV, are not identical with the words of v. 12, but which in the Hebrew read, "A mortal in his/her/their pomp does not *understand* [Hebrew *bîn*]," and though in both ancient and modern translations there has been a marked tendency to make verses 12 and 20 the same, and to see them as some sort of refrain, I prefer to read them as in the Hebrew, retaining

---

4. Anderson, *Psalms*, vol 1, 380, says of Ps 49:15, "it may be more appropriate to speak of a daring hope than of an established doctrine of afterlife." See also Johnston, *Shades of Sheol*, 202–4.

the differences.[5] Refrains they may be, but not identical ones, not an unknown phenomenon. However, I suggest that rather than using the word "refrain" of them, we perhaps do better to understand them primarily as summarizing expressions of the two points being made by the psalmist in his contribution to the riddle of the matter we have come to call theodicy. We may even go as far as saying that we admire the literary and theological variations on the overall theme of the psalm in these summarizing verses—they do share a common form, yet within that common form there is the change from "abiding" to "understanding" between vv. 12 and 20.

The particular point, surely, that the psalmist is seeking to make in v. 20 concerns the apparent lack of *understanding* on the part of those who put their trust in wealth and possessions. The Hebrew word (*bîn*) here translated "understanding" is characteristic of Old Testament wisdom-tradition vocabulary, indicating understanding, perception, comprehension, something that comes to a person through careful consideration. And what comes through such consideration here being spoken about is the *understanding* that far more precious, of far more worth than worldly possessions is the relationship between the pious person and God. While those who trust in their riches are "foolhardy" (NRSV, v. 13, "self-confidence, stupidity"), the one who trusts in God is the one who has the real *understanding* about life.

What, then, does this psalm contribute to the "riddle" of theodicy? What music (v. 4) does it bring to our ears? There is awareness here of imbalance in the world between those who possess and those who lack the world's wealth, but it also calls us to consider where in fact the real, the true, wealth for a person is to be found. The person whose whole trust is in earthly wealth will neither "abide" nor will they offer any evidence that they have come to real *understanding* of the ways of God with his people. On the other hand, those whose trust is in God *will* "abide," and *what* understanding of God and his ways they truly have!

---

5. Both LXX and Vulgate (Latin) translations made vv. 12 and 20 the same, the former "understand" and the latter "abide." So also in recent times both are rendered "abide" in NRSV, while REB has "short-lived" for both.

5

New Light on Suffering

Isaiah 53

> But he was wounded for our transgressions,
> crushed for our iniquities;
> upon him was the punishment that made us whole,
> and by his bruises we are healed.
> (Isa 53:5)

This is a particularly striking verse occurring within a whole passage that is remarkable for its radical and striking thoughts. That passage is Isa 52:13—53:12 (which henceforth for the sake of convenience I shall call Isa 53), being the fourth of four pieces in Isa 40–55—the others being 42:1-4; 49:1-6; 50:4-9—which have for many years been called "Servant Passages," or perhaps more frequently, "Servant Songs." First, something must be said about the biblical material in which these four passages are embedded.

The book of Isaiah is a long and complex work, its various parts appearing to come from different periods of Israelite history, though in the case of some of these parts just which periods of history they come from is not easy to decide.[1] However, with chapters 40–55 the situation is rather more straightforward than it is with other parts of the book,

---

1. For a basic guide to the arrangement, parts, theological thought, authorship, and possible historical settings see the three Old Testament Guides to the book of Isaiah: Barton, *Isaiah 1–39*; Whybray, *The Second Isaiah*; Emmerson, *Isaiah 56–66*.

for these chapters give all the appearances of coming from the closing years of the exile in Babylon when Cyrus the Persian had completed those spectacular conquests that culminated in his 539 BCE entry into Babylon in military triumph.[2]

The central theme of these joyous chapters, Isa 40–55 (whose anonymous author scholars often refer to as "Second Isaiah"), is that through the might and will of the Lord God of Israel, the people of Israel—at present languishing in exile in Babylon—will experience something of a new exodus of God's people whereby they are enabled to end their captivity and go back home, to Jerusalem. To be more specific, the message of Isa 40–55 (and indeed of the whole of the book of Isaiah) is focussed on God, God's people, and the earthly city of Jerusalem,[3] or as that is expressed by Goldingay and Payne concerning Isa 40–55, "your God," "my people," these being focussed on Jerusalem-Zion.[4]

Yet within these most joyful chapters—undoubtedly collectively the most joyful chapters within the whole of the Hebrew Bible—are set four passages that appear to cast a distinctly sombre light, making a real contrast in tone and mood with the surrounding material. These days it is generally thought that these four passages do come from the same author as that surrounding material,[5] and they have been the subject of enormous scholarly labors to understand them, fathom their meanings, and discern their significance both in the context of the development of the thought of the Hebrew Bible and also for what they contribute to the belief and worship of Jews and Christians.[6] A particular aspect of this whole study of these four passages concerns the matter of who the servant is; to be more precise, who it was that the author of these poems had in mind when he wrote them. Many have been the suggestions offered as to this identity, and it is a matter that I shall refer to later.

---

2. For these and other details see Whybray, *Isaiah 40–66*, 20–38; Whybray, *The Second Isaiah*, 8–12; Thompson, *Isaiah 40–66*, xix–xxviii.

3. See, e.g., Thompson, *Isaiah 40–66*, xix–xxv.

4. Goldingay and Payne, *Isaiah 40–55*, vol. 1, 49–54.

5. See North, *The Suffering Servant in Deutero-Isaiah*, 156–91; Whybray, *Isaiah 40–66*, 20–22.

6. See, for example, North, *The Suffering Servant in Deutero-Isaiah*; Bellinger and Farmer, *Jesus and the Suffering Servant*; Janowski and Stuhlmacher, *The Suffering Servant*.

The first two of these servant passages are to be found in Isa 42:1–4 and 49:1–6, and although commonly referred to as being about a suffering servant are not in fact about a servant who suffers. Rather here, the servant is the one who is given a new mission, a greater mission, in fact a more international mission than he has had hitherto. In Isa 42:1–4 the talk is of the servant whom the Lord upholds, in whom he delights, and upon whom he has put his spirit, bringing forth justice to the nations (42:1), a task that he will carry out in a spirit of gentleness and care (42:2–3), and discharge with faithfulness, until he has established "justice in the earth." Further, "the coastlands" wait for his teaching (42:4). Just what are the intended meanings of the "justice" and "coastlands" are not explained to us in the text.

The second passage (Isa 49:1–6), in which the speaker is the servant himself, makes it clear that an earlier work he had been given was that of being a servant to Israel, but now, in spite of his feelings that he had failed at this task, is being given a much greater and wider ministry, nothing less than of being a light to the nations, that the Lord's salvation may reach to the ends of the earth (49:6). According to verse 3, the servant, or at least *this* servant, was in fact, "Israel, in whom I [the Lord] will be glorified."[7]

However, when we come to the third of the servant passages (Isa 50:4–9), there is talk of the servant suffering. Here once again it is the servant who is the speaker, and here he records how he has had to contend with those who struck him, pulled out his beard, insulted and spat upon him (50:6). Yet with the Lord's help the servant knows that he will prevail, neither being disgraced nor put to shame (50:7–9). Rather, the way of life that the servant's enemies have chosen is one that has neither substance nor future, for, "All of them wear out like a garment; / the moth will eat them up" (Isa 50:9b).

The fourth of these so-called "servant passages" is Isa 52:13—53:12, and is on a totally different scale compared with the earlier three—in length of composition, in depth and (apparently) originality of thought. We need to consider it part by part, and for each of these parts I shall offer a translation, one that will in some places be different from that found in NRSV. The first part is Isa 52:13–15, and this appears to give

---

7. Although some have argued that the word "Israel" has been added to the text, there is in fact little textual warrant for doing so. See, e.g., Goldingay and Payne, *Isaiah 40–55*, vol. 2, 158–60.

us a summary of certain aspects of what will follow in the remainder of the composition.

> 13 See, my servant shall prosper;
> he shall be exalted and lifted up,
> and shall be very high.
>
> 14 Just as there were many who were astonished at you
> —so marred was his appearance, beyond human semblance,
> and his form beyond that of mortals—
>
> 15 so shall he startle many nations;
> kings shall shut their mouths because of him;
> for that which had not been told them they shall see,
> and that which they had not heard they shall contemplate.[8]
>
> (Isa 52:13–15)

This passage would appear to give something of an overview of what happened to the servant, the details of which will be fleshed out in the verses that follow. We are given the impression that it is intended to serve as an introduction, rather like an overture, to what is to come. If we abide by the decision spoken about in part 1 of footnote 8, that we retain the reading in 53:14—"Just as there were many who were astonished at *you* / so marred was *his* appearance . . ."—then we have to

---

8. There are just two textual matters to note here, and one comment to be made. 1. In the first line of v. 14 the Hebrew has "astonished at you" which is strange in view of what precedes and follows. It is therefore frequently emended to "at him" (as in NRSV), a reading that is found in the Syriac and the Targum. Thus Blenkinsopp, *Isaiah 40–55*, 346, accepts the emendation, saying, "it fits the context better." On the other hand, Goldingay and Payne, *Isaiah 40–55*, vol. 2, accept it as an example of a change of grammatical person found also in Isa 1:29–31 and 42:20. Further it should be noted that LXX, Vulgate, and the Isaiah scrolls found at Qumran all have "at you," so perhaps this is a case when we should accept the more difficult reading. Apart from that we can give some explanation for it as reflecting something of the observations of the unnamed "we" who comment in 53:4–6 on the significance of the death of the servant. 2. The Hebrew behind the verb "startle" in v.15 is not easy, but the earlier rendering "sprinkle" (as in a sacrificial rite, and which would indeed link up with what seems later spoken of in 53:10) poses grammatical problems (see the comments of Blenkinsopp, *Isaiah 40–55*, 346–47; Whybray, *Isaiah 40–66*, 170; but compare Goldingay and Payne, *Isaiah 40–55*, vol 2, 294–95). 3. The above two points alert us to the fact that with the whole passage, Isa 52:13—53:12, we are dealing with a very difficult text, one that is without parallel in the Old Testament, in which clearly the writer was seeking to speak of things that were both new and radical, perhaps searching for the appropriate words. As I said some years ago about this passage: "What on the surface seems reasonably straightforward turns out on closer examination to be nothing of the sort" (Thompson, *Isaiah 40–66*, 102).

say that there are apparently two speakers in this short passage. At the beginning (52:13) it is the Lord who speaks, but it would appear to be the "we," whose various assessments of what was happening to, and in, the servant we shall read about in what follows, who speak in v. 14. It could be that v. 15 is intended to be understood as coming from either the "we," or else from God. Something will be said about the "we" in the discussion of 53:1–3 that follows shortly.

Isaiah 52:13–15 begins, then, by speaking of the prosperity and exaltation of the servant (52:13), and then goes on to talk about the remarkable effect that his appearance had upon people, such that even kings were forced into silence, and whole nations were startled at him. Just why they had this sort of reaction we have perhaps to remain agnostic, for while the translation of v. 14 above—"so marred was his appearance"—is indeed one possible way of translating the Hebrew, it is not the only one. Thus, for example, while NRSV offers, "so marred was he beyond human semblance," the translation of REB (which also includes some rearrangement of the text) is, "and kings curl their lips in disgust."[9] What, however, is clearer is that the reader is being prepared for a surprise: "for that which had not been told them they shall see, / and that which they had not heard they shall contemplate" (Isa 52:15b).

The passage continues in Isa 53:1–3, verses which detail the sufferings of the servant, and which may be translated (with some variations from NRSV) as follows.

> 1 Who has believed what we have heard?
> And to whom has the arm of the Lord been revealed?
>
> 2 For he grew up before him like a young plant,
> and like a root out of dry ground;
> he had no form or majesty that we should look at him,
> nothing in his appearance that we should desire him.
>
> 3 He was despised and rejected by people;
> a man of suffering, knowing infirmity;
> and one from whom people hide their faces
> he was despised, and we held him of no account.
> (Isa 53:1–3)

In these verses the "we" constitute an un-named group of people, but their role in the passage is to recount a series of remarkable things that

---

9. See the discussion in Goldingay and Payne, *Isaiah 40–55*, vol. 2, 290–94.

they have observed about "him," presumably the servant, the one specifically spoken of in 52:13. The passage opens with two startling rhetorical questions: the first is, "Who has believed what we have heard," and is perhaps intended to be understood in the sense, "Whoever would have believed..." That is, the "we" appear to have some remarkably surprising information to pass on, news that is almost bound to be a real challenge to belief on the part of the hearers. The second question concerns a specific manifestation of the Lord's strength, "strength" here in the Hebrew being indicated through the word "arm." This divine strength is about to be demonstrated in a most unlikely human life, and we are surely being pointed to the "servant," the one spoken about in the words that follow, 53:2–3, the one who gave all the impressions of being utterly unworthy of any serious attention, one in short that the "we" "held... of no account" (v. 3). Verses 2–3 set out what must have been the first impressions that were gained by the speakers about this servant person, but it turns out to be an initial impression that in the light of further observations must be modified—in fact drastically, even radically modified.

The text continues with talk about healing and forgiveness, as follows, and here (once again, with some differences from NRSV) we seem to be approaching the heart of the matter that makes for such a remarkable theme within this passage.

> 4 Surely he has borne our infirmities,
> and carried our diseases;
> yet we considered him stricken,
> struck down by God and afflicted.
> 5 But he was wounded for our transgressions,
> crushed for our iniquities;
> upon him was the punishment that made us whole,
> and by his bruises we are healed.
> 6 All we like sheep have gone astray;
> we had each turned to our own way,
> and the Lord has laid on him
> the iniquity of us all.
> (Isa 53:4–6)

It may reasonably be assumed that the intended meaning of the second part of v. 4, "yet we considered him stricken, / struck down by God and afflicted," was along the lines that it looked as if this man had sinned, and that his being thus stricken was nothing less than the judgment of God upon him. Yet elsewhere in these few, but theologically heavy-laden, verses the speaker, speaking as if on behalf of the "we," expresses the belief that the sufferings the servant bore were in fact the sufferings that they, the "we," should *themselves* have borne for their own sins. What is being spoken about here is some sort of exchange taking place, the sins of others are being taken by one person so that the many may have "healing" and "wholeness" (v. 5b). The point is made a number of times through the grammatical usage of the personal pronouns, thus, "Surely *he* has borne *our* infirmities, / and carried *our* diseases" of v. 4a. And it continues in the following verses: "*he* was wounded for *our* transgressions, / crushed for *our* iniquities" in v. 5a, and so on in vv. 5b and 6.

The thought in these verses, of some sort of exchange of sins of a number of people with one human life, is not entirely new as far as the Old Testament is concerned, for it was *perhaps* something of this order that is being spoken about in Exod 32:32. The situation is that Moses has prayed for the forgiveness of God for his people who have sinned so grievously in their making of, and then bowing down to and worshipping, the golden calf in the desert at the foot of Mount Sinai (Exod 32:1–14). Now Moses prays again to God (Exod 32:31–32), at the end saying, "But now, if you will only forgive their sin—but if not blot me out of the book that you have written" (Exod 32:32).

Now this text is not entirely straightforward, and it may be that some word in the Hebrew is missing; further, it may be that the writer was having some trouble in trying to express what he wished to say.[10] However, it may be that what is being intended is that Moses is offering his own life in order that his people may have forgiveness; he is offering to give himself that his people may go free, one life that the many may live.[11]

Difficult though it may be to date the thought of Exod 32:32, it is not beyond the bounds of possibility that it did come from exilic times, that is from around the same period in which the Isa 53 text is to be

---

10. For details see Thompson, *I Have Heard Your Prayer*, 109–10.

11. An alternative understanding would be that Moses was being portrayed as saying that unless God will forgive the people their sin, then he, Moses, does not wish to have further part in the enterprise. That is, in that situation Moses was intending by his words "blot me out" the sense "count me out, forget about me, I no longer wish to be part of all this."

dated. In that sense, it may be that both texts were striving to express something about forgiveness of sins through the giving of a life of a human being. If this is so, then here there is something significantly new being said about a possible understanding of suffering. Perhaps we have had something of an insight into such a thought in the words that a writer put into the mouth of Joseph when he said to his brothers, "And now do not be distressed, or angry with yourselves, because you sold me here; for God sent me before you to preserve life" (Gen 45:5).[12]

Isaiah 53:7–9 speaks of the fate of the servant, and the following translation may be offered of these verses.

> 7 He was oppressed, and he was afflicted,
> yet he did not open his mouth;
> like a lamb that is led to slaughter,
> and like a ewe before its shearers is silent,
> so he did not open his mouth.
> 8 Without protection and without justice he was taken away,
> and who would have considered his future?
> For he was taken away from the land of the living,
> for the transgression of my people, for them he was stricken.
> 9 And they made his grave with the wicked,
> and with the rich in his death,
> although he had done no violence,
> and there was no deceit in his mouth.[13]
> (Isa 53:7–9)

The theme of the servant's suffering, now with added details, continues. The depths of the suffering is very much brought out in v. 7, while in v. 8 we learn something new, namely the lack of protection and justice for him, and there would appear to be the implicit suggestion that he should have had these, that is, what took place did indeed amount to "a perversion of justice." And why should this have happened? The point is made that this was not because the system and the correct way of doing things had failed, but it was because benefit would

---

12. See above, 78–80.

13. These are some of the most difficult verses to translate in this chapter of translational difficulties. The above translation, intended to be literal rather than elegant and so convey something of the feel of these verses, incorporates a number of changes to the received Hebrew text, these being too many to warrant each having a mention. For full details see the textual notes in, e.g., the works of Blenkinsopp, *Isaiah 40–55*; Goldingay and Payne, *Isaiah 40–55*, vol. 2; North, *The Second Isaiah*.

flow to others as a result of what was happening to this one person, the servant. As the matter is expressed in the text, "for the transgression of my people, for them he was stricken" (Isa 53:8).

Thus in earthly-life terms the servant's grave was with those who were accounted "wicked,"[14] even though it is affirmed that he had committed no violence, and nor had he spoken deceitfully. Thus this part of the passage ends on an entirely positive note as regards the servant's actions and words, as if perhaps intended to indicate that the ignominious death of the person was not due to his own sins and shortcomings. We continue then with the passage, which may be translated in the following way.

> 10 But the Lord desired to crush him with grief.
> When you make his life a guilt offering,
> he shall see his offspring, he will prolong his days;
> and the will of the Lord will prevail through him.
> 11 Out of his distress he will see light;
> he will be satisfied through his knowledge.
> The righteous one, my servant, shall make many righteous,
> and their iniquities he will bear.
> 12 Therefore I will allot him a share with the many,
> and he shall divide the spoil with the strong;
> since he poured out his life to death,
> and was counted with the transgressors;
> for he bore the sin of many,
> and interceded for the transgressors.
> (Isa 53:10–12)

Once again various changes in rendering will be observed between what is offered above and the standard Bible translations of these days. It is in these few verses that the greatest difficulties occur in the translation and

---

14. The further words here "and with the rich in his death" are problematic, for they appear to be suggesting that "the rich" are to be equated with "the wicked," which though it may sometimes be true we would tend to judge that it is not necessarily so. Payne and Goldingay (*Isaiah 40–55*, vol. 2, 316–17), citing examples, argue that for the Old Testament the equation of the two is less odd than it is for us, and thus retain the text as it stands. Others, finding this collocation of words difficult, make a small emendation to the Hebrew from "rich" to "evildoers" (so, e.g., Blenkinsopp, *Isaiah 40–55*, 348, note y), but it has to be said that there is minimal support for this in the Versions, LXX having "rich" (*plousious*), and similarly Vulgate (*divitem*). I thus retain the reading in the Hebrew, and accept that there may remain a problem of unresolved meaning and its interpretation.

interpretation of the text that we have before us.[15] No doubt a considerable reason for this difficulty lies in the fact that the writer is trying to say new things, but for us it is perhaps also because the passage is in poetry, and poetry tends to have an allusiveness rather than precision and specificity in what it is intended to express. This, of course, is a real part of the glory and genius of the medium of poetry, but at the same time it does cause us some difficulties in seeking to fathom what an author of long ago, living in very different conditions and settings from ours, was endeavoring to say. Further, there is a temptation for Christian readers to read into this passage understandings of vicarious suffering such as they believe that Jesus endured—which may be the understanding that the author of the passage had, but equally may not be so.

It seems clear that the talk in this whole passage is of the servant actually dying. This may appear to be laboring a straightforward matter, but there is a minority of scholars who have argued that this is not so, and that, on the contrary, the talk of "death" is intended to indicate a "death-*like*" situation, one in which the servant, we might say, was "as good as dead." In recent years this was argued by R. N. Whybray in two studies.[16] If the servant did not actually die, then that does have a considerable effect on the way that we interpret the passage. However, the whole thrust of words such as "cut off from the land of the living" (v. 8), "his grave with the wicked / and his tomb with the rich" (v. 9), "poured out himself to death" (v. 12) would all appear to be speaking about an *actual* death.[17]

Then second, this text would appear to be speaking about a purposeful death on the part of the individual who is the principal subject of this passage. In particular it appears intended to speak about vicarious suffering and death, that the one spoken of *himself* died that others may live. This is made particularly clear in 53:4–6, where in phrase after phrase the point is made that the servant in his death took upon

---

15. An example of this is in the second line of v. 10. The Hebrew seems to say that it was the Lord who made the servant an offering for sin, and so NRSV renders it, and so do I above. But the Hebrew is not straightforward, and so, e.g., REB has the servant offering himself.

16. Whybray, *Isaiah 40–66*; Whybray, *Thanksgiving for a Liberated Prophet*.

17. Crenshaw, *Defending God*, 145, says "the reference in v. 9 [is] to a grave and burial with the wicked. It therefore seems best . . . to understand the language about death literally."

himself the sins that others would in the normal course of events have been expected to bear, to live with. Instead, we are told, the Lord laid upon the servant "the iniquities of us all" (Isa 53:6). Perhaps we are to understand the "all" to represent the "we," those speakers whose words are recorded in this verse. That is to say, what is being spoken about here is an exchange of sins whereby those who are guilty may be forgiven. That is, one person takes upon himself the sins of others, in fact the sins of many—as it is expressed at the end of Isa 53:6 "of us all."[18]

What the prophet is attempting to speak about here does, I believe, receive some clarification from various words, expressions, concepts employed in the passage. It seeks through reference to three known practices, religious observances, ceremonies to speak of the forgiveness of sins.

1. Isaiah 53:6, with its words "and the Lord has laid on him / the iniquity of us all," would appear to be intended to bring to our minds the ritual of the scapegoat about which we read in Lev 16. In this ceremony the sins of the people were symbolically laid upon the head of a goat that was then sent away into the wilderness; that is, to a faraway place. Thus it was believed sins were forgiven—that is taken away, literally and physically.[19]

2. The language of the pre-exilic temple cult is clearly recalled in the talk in 53:10 about "guilt offering" (Hebrew ʾāšām). This word, which occurs some forty-eight times in the Hebrew Bible, makes its most frequent appearances (thirty-two times) in texts that come from the priestly tradition. Although we may not be entirely sure just what each sacrifice was for vis-à-vis another sacrifice, it seems clear that the ʾāšām sacrifice was believed to be effective in making atonement "for all cases of gross negligence,

---

18. I find the argument of Orlinsky, *Studies on the Second Part of the Book of Isaiah*, 51–59, both curious and unconvincing. He maintains that the talk in Isa 53 is not about vicarious suffering, speaking of such being a theological and scholarly fiction. He accuses scholars of just accepting various verses in the passage as indicating the thought of vicarious suffering, but he does nothing to explain what these verses are intended to indicate if it is not vicarious suffering.

19. The ritual of the scapegoat is of wide provenance. See, e.g., Frazer, *The Golden Bough*, 736–56, "Public Scapegoats." In the post-exilic period it was known about, being spoken of by Philo of Alexandria (see e.g., Hayward, *The Jewish Temple*, 137–38), and in the Mishnah, in *Yoma* (see Danby, *The Mishnah*, 162–72). See also Sanders, *Judaism*, 141–43.

and ultimately as a guilt-offering in difficult cases."[20] We learn something of the rite of this sacrifice through Lev 7:1–10, in particular that it is an offering of a slaughtered animal, and that it is most holy. But there is nothing in Lev 7:1–10 about the sacrificial offering being a *human* life.

3. Second Isaiah uses the illustration of intercession. This occurs in Isa 53:12: the servant "made intercession for the transgressors." In Old Testament thought not all forgiveness of sins is believed to be effected through either offerings or sacrifices, but frequently can be achieved through intercession. Solomon's prayer at the dedication of the temple in 1 Kgs 8 is at one level an extended list of situations where the people ask for God's forgiveness, yet somewhat surprisingly there is nothing here about offering sacrifices. Rather the talk is of praying to God in that place, or at least towards that place, and asking for forgiveness of the particular sin under review. Further examples are to be found in what we are told about Moses, how he prayed to God that his people might be forgiven their sins (Exod 32:11–13, 31–32; Deut 9:18–21), and further with the intercessions that Amos is portrayed as having made to God for his people in situations when divine judgment is upon them for their sins (Amos 7:1–6).[21]

Thus, I suggest, what we have in Isa 53 in this fourth passage about the "servant" is the servant portrayed as taking his people's sins upon himself, the writer using these three pictures to illustrate the new thoughts that he is introducing. He is seeking to say that through what the servant did, the end result was, or would be, of the same order as when the scapegoat—the priest having laid his hands upon its head—was sent off into the wilderness, as when an ʾāšām (guilt offering) sacrifice was made, as when one interceded for the sinners. Through these acts, these holy rites, God was being asked, implored, entreated to forgive his people their sins. That is, the sufferings spoken about in Isa 53 that the servant bore are not spoken about as being of either a futile or an incomprehensible nature, but were intended for the real purpose of seeking to bring about the divine forgiveness of sins. Here surely is the

---

20. D. Kellermann, article "ʾāšām," *TDOT*: 1, 429–37, see 434. See also Gaster, "Sacrifices and Offerings, OT," *IDB*: 4, 152.

21. For such intercessions see Thompson, *I Have Heard your Prayer*, 89–118.

Old Testament setting before us an example of what can only be called *purposeful* suffering. This is an entirely different approach to suffering from anything we have encountered hitherto in this study.

We should also take note of a further fact, namely that the servant as portrayed in this chapter was given by God a life after he had passed through death. The text is frustratingly short on details, but the thought of 53:10b and 11a would appear to indicate the concept of a life after death. Isa 53:10b has "he shall see his offspring, and shall prolong his days," while 11a reads, "Out of his anguish he shall see light."[22] It does appear that some sort of post-mortem existence is being spoken about here, but no details are given. It is nevertheless a point that the student of the Old Testament's approach to issues of human suffering should take note of. Here is something akin to those expressions found in Pss 49:15 and 73:23–24, expressions perhaps of an emerging belief that with God there is for a person the possibility of a relationship that can transcend death. Yet, to make the point yet again, as it is in Pss 49 and 73, so it is also in Isa 53, that no details of this future existence are given.[23]

However, there is a further aspect of Isa 53 that calls for notice in the context of this study. It is something that I am convinced is within this text and that comes out of the whole experience of the exile. It is that the whole tendency of this passage is of a religious life that is not surrounded by privilege and favor. Rather, it is that something radical has taken place in the mind of the prophet through all that he has experienced in his Babylonian captivity. He is seeking to say through his prophecy that he has come to new understandings of God. These are both new and radical understandings of God, for the prophet has done nothing less than discover the presence, the purposes, the plans of God while he has been away in a foreign and strange land. It is surely no coincidence that this prophet who can present pictures of a servant who suffers, can also—and first!—present us with two pictures of a servant who has a mission to a wider world, in fact nothing less than a vision of the call to establish justice in the earth, and in which the coastlands are envisaged as waiting for his teaching (Isa 42:4). Further, the earlier mission to Israel must now give way to the call to be "a light to the nations,"

---

22. The Hebrew has "life," but both the Isaiah scrolls from Qumran and also LXX have "light," and so this reading is widely accepted these days.

23. See North, *The Second Isaiah*, 243: "It must suffice that Isa. liii did . . . conceive of a man returning from the world of the dead."

for there is a call from the Lord that his "salvation may reach to the end of the earth" (Isa 49:6). Does this not read as if the prophet is saying that the "outsiders" must now have priority time?

I believe that the prophet here is speaking about the fact that henceforth the people of Israel must live without special privileges. In times past, in the days before the exile, they were able to enjoy the benefits and the privileges of self-rule, when they were ruled by their own kings, and when, further, certain other nations had politically, militarily, and maybe even religiously, to take notice of them. In those times they could surely believe that their God was the Lord of battles, that he had a particular care for his people, and in those times they could ask serious existential questions about why they were suffering some indignity or a certain set-back. Perhaps the Second Isaiah had theologically moved on from there, and had come to understand that he and his people must now find the presence of God for themselves in this situation of lack of privilege, both then and also in future days.

For though it may be observed that this is the prophet who can present his people with the thrilling message that they can go home to Jerusalem, that for this the desert will be transformed, and that in the fullness of time the at-present derelict and tumbledown city of Jerusalem will be rebuilt and made beautiful, yet I do not believe that this prophet was so politically naive as to believe that Cyrus the Persian would give them political carte blanche when they were settled back in their homeland. This prophet must have realized that he and his people were now a subject people, and further that subject people they would remain. They were now living in the days of greater and more extensive empires, those of far greater power and might, than had been known in days gone by. Thus this prophet could speak to his people about servanthood and suffering, and perhaps now be less concerned than others of his people had been to question why God's people had to endure times and experiences of suffering—especially of exile away from home.

Who then was the "he" of Isa 53, the one we are accustomed to call "the servant"? The search for the identity of the servant has certainly been long and tortuous, and most of the basic possibilities were set out by Christopher North in the middle of the last century.[24] It seems to me

---

24. North, *The Suffering Servant in Deutero-Isaiah*. See now, Blenkinsopp, *Isaiah 40–55*, 355–57.

that these four passages in the prophecies of the so-called Second Isaiah (Isa 42:1–4; 49:1–6; 50:4–9; 52:13—53:12) are intended to be four pictures of how it will be in future days that the life of the people of God will be lived out, and the work of God done on earth. That life may well be one that lacks earthly privileges, and that work will involve mission. Further, there will also be the experience of suffering on the part of the devotees of the Lord God of Israel.

Here then, as far as the Hebrew Bible is concerned, is a new approach to the theodicy questions. In fact, it might be said that those difficult questions raised by the experiences of the exile in Babylon—Why did such things happen for these chosen people of the God who was the creator of the whole earth? Where was their God of justice when Jerusalem was falling to the Babylonians?—would issue for the Second Isaiah in a theodicy which spoke of ongoing life for the people, both individually and corporately, but which also had within it the warnings of lack of privilege, and the call to live *among*, even maybe *under*, rather than *over*, the nations; that is, servanthood and suffering.

Psalmic Interlude 4

"I saw the prosperity of the wicked" (Psalm 73)

"Some things are best communicated by personal testimony," says James Crenshaw in his essay on this psalm "Standing Near the Flame: Psalm 73":[1] here indeed is presentation in the first person. The psalm begins by stating the general principle that says human suffering is due to human sinfulness, that the Lord is good to those who are upright and pure in heart. Not however in the experience of this psalmist.[2]

> Truly God is good to the upright,
> to those who are pure in heart.
> But as for me, my feet had almost stumbled;
> my steps had nearly slipped.
> For I was envious of the arrogant;
> I saw the prosperity of the wicked.
> (Ps 73:1–3)

Verses 4–9 flesh out the psalmist's complaint regarding what he has observed to be the good life that arrogant and apparently wicked people are able to enjoy. These people appear to suffer neither pain nor trouble, rather "their bodies are sound and sleek . . . they are not plagued like other people" (vv. 4–5). Thus they are proud and violent, full of conceit, they scoff and speak with malice, they threaten oppression. Verse 9 with

---

1. Crenshaw, *A Whirlpool of Torment*, 93–109, see 93.

2. On Ps 73, apart from the usual commentaries, see Crenshaw, *Defending God*, 154–56; Lindström, "Theodicy in the Psalms," 299–300; Kraus, *Theology of the Psalms*, 168–75; Westermann, *The Living Psalms*, 132–45.

its talk of the wicked setting their mouths against heaven, their tongues ranging over the earth, may best be understood by reference to Ugaritic texts. "It is possible," says Curtis, "that the wicked are being likened to a great monster, or perhaps to Mot, the god of death who, in the Ugaritic texts, may be described as having 'a lip to the earth, a lip to the heavens . . . a tongue to the stars.'"[3]

In vv. 10–14 are two reactions occasioned by this apparent power and prosperity, this arrogance and the oppressive presence of these wicked ones. The first is that of "people" in general, but it has to be admitted that the text of v. 10 is not easy to understand: its burden may be that because of their power and wealth the wicked find themselves honored, even perhaps, unfortunately, being regarded as models for others to emulate. Maybe, further, it is such reactions that then fuel the arrogance of the wicked, leading them into even more arrogant attitudes, so much so that they become arrogant even towards God (v. 11)! All this leads the psalmist to his rather plaintive cry,

> All in vain I have kept my heart clean
> and washed my hands in innocence.
> For all day long I have been plagued,
> I am punished every morning.
> (Ps 73:13–14)

The psalm records the psalmist seeking to deal with all this (and this is perhaps what v. 15 is saying) by drawing strength from the fellowship of believers, and from those traditional ways in which they are accustomed to think about such matters—namely by the notion of punishment for the wicked and rewards for the righteous. But then (v. 16) the problem was still with the psalmist, still there on his mind, and he finds himself unable to come to clarity of thought and understanding. That is, the psalmist has sought an intellectual answer to his problem, but has not succeeded.[4]

---

3. Curtis, *Psalms*, 152.

4. David Clines in his discussion about Job 3:1–26, in regard to that passage being in the style of the individual lament psalms with their characteristic question "why?," says, "The 'why?' question belongs to the psalmic language, where it never signifies a desire to discover a reason intellectually" (Clines, *Job 1–20*, 99). While Ps 73 may not literally be a "why?" psalm, it is nevertheless one in which questions about human life and trust in God, and about the Lord's ordering of human life, are being posed, and v. 16 does suggest that the psalmist *has* sought an intellectual answer to his questions

A remarkable turning point in this psalm comes with verse 17:

> Until I went into the sanctuary of God;
> then I perceived their end.
> (Ps 73.17)

We cannot know just which "sanctuary" is intended here.[5] The suggestion that the words "sanctuary of God" (*miqděšê-ʾēl*) be understood as "the sphere of God's holiness, the holy mysteries of God"[6] may seem somewhat forced, and yet the crucial thing here being pointed to is that light began to dawn for this psalmist as that person turned away from self and towards God. Whether it was through holy place or whether through contemplation of God, the feelings and outlook of the psalmist changed. This person saw, or at least began to see, things and people around him in a different way—perhaps even in a radically different way.

For the great insight that this psalmist came to through his twin experiences of observing the worldly wealth and successes of the wicked and arrogant ones around him, and his calling to mind the being of God, lay in coming to appreciate how profoundly greater was the latter than the former. Thus, in that moment, the psalmist understood what an ephemeral existence is lived by those who put their trust in riches, whose surety is in what they can do and gain; they live without firm foundations and are in a dream-like existence. Thus:

> . . . until I went into the sanctuary of God;
> then I perceived their end.
> Truly you set them in slippery places;
> you make them fall to ruin.
> How they are destroyed in a moment,
> swept away utterly by terrors!
> They are like a dream when one awakes;
> on awaking you despise their phantoms.
> (Ps 73:17–20)

In contrast how great are the resources that the psalmist has, for he comes to understand (or indeed, to understand once again) that in his

---

about the prosperity of the wicked. This approach has not helped him, such intellectual activity seeming to him "a wearisome task."

5. The options are set out by Tate, *Psalms 51–100*, 229, "the Solomonic temple, the ruined temple site after 587 BC, the post-exilic temple, or simply a family 'holy place.'"

6. So Buber, "The Heart Determines: Psalm 73," 113.

life he is, or he can be, with God continually, and that God holds his right hand, guiding him with his (God's) counsel (vv. 23–24a).

What are we to understand by the words of v. 24b, "and afterwards you will receive me to glory/with honor"? In the Hebrew that line has just three words, and there are difficulties with the interpretation of all three of them, as follows.

1. It is not clear whether "afterwards" (*ʾaḥar*) is intended to refer to a later stage of this life, or to a life after earthly life, that is to a post-mortem existence.
2. In the Hebrew of this verse the word *kābôd*, which can mean either "glory" or "honor," does not have a preposition, "to" or "with." Further, this word does not appear to be used elsewhere in the Hebrew Bible of heaven; that is, of a post-mortem existence of a human being.
3. The verb *l-q-ḥ* can mean "take" or "receive," and it is one that we have come across before.[7] It is used in Ps 49:15, to express a psalmist's belief that God will ransom his life/soul from the power of Sheol, and will "receive" him, and it is also used in the Hebrew Bible of Enoch of whom it is recorded that he did not "die" but rather was "taken" by God (Gen 5:24). This verb, then, does perhaps give at least some possible suggestion that the psalmist is thinking of a post-mortem existence.

Whether or not the psalmist here is seeking to speak of a life after death is hard to say. The evidence, one way or the other, is mixed and perhaps we have to accept that.[8] However, what the psalmist *has* certainly reached is the stage at which he can return to life in a spirit of confidence and hope in God, certainly with an adequacy of what he needs for the next stage of his life. To be sure, the remaining words of the psalm are ones of deep personal assurance, which some have described as "credo," but which equally can be regarded as "proclamation."[9]

> Whom have I in heaven but you?
> And there is nothing on earth that I desire other than you.

---

7. See above, 82–83.
8. See Johnston, *Shades of Sheol*, 204–6.
9. Thus Terrien, *The Elusive Presence*, 316, observes that this psalmist "began a song on the issue of theodicy and ended it as a credo on the eternal presence."

> My flesh and my heart may fail,
> but God is the strength of my heart and my portion forever.
> (Ps 73:25–26)

Whether or not this psalmist has gained any insight into a post-mortem existence in the presence of God we have to leave unresolved, but in the context of this work that is perhaps not too serious. What is clear is that the psalmist has come to a real accommodation with his problem of the worldly progress and prosperity of those wicked and arrogant ones he had perforce to observe. He proclaims for himself, and to all who will listen to him, realities that are greater by far than any apparent injustices on earth. These are the realities of his relationship with God.

> But for me it is good to be near God;
>   I have made the Lord God my refuge,
>   To tell of all your works.
> (Ps 73:28)

6

The Great Debate

The Book of Job

Where does one begin in talking about the Book of Job? What is there left to say about this supremely great work, apart from making the observation that one who essays to write on it has indeed stood "on the shoulders of giants"?[1] Thomas Carlyle (1795–1881) wrote in glowing terms of the book of Job.

> A Noble Book; all men's Book! It is our first, oldest statement of the never-ending Problem,—man's destiny, and God's ways with him here in this earth. And all in such free flowing outlines; grand in its sincerity, in its simplicity; in its epic melody, and repose of reconcilement. There is the seeing eye, the mildly understanding heart . . . Sublime sorrow, sublime reconciliation; oldest choral melody as of the heart of mankind;—so soft, and great; as the summer midnight, as the world with its seas and

---

1. This famous quotation is from Isaac Newton (1642–1712), "If I have seen further, it is by standing on the shoulders of giants", and quoted by Clines, *Job 1-20*, x. It had been written by Newton in a letter to Robert Hooke in 1675/6, but seems to have originated with Bernard of Chartres (died c.1130) who spoke of our being like dwarfs on the shoulders of giants, so that we can see more than they, and things at a greater distance, not by virtue of any sharpness of sight on our part, or any physical distinction, but because we are carried high and raised up by their giant size. Thus John of Salisbury, *Metalogicon*, ch. 4, and—it may be added—so it seems to one who presumes to bring some insights in yet another study of the book of Job.

stars! There is nothing written, I think, in the Bible or out of it, of equal literary merit.[2]

In an understanding spirit regarding Carlyle's 1905 usage of non-gender inclusive language, we can perhaps go along with the main themes of his encomium over the book of Job and, as a way into the book, consider his words "oldest statement" and "simplicity," both of which call for comment.

First then, what are we to say about the date of the book of Job? While Job, his family and friends are portrayed as living in a somewhat patriarchal setting, the work seems most likely to have come from a late period of Israelite history. The language and also some of the details of life mentioned suggest a late work.[3] Nevertheless, it needs no special pleading to say that the book is dealing with issues that are relevant and pertinent for any age, and that there is thus an "agelessness" about the work. For this reason I shall not pay any further attention to the date of the work.

Then Carlyle's "simplicity": While indeed there is a basic simplicity about the architecture of the book, insofar as a problem is stated, there is then a great debate about it. Eventually the Lord gives his divine word about the issues and the book ends with a now-calm Job—and indeed a greatly re-enriched Job. Even so there are some less-than-simple aspects to it. There are many difficulties with the Hebrew of the book, as a glance at the marginal notes in NRSV and REB make clear. There are many words in the book of Job that only occur in this book, many of these also making their once-for-all appearance in the Hebrew Bible. In a considerable number of cases we cannot be sure of their intended meanings.

Further, while the layout of the book may be straightforward, we are presented with difficulties at various stages. In the first place it is not easy to see how all of chapter 27 can come from Job, as in verses 7 onwards un-Joban statements are being presented, hardly consonant with what he has been saying earlier. Does 27:7–23 then make up the otherwise missing third speech of Zophar? It could also belong to Bildad's suspiciously short speech in 25:1–6; at any rate to judge by the tenor of its argument it would seem to come from one of the friends of Job rather than from Job.

---

2. Carlyle, "The Hero as Prophet," *On Heroes*, 49. I am indebted to Gordis, *Book of God and Man*, 3, for these words.

3. For further details see Crenshaw, "Job," 332.

Then second there is a question concerning the place in the book of Job of chapter 28, the passage about wisdom. This is in a different style of writing from the surrounding material, and it exudes a sense of calmness in the midst of somewhat frenetic debate. Yet in the context of the whole work it has something to say about true wisdom in the world, and thus it will be regarded in this present work as a part of the book of Job. In the third place, there are the extensive speeches of Elihu in chapters 32–37 which, from a literary point of view, could be taken out and the work be seen to continue where it left off. Thus some commentators do not take the Elihu speeches with much seriousness,[4] but that is not the approach in this work. After all, either sooner or later, they were added to the work and are now part of it. My understanding is that these speeches have their point to make, which I believe to be worthy of consideration.

The outline of the book of Job is as follows. The work opens in 1:1—2:13 with a Prologue in which the speaker is an individual who is generally the Narrator. This Prologue sets out the complete change in fortunes and lifestyle that the man Job experiences in a very short time. Job is portrayed as being devout and God-fearing, having good health and being blessed with a large family and many possessions. Yet suddenly all this changes, and Job loses just about everything, his health, most of his family, his possessions, and his livelihood. Thus it is that Job's three friends, Eliphaz, Bildad, and Zophar, come to sympathize with Job and after a lengthy time of silence they give to him the benefit of their thoughts as to the cause of Job's misfortunes, none of which Job can accept. Thus a very extensive dialogue takes place in which Job speaks, and then a friend responds, then Job and another friend, and so on until all have had their "say." That makes up what is called the First Cycle of speeches. Then the process begins again making the Second Cycle, and—as if for good measure—a Third Cycle follows. After that, in chapter 28 we have something different in the poem on Wisdom, after which Job makes his long, final speech (chs 29–31).

With chapter 32 a new person appears on the scene. This is Elihu, who announces himself as a young man, and who goes on to make four speeches giving expression to his views on the matter of Job's sufferings. Then we go from Elihu to the Lord, for in 38:1—40:2 the Lord appears

4. See, for example, Gibson, *Job*, 268–81, who relegates his comments on them to an appendix.

and speaks to Job. Job answers briefly but very humbly (40:3–5), and then the Lord launches into another lengthy speech (40:6—41:34), which Job answers, once more with brevity and great humility, in 42:1–6. The book comes to a calm end with an Epilogue (42:7-17) in which the narrator speaking in the name of the Lord roundly condemns the friends for their misguided counsel to Job, and who then goes on to recount the reinstatement of Job and his fortunes, and his new and even larger family.

All this may be set out in the following way.

The Prologue (1:1—2:13)—Narrator
The Debate (3:1—42:6)

    1. Job and his Friends,

        First Cycle of Speeches
        Job (3:1-26)
            Eliphaz (4:1—5:27)
        Job (6:1—7:21)
            Bildad (8:1-22)
        Job (9:1—10:22)
            Zophar (11:1-20)

        Second Cycle of Speeches
        Job (12:1—14:22)
            Eliphaz (15:1-35)
        Job (16:1—17:16)
            Bildad (18:1-21)
        Job (19:1—29)
            Zophar (20:1-29)

        Third Cycle of Speeches
        Job (21:1-34)
            Eliphaz (22:1-30)
        Job (23:1—24:25)
            Bildad (25:1-6)
        Job (26:1—27:6)*
            Zophar (27:7-23)*

    2. The Poem about God's Unfathomable Wisdom (28:1-28)

    3. Job's Final Speech (29:1—31:40)

4. The Contribution of Elihu
    Elihu (32:1—33:33)
    Elihu (34:1-37)
    Elihu (35:1-16)
    Elihu (36:1—37:24)
5. The Speeches of the Lord
    The Lord (38:1—40:2)
        Job (40:3-5)
    The Lord (40:6—41:34)
        Job (42:1-6)

The Epilogue (42.7-17)—Narrator

* The above arrangement of speeches represents a change to the biblical text, which has all of chapter 27 as a part of a speech by Job (and thus putting into Job's mouth thoughts characteristic of the friends), and lacks a third speech of Zophar.

The subject of the book of Job is clearly suffering; that is the reality confronting us on virtually every page of the book. Job is the one who suffers, for all manner of ills have come upon him, both suddenly and inexplicably. Why is Job suffering all these misfortunes? That is what the book is about. Further, Job is portrayed as believing that he is an innocent sufferer; he cannot believe that he has sinned to such an extent that he has brought all these sufferings upon himself.

Although suffering may be the subject of this Old Testament book, it has to be said that in spite of all that is said within it, *the book as a whole does not come up with any single solution to the problem of suffering*. That is, it is not able to come up with one all embracing theodicy. What, however, the book does do is to present a series of views and opinions as to why it is that Job suffers so greatly. I understand the book as intended to present us with this range of possible answers to the vexed question about why it is that a God-fearing and apparently devout man must endure such depths of suffering. Thus we are presented with various possible answers—and also some non-answers!—to questions about suffering that have been raised. So the reader/hearer of the book is enabled to consider all these possibilities, and then accept or reject as seems appropriate. In this way there are laid before us in the book of Job a series of theodicies—those in the Prologue and the Epilogue, in the great series of speeches uttered by Job and his three friends, Eliphaz,

Bildad, and Zophar, in the poem about God's unfathomable wisdom (ch. 28), in the speeches of Elihu, in the two great speeches of the Lord—and we are invited to "take and read."[5]

What also we have in the book of Job is talk about how a suffering and God-fearing person carries on in spite of their suffering, and how they continue to believe in God. Yet before the book ends the Lord will make his appearance to Job, and for the suffering man the encounter with God will change everything. Thus, in spite of Job's questions never being adequately answered, as far as he is concerned we do in the end read of a satisfied man, but satisfied through the encounter with God rather than with human talk and rational discourse on theological matters. We consider in turn each of these various parts of the book of Job, asking of each whether it offers a theodicy.

The Prologue (Job 1:1—2:13)

These thirty-five verses tell us of the great change of fortunes that came to Job and his wife. At the beginning we are told that Job "was blameless and upright, one who feared God and turned away from evil" (1:1). We read about the family and prosperity of Job, about his seven sons and three daughters (1:2), about his animals and servants, both alike possessed in such numbers "so that this man was the greatest of all the people of the east" (1:3). Further, as regards his religious observances Job, we are told, was punctilious (1:5).

Now we appear even within these five opening verses of the book of Job to be in the thought world of that Old Testament emphasis which avers that when people live just and devout lives then they will prosper and enjoy the good things of life. And conversely, those who are wicked and do not live in the fear (that is, "reverence") of the Lord will not enjoy the good of the land and are likely to have to endure suffering. Thus it was indeed for the Job and his family of the first five verses of the book that bears his name, for here they are portrayed as living righteously, devoutly—and thus enjoying the sweet savor of success.

But the book is about to go on and raise questions that will seriously challenge this particular explanation for the prosperity of some, and the sufferings of others, in the world. For all too soon—and this

---

5. On studying the book of Job as a "polyphonic text" see Newsom, *The Book of Job*.

while Job is portrayed as remaining a righteous and devout person—he will lose most of his share of the good things of life, his servants and his animals (1:13–17), and then his sons and his daughters (1:18–19). This is to say that in the Prologue to the book a serious blow is being struck at that most common of Old Testament explanations for the reality of human suffering, namely that suffering is due to human sinfulness while human prosperity comes as a direct result of godly and righteous living. For the fact is that the sufferings that here come so suddenly upon Job are in no way portrayed as being a "deserved calamity"![6]

Then, what are we to say about "the satan" who features in the Prologue, no fewer than fourteen times (1:6, 7 [twice], 8, 9, 12 [twice]; 2:1, 2 [twice], 3, 4, 6, 7)? In each of these occurrences the name comes with the definite article, "*the* satan," and this figure is portrayed as being, along with "the sons of God" (NRSV "heavenly beings"), part of the "divine council," such as we read about in 1 Kgs 22:19–22; Dan 7:9–14, and elsewhere in the Old Testament. That is, "the satan" here is portrayed as being part of the divine entourage and we need to bear in mind that the concept of "Satan" that we encounter in texts that come from later times—from the Intertestamental period and also in the New Testament, in for example Mark 1:13—is a being who is ranged against God and is a force for evil.[7]

The satan of Job 1–2 is portrayed as being used by God to "test" Job. In fact, the satan and the Lord have something of a wager as regards the righteousness of Job: does Job really serve the Lord for purely disinterested motives, or does he not rather serve God because he perceives that is how he will gain the most benefit (1:8–12; 2:1–7)? Thus are portrayed the great sufferings that come upon Job. Now if we take this task of the satan, and the conversation between the Lord and the satan literally, we have a problem, for in that case, as Whybray observes, "It cannot be said that Yahweh comes well out of the encounter."[8] Indeed, the conception of God here in this prologue is of a somewhat capricious God, one who

---

6. We may notice in passing that the first of these tragedies is due to human warlike activity, and so in modern terminology would be referred to as an evil act, while the second was due to a great wind, what would come to be known as a "natural disaster." Thus already we are being introduced to two different types of human suffering.

7. For Satan, and the changing understanding of him in the Scriptures see, e.g, Gibson, "Satan," in *EDB*, 1169–70.

8. Whybray, *Job*, 29.

will stoop to using his people on earth rather in the role of his pawns as he and one of his entourage are enabled to see which of them is right about the particular religious belief that Job holds. Does Job reverence the Lord expecting nothing in return (so God), or does he reverence the Lord in order that things in his life will go much better (so the satan)? Thus a trial by suffering is portrayed as being set up, or at least being allowed, by none other than the Lord.

This is hardly a worthy picture of God. Indeed, I suggest that it is not a mainstream Old Testament view of God, for we do not come across such a view being propounded elsewhere in the Hebrew Bible. This is an understanding of God which must appear to us to be much more in tune and accord with, for example, Greek traditional understandings of the gods and their various antics and strivings over their interrelationships one with another and with their peoples on earth. However, it might be said that here in the opening chapters of the book of Job we are presented with a solution to the question as to why it is that there is so much suffering, in particular innocent suffering, for the people of earth. It is, so it might be argued from a superficial reading of Job 1–2, for the reason quite simply that God and his divine council have arranged that there will be suffering for Job.

This I suggest must be resisted, in the first place for the reason that I have already presented, namely that this is an understanding of the relationship of God and his people with roots outside of the Hebrew Scriptures and traditions. In the second place, it is to be observed that this scene in heaven, with its conversations, and the associated wager, are not referred to again in the book of Job. As a part of that, the figure and personality of the satan in particular is not mentioned again in the book. That is, they are hardly integral parts of the argument of the book, and I do not think that they can seriously constitute an explanation and justification for certain of the sufferings of the people of earth. That is to say, we should not think of any theodicy being set forth here in the Prologue to the book—or at least if we do, then it is a theodicy that is to be rejected.

Rather, we do well to regard these two opening chapters of the book as being material that the author had, so to speak, to hand. Let us think of the content of these chapters in the terms in which frequently they have been described, as a "folk tale," a piece of material that was known by the author (and possibly by those for whom he was writing?)

and that it was used for the purpose of setting the scene for what is to follow.⁹

But what about immediate reactions to these matters? There are set forth in these chapters the reactions of both Job and his wife to this series of calamities, and also what some of the friends of Job did. First there is Job, and he is portrayed as reacting to the news of the disasters with remarkable calmness and patience—a reaction that included even the worship of the Lord. "Then Job arose, tore his robe, shaved his head, and fell on the ground and worshipped. He said, 'Naked I came from my mother's womb, and naked shall I return there; the Lord gave, and the Lord has taken away; blessed be the name of the Lord'" (Job 1:20–21). The narrator adds, "In all this Job did not sin or charge God with wrongdoing" (1:22). This is one reaction to the experience of suffering that a believer in God may have. It is hardly a reaction that is to be expected in the case of a person who has been so grievously affected by loss and deprivation in their life, but nevertheless it is portrayed as being Job's *first* reaction. However, as we shall come to see, it is by no means the final reaction of Job and, before we get far into the book, we shall find Job saying very different things, so much so that later it is as if a different Job is speaking. But for the present the Job of the Prologue is Job the silent and patient one. Even when Job became afflicted with "loathsome sores . . . from the sole of his foot to the crown of his head" (2:7), he still retained his patience—"He took a potsherd with which to scrape himself, and sat among the ashes" (2:8).

Then there is the reaction of Job's wife, who we are told said to her husband, "Do you still persist in your integrity? Curse God, and die" (2:9).¹⁰ This is a different reaction from that of Job, and is an entirely understandable one. In fact, in the course of time Job himself will move

---

9. Katharine Dell, *Shaking a Fist at God*, 21–22, making reference to the play *JB, A Play in Verse*, 1957 by A. MacLeish, says helpfully, "We can . . . see the whole prologue section as forming the 'outer play' within which the 'inner play' (the dialogue) takes place."

10. Both here at Job 2:9, and also earlier at 1:5, we read in, e.g., NRSV, "curse," whereas in both cases the Hebrew reads "bless" (*b-r-k*). In all probability the Hebrew had earlier read "curse," but because that was deemed to be unacceptable in address to the Lord was probably changed by a later hand to the polite and reverential "bless." We also may note at this point that while according to the Hebrew text the comment of Job's wife is brief, and nothing if not straight to the point, in the LXX it has been very considerably expanded. For a translation of the LXX of 2:9 see Clines, *Job 1–20*, 53.

closer to it. However the Job of chapter 2 is portrayed as being censorious to his wife for her comments and for voicing her existential reaction to these calamities with her "Curse God, and die." Job responds to his wife, "You speak as any foolish woman would speak. Shall we receive good at the hand of God, and not receive the bad?" (2.10). The words of Job seem harsh to us and our twenty-first-century sensibilities, but we should perhaps understand the word "foolish" (*nĕbālâ*, a word that we shall come across again in the book of Job) as meaning "impious," perhaps not anything more than indicating "speaking out of turn." For the sense of the words is that Job is critical of his wife not for actually *being* foolish but rather for speaking *like* a foolish person, maybe in the manner in which some class or group of foolish people would be expected to speak.[11] Meanwhile, the narrator tells us that in all this Job did not sin with his lips (2:10). What he was thinking is not stated, and may indeed have been a different matter, and perhaps we cannot be quite as confident as Calvin was when he said "that he [Job] did not imagine that God did anything which was not just and equitable."[12]

We are then introduced to three friends of Job, who, having heard of all the misfortunes that had befallen him, met together and came to console and comfort him (2:11–13). These were Eliphaz the Temanite, Bildad the Shuhite, and Zophar the Naamathite, and we shall hear a good deal more of them—and from them—before our study of the book of Job is finished. So appalled were these man at the Job they saw—even from a distance!—that they raised their voices, wept aloud, tore their robes and threw dust in the air upon their heads. In an expression of profound sympathy they sat with him on the ground for seven days and seven nights, "and no one spoke a word to him, for they saw that his suffering was very great" (2:13). However, at the conclusion of those seven days and nights these three friends would embark upon saying very much indeed to Job, and their words, along with those of Job before and after they each made their various utterances, make up a large part of the Debate (3:1—42:6) in the book of Job.

---

11. See Clines, *Job 1–20*, 53–54 for a discussion of what this group or class of people might possibly have been. About Job's wife see also Gibson, *Job*, 24–25, "A Note On Job's Wife."

12. Calvin, *Sermons from Job*, 29.

The Debate (Job 3:1—42:6)

The scene has now been set, and what follows is the expression of a range of views portrayed as being called forth by the sufferings of Job, but which are in reality a series of possible responses to the sufferings of devout people. In the case of some of these, in particular with the speeches of the three friends, Job makes a response to what has been offered by another person, but in other cases there is no response from Job. In this Debate, and this is the major and central part of the book, we have the contributions of Eliphaz, Bildad, and Zophar, of the unknown author of the chapter (28) about God's unfathomable wisdom, the advice of Elihu, and finally the Speeches of the Lord—to the second of which Job does respond, yet how differently from the ways he has responded to the speeches of the earthly ones! However, all this great debate is portrayed as being set in motion by the words of Job himself.

Job Speaks (3:1–26)

This is no longer Job with the apparently endless patience of the earlier chapters. Rather, following the seven days and seven nights of silence (2:13), "After this Job opened his mouth and cursed the day of his birth" (3:1). And we do need to hear what it is that Job has to say at this point, for not only does this provide the starting-point of what will be an extended conversation between Job and his three friends, but also because this is a remarkable passage. It is remarkable in the first place in that it is widely regarded as something of a literary masterpiece, but for our purposes perhaps more important it is a remarkable and open statement coming from the depths of Job's inner being, and addressed directly to the Lord. Cursing the day of his birth (3:1), Job says:

> Let the day perish on which I was born,
> and the night that said,
> "A man-child is conceived."
> Let that day be darkness!
> May God above not seek it,
> or light shine on it.
> (Job 3:3–4)

What Job says here sounds remarkably like one of the so-called Confessions of Jeremiah in which the prophet cries out to God about the grievous sufferings that his following of God has brought upon him (Jer 20:14–18).[13] It is highly likely that the book of Job is here taking up and using in a direct way the lament of the prophet about his lot in life, applying it to Job's troubles. This taking up of words found elsewhere in the Old Testament is found in other parts of Job. Here, with the use of the words from Jeremiah we have a quotation "in agreement." We shall later come across the employment of words from Ps 8 concerning the place of rare and remarkable privilege that God has given to the humans in the total world set-up, but in those cases the words of Ps 8 will be quoted in a sense of deep irony: what sort of privileged life is this when it involves such suffering, abuse and rejection (see Job 7:17–18)?[14]

In chapter 3 the passage continues with talk of light and darkness, and we are surely being invited to savor the language of light and darkness, of creation and death, of crying in joy and cursing in despair (3:4–10). In v. 11 Job reverts to the matter of his coming into the world, and laments that he ever was born—and here we have examples of the characteristic use of the "why?" in the Old Testament laments:[15] why did he not die at birth? (v. 11), why were there knees to receive him and breasts to feed him? (v. 12). If only he were dead and therefore at rest (vv. 13–19)—where the small and the great are, and the slaves are free from their masters (v. 19). Then some more laments, each prefaced with "why?" (vv. 20–23), until finally Job speaks of his sighing and groaning, and the fact that all he has feared and dreaded has come upon him (vv. 25–26). All this results in his present situation, which he sums up in the moving words,

> I am not at ease, nor am I quiet;
> I have no rest; but trouble comes.
> (Job 3:26)

Thus says Habel, "Job summarizes his plight. He can find none of the repose he had envisaged in the realm of the dead. Instead of a threefold exaltation on discovering his grave (v. 22), he endures a threefold absence of peace, rest, and quiet. One thing dominates his life—*rōgez*, 'turmoil' (cf. v. 17). His inner being is in chaos and his world in

---

13. See above, 49–55. As regards the lament tradition and the book of Job see Westermann, *The Structure of the Book of Job*.

14. On this see Mettinger, "Intertextuality."

15. See above, 31–34.

confusion."[16] Will his friends, who now break their seven day and night silence, be able to help him?

The Friends of Job Speak (4:1—27:23)

It might be thought that the friends of Job would have done well to stay silent, for from a pastoral point of view they apparently were doing fine when they sat with Job in silence. They were with him in his bereavement and loss, in his turmoil and confusion. From a pastoral point of view no doubt that was what was needed. But, of course, the book of Job is neither a treatise about, nor a record of, pastoral practice, but rather a theological discussion attempting to give some explanation for the fact of suffering in the world, and in particular in the life of a devout follower of the Lord. So inevitably we must hear what these friends of Job have to say.

What the friends—Eliphaz, Bildad, and Zophar—have to say takes up a large portion of the whole book of Job, and is presented in what has been called three cycles of speeches. In the first cycle (Job 3:1—11:20) after Job has spoken (3:1–26, the speech spoken of above) there is the response of Eliphaz (4:1—5:27), then Job speaks again (6:1—7:21) followed by Bildad (8:1–22), then once again Job (9:1—10:22) followed by Zophar (11:1–20). That is the so-called first cycle of speeches, and the second cycle, found in Job 12:1—20:29, follows very much the same format.

As has been observed, the third cycle presents certain problems. It begins all right with Job's speech (21:1–34) followed by Eliphaz (22:1–30), then Job again (23:1—24:25) followed by a very short speech by Bildad (25:1–6). However, according to the text Job continues with another lengthy speech in 26:1—27:23. The problem is twofold: first, there is no speech of Zophar; second, there is material attributed to Job in chapter 27, especially in vv. 7–23, that just does not sound like Job's talk, but which does exhibit the viewpoint of the friends. Along with others I therefore regard Job's third speech as running from 26:1 to 27:6, and the remainder of chapter 27 (vv. 7–23) as being the otherwise missing third speech of Zophar.[17]

---

16. Habel, *Job*, 112.

17. This is only one of a number of possible solutions to this conundrum. For a much more elaborate one, which also involves chs. 23–25, see Clines, *Job 21–37*, 572–677.

It is possible to handle all the speeches of the three friends together for the reason that not only are the three friends saying much the same thing, though each has his particular mien, but also because the thinking of them does not appear to advance as the debate continues, nor do they come up with any really new thoughts. By contrast, Job's thought moves on and, as the debate proceeds, he has new things to say. Thus we shall need a further section below on the views of Job in order to take into account his own developing thoughts and growing passion.

We consider, then, the first of the speeches of the friends, that of Eliphaz in 4:1—5:27. Very probably Whybray is correct when he says that Eliphaz "is clearly intended to be seen as the leader of the friends and their chief speaker; his speeches are longer and more wide-ranging than those of the others."[18] At any rate Eliphaz opens his speech with an expression of apparent humility, and the acknowledgement that Job is one who has fame as a man who has instructed and strengthened people, who has supported the stumbling, and made firm the feeble knees (4:2–4). But now, so it appears to Eliphaz, impatience and dismay have come over Job, so that Eliphaz questions what has happened to Job's fear of God and his integrity (4:5–6).

And with that Eliphaz launches into what will henceforth be the main theme not only of his own three speeches, but also of those of the other friends as well. He avers that in God's world there is justice, and that therefore innocent people will survive, but that wicked people cannot expect to receive the good things of life. This is a conventional theology found in various places in the Hebrew Bible, as we have already seen, in particular in the Deuteronomistic History, in the books of the prophets, in the book of Proverbs, and elsewhere.[19] Yet it has to be said that here Eliphaz makes a very full explanation of the theory, and with considerable poetic beauty and force. His basic thesis is set out in 4:7–9:

> Think now, who that was innocent ever perished?
> Or where were the upright cut off?
> As I have seen, those who plow iniquity
> and sow trouble reap the same.
> By the breath of God they perish,
> and by the blast of his anger they are consumed.
> (Job 4:7–9)

18. Whybray, *Job*, 41.
19. See above, 7–21.

And then, in a passage of considerable beauty (alas that its main point is so mundane!) in which he speaks of the revelation granted to him in vision in the night Eliphaz works up to ask the question, "Can any mortal be righteous before (the implied perfection of) the Lord?" Therefore, *ipso facto*, how can Job possibly protest his innocence?

> Can mortals be righteous before God?
> Can human beings be pure before their Maker?
> Even in his servants he puts no trust,
> and his angels he charges with error;
> how much more those who live in houses of clay,
> whose foundation is in the dust,
> who are crushed like a moth.
> Between morning and evening they are destroyed;
> they perish forever without any regarding it.
> Their tent-cord is plucked up within them,
> and they die devoid of wisdom.
> (Job 4:17–21)

Eliphaz goes on to admit that human life does indeed come with its full tally of suffering, "but human beings are born to trouble / just as sparks fly upward" (5:7), going on to say what he would do were he in Job's shoes, namely commit his cause to God (5:8–16). Eliphaz is confident that God "sets on high those who are lowly, / and those who mourn are lifted to safety" (5:11). Then he has a new thing to say to Job, making the point that suffering can be understood as a divine discipline, and that particular manifestation of the work of God in the life of an individual must be a source of some happiness for that person.

> How happy is the one whom God reproves;
> therefore do not despise the discipline of the Almighty.
> (Job 5:17)

This is a variation on a theme found elsewhere in the Old Testament (see Ps 94:12a; Prov 3:11a; cf. Amos 4:6–11), and which will reappear, as we shall see, in a much more developed form in the speeches of Elihu (Job 32–37). However, just how appropriate this advice is for Job at this stage is questionable, for Job is not convinced that he has sinned. Further, says Eliphaz, although God may wound, he also binds up, although he strikes he heals (5:18). To make sure that the matter is understood he gives a series of examples for Job's consideration (5:19–26), ending with the observation that he and his group, "we," whoever they are—perhaps the "wise," representatives of the wisdom tradition—know these things to be true, so let Job also be sure about them:

> See, we have searched this out; it is true.
> Hear, and know it for yourself.
> (Job 5:27)

Eliphaz's second speech is in Job 15:1–35, and he really has nothing new to offer to the debate,[20] but what he says (again) is in a tone and spirit markedly more harsh and pugnacious. He opens his address to Job with the judgmental words on one who seems to think that he has wisdom in these matters (15:2), and goes on to present his viewpoint once again, that is, if a person is suffering then they must have sinned, and that is sufficient explanation for the trials Job has experienced:

> The wicked writhe in pain all their days,
>   through all the years that are laid up for the ruthless . . .
> For the company of the godless is barren,
> and fire consumes the tents of bribery.
> They conceive mischief and bring forth evil
> and their heart prepares deceit.
> (Job 15:20, 34–35)

Eliphaz's third speech is in Job 22:1–30, and here he does have something new to say, and at the same time to say it with a new note of combativeness: he will speak about Job's sins. And this is perhaps all he can speak about because any thoughts that he has on the subject of theodicy revolve around the facts that the innocent prosper and the wicked suffer. If Job is suffering then he must therefore be a sinner, and if Job cannot see his sins, then they need to be pointed out to him. Thus Job gets a strong lecture from Eliphaz about the fact that he is a sinner. J. C. L. Gibson says of this contribution of Eliphaz, "his speech is the speech of a devout man turned hunter of heretics, and the sparks of malice and hypocrisy fly from it in all directions."[21] Thus from the

---

20. Clines, *Job 1–20*, 346, observes about this second speech of Eliphaz, "Is there any inherent reason in the dynamics of the book why a second and third cycle of speeches should unfold? The friends have no new points to make, so their speeches are in themselves otiose." He goes on to say, "But Job, ever divergent and exploratory, has yet a lot of ground to cover, and the immovability of the friends' theologies is a necessary backdrop to his perpetual shifting of position and perspective."

21. Gibson, *Job*, 173.

statement, "Is not your wickedness great? / There is no end to your iniquities" (22:5), up to—and beyond—"Agree with God, and be at peace; / in this way good will come to you" (22:21), Eliphaz lays into Job about his sinfulness. Yet the trouble, as we shall come to see, is that Job is not convinced that he is a sinner.

In each of the three cycles of the speeches of Job's friends the second speaker is Bildad, but alas he does not have anything new to contribute after what Eliphaz has already said.[22] Thus in his first speech (Job 8:1–22) Bildad opens with the subject of the sinfulness of Job's children, and he advises Job to make supplication to the Lord.

> Does God pervert justice?
> Or does the Almighty pervert the right?
> If your children sinned against him,
> he delivered them into the power of their transgression.
> If you will seek God
> and make supplication to the Almighty,
> if you are pure and upright,
> surely then he will rouse himself for you
> and restore to you your rightful place.
> Though your beginning was small,
> your latter days will be very great.
> (Job 8:3–7)

How ephemeral, says Bildad, is the house of the wicked (8:14–19), but Job can be very sure that "God will not reject a blameless person, / nor take the hand of evildoers" (8:20), and that therefore "He will yet fill your mouth with laughter, / and your lips with shouts of joy" (8:21). In his second speech (18:1–21), Bildad, at considerable length, and for the benefit of his hearer(s), in much detail, speaks of the destruction of the wicked and the terror that will come upon them. There is hardly a shred of comfort here for Job in his toils, nor anything new to say to those who seek some light upon the theological problem of the sufferings of the devout. And nor is there in the third of Bildad's speeches, which is brief and is to be found in Job 25:1–6, where his theme is the majesty and the purity of God, so that,

---

22. Gibson, *Job*, 70, expresses it well: "In Dickens' novel, *Dombey and Son*, it is said of a certain Mr. Feeder, B.A., that 'he was a kind of human barrel-organ, with a little list of tunes at which he was constantly working, over and over again, without any variation.' That is almost true of all three friends from this point on."

> If even the moon is not bright
> and the stars are not pure in his sight,
> how much less a mortal, who is a maggot,
> and a human being, who is a worm!
> (Job 25:5–6)

The third of the friends is Zophar, and his first speech is in 11:1–20. His style is nothing if not blunt and to the point; he gives the impression that he is a "plain speaker," one who as we say does not "mince his words." Peake says that "Zophar is a rougher type of man than the more dignified Eliphaz or the gentler Bildad . . . He is the most rasping disputant of the three," while Whybray observes, "Zophar's tone is clearly more acerbic, even hostile, than that of the previous speakers, who have shown more sympathy with Job."[23] Thus Zophar launches his assault upon Job, making it clear that in his (Zophar's) eyes Job must be a sinner:

> 4 For you say, "My doctrine is pure,
> and I am clean in your [God's] sight."
> 5 O that God would speak,
> and open his lips to you,
> 6 and that he would tell you the secrets of wisdom!
> For wisdom is mysterious.
> Know then that God exacts of you less than your guilt deserves.
> (Job 11:4–6)[24]

The point that Zophar seeks to make—forcibly—is that Job is a sinner, and that he should think himself fortunate that God is not being more judgmental towards him. Further, the things and ways of God are mysterious (11:6, 7–10), unfathomable by those who are somewhat stupid, lacking understanding (v. 12)—which Zophar seems to be suggesting Job appears to be. Therefore, let Job reorient his life ("look into your heart"), and pray to God ("stretch out your hands towards him"), put

---

23. Peake, *Job*, 125; Whybray, *Job*, 68.

24. It will be noticed that the above translation differs a little from that of NRSV. In v. 4 the word NRSV translates "conduct" is much more likely to mean "doctrine" (as I have rendered it) or "teaching" (as NRSV margin). In v. 6 the word translated in NRSV "many-sided" would at least be better as "two-sided", but perhaps means "mysterious", as I have rendered it. The last line of v. 6 may mean either "Know that God exacts from you less than you deserve" or "Know that God overlooks part of your guilt."

away iniquity (11:13–14), and then there will be a dramatic change for him in his life,

> And your life will be brighter than the noonday;
> its darkness will be like the morning.
> And you will have confidence, because there is hope;
> you will be protected and take your rest in safety.
> You will lie down, and no one will make you afraid;
> many will entreat your favor.
> (Job 11:17–19)

But, of course, the trouble is that this does not seem to fit with the facts, for as far as Job was concerned, and as far as we have been told, Job was not a great sinner. So, should Zophar, so full of talk (as Zophar accuses Job in v. 2) be vindicated?

Job will indeed respond to this (12:1—14:22), but for the present we need to hear what further pearls Zophar has to lay before us.

Zophar's contribution to the second round of speeches is in Job 20:1–29, where his speech beginning with the peremptory "Pay attention!" (v. 2), falls into three parts: (a) The wicked will perish (vv. 4–11); (b) The wickedness in a person is like "the venom of asps" (v. 14) having no lasting benefit (vv. 12–23); (c) A terrible end is appointed for the wicked (vv. 24–29). Zophar appears to be passing on some standard and generalized teaching to Job; notably he is short on specific address to Job, failing to make particular application to his situation. The only exception to this would seem to be in v. 19, though it has to be said that we do not hear of such specific sins being committed by Job. Rather, what Zophar has said to Job has been in the nature of a rhetorical "set piece."

The text of Zophar's third and final offering appears to have had a hazardous transmission history, and it is reconstructed here as being found in Job 27:7–23.[25] We are already well familiar with the theme, here expressed as uncompromisingly as ever, namely, "what is the hope of the godless when God cuts them off?" (v. 8), the portion of the wicked under God is nothing less than certain destruction (vv. 13–23). There is naught here that advances the argument the friends have already presented, and certainly naught by way of comfort for the suffering Job.

What then in summary can we say about the contribution the three friends of Job, Eliphaz, Bildad, and Zophar, make to the enigma of the

---

25. See above, 106, 117.

devout who suffer. What is there in the multitude of words in their nine speeches that contributes to the discussion in the book of Job about the sufferings of Job? The fact is that the friends are offering no more than two reasons to account for Job's situation, one of these being made with great emphasis a number of times, the second but once. The principal theme of the friends is that Job must have sinned, and that is why he is suffering so grievously. For these are devoted and rather slavish followers of the belief that sin leads to suffering, while it is righteousness that leads to life. Further, they state, and restate, and once again state, this in their speeches—in spite of the fact that Job, as we shall come to see, will protest and go on protesting that any sin of his cannot have led to the scale of sufferings that he has had to face, and now must go on enduring. Bildad offers a variation on this theme in his suggestion that maybe it is the sin of Job's children that has brought these toils upon their father (8:1–22). The only other consideration that these men can offer is voiced by Eliphaz, and is that suffering is a divine discipline and therefore as a manifestation of the work of God within the life of an individual person is to be welcomed, embraced and not to be despised (5:17). In this view, "suffering may be seen not as something that puts a gulf between a human being and God but as something that binds them together."[26]

We shall return to consider this contribution of the friends of Job in the context of the other contributions in the book, and to any ongoing worth it may have, but meanwhile we need to attend to the various speeches of Job himself, being uttered in response to his friends' contributions.

Job Speaks Again (6:1—27:6)

We last considered Job when he was making the speech that began, "After this Job opened his mouth and cursed the day of his birth" (3:1), a powerful and heart-rending speech that culminated in the words, "I am not at ease, nor am I quiet; / I have no rest; but trouble comes" (3:26). After this Eliphaz makes his first speech (4:1—5:27), and then follow Job's words in 6:1—7:21, at times angry words, for Job is angry about the treatment he has received both from God and also from his friends. He feels a sense of rage before God, for "the arrows of the Almighty

---

26. Clines, *Job 1–20*, 148.

are in me" (6:4), and he would rather die than go on in these sufferings (6:8–9). And this, in spite of the fact that Job believes he has been faithful to the Lord, "for I have not denied the words of the Holy One" (6:10).[27] Yet the anger of Job is also directed against his friends who, Job feels, "are treacherous like a torrent-bed, / like freshets [so NRSV, "seasonal streams"] that pass away" (6:15). This was how Jeremiah in an hour of need is recorded as having felt about the care of God for him (Jer 15:18). With Job the words are against his friends, who he feels have falsely accused him of sins, having failed to offer true friendship to him, and he ends with a moving appeal to them that they will understand what depths of despair he is in (6:28–29).

The second part of this speech of Job (7:1–21) is directed against God. Job complains that human beings have been given a hard and difficult road to travel in life (7:1–5), their brevity being matched by their lack of hope, "My days are swifter than a weaver's shuttle, / and come to their end without hope" (7:6). Movingly he speaks of the lack of hope when death comes (7:7–10). Yet even during life he feels that God has not understood his servant's wretched lot, but has pursued him without mercy (7:11–16), while in 7:17–18 he turns the language of Ps 8:4–5 somewhat on its head and reuses with irony and bitterness to express his feeling that God is not relating to him in a spirit of justice and care.[28] If Job has been such a sinner (presumably in the way that Eliphaz has suggested he is, 4:1—5:27), why cannot God forgive him here and now? For all too soon Job will be dead and beyond even God's reach (7:21).

Job next speaks in 9:1—10:22, a long speech that follows Bildad's offering in 8:1–22, but which neither answers nor responds to it. Job realizes that a mortal cannot be just before God (9:2), and that he is puny indeed alongside the surpassing greatness of the Lord (9:5–12). What then can Job do?

> How then can I answer him,
> choosing my words with him?
> Though I am innocent, I cannot answer him;
> I must appeal for mercy to my accuser.
> (Job 9:14–15)

---

27. About this and other such speeches of Job, D. Soelle, *Suffering*, 115, says, "In reports from those who are interrogated and tortured over a long period of time there are similar experiences of self-destruction, self-hatred, and loathing."

28. See the contribution of Mettinger noted in note 14 above.

The last word in this quotation, "accuser," indicates "an adversary at law," and Job here is likening his situation to one who is involved in a case at law—except that in Job's situation his accuser is none other than God! This is the accuser who can crush a human (9:17), who can destroy both the blameless and the wicked (9:22). Further, for Job—he whose "days are swifter than a runner; / they flee away, they see no good" (9:25)—"There is no umpire between us, / who might lay his hand on us both" (9:33). This word "umpire" (*môkîaḥ*) indicates one who might "mediate" between the parties in this (envisaged, imaginary) court case, the diminutive Job and the mighty God. Alas, the darkening mood of Job is that there is no such person available to help him. Rather, Job feels totally on his own, his friends being no proper friends, and God apparently against him.

Thus it is that when we come to the second part of this speech (10:1–22) the person addressed in the words of Job is no longer one of the friends, or the friends collectively, but is now God himself. Moreover, the talk is outspoken, for Job "will speak in the bitterness of [his] soul" (10:1). The speech is reminiscent of the Psalms of Lament, and of the so-called Confessions of Jeremiah that we have already considered,[29] yet perhaps if anything even bolder than they are, the word "accusatory" is not inappropriate.[30] For here God is condemned as the one who has made Job, "and now you turn and destroy me" (10:8), boldly addressing God as the one who has poured him out like milk, curdled him like cheese (10:10). Thus Job works up to the climax of his speech, with its,

> Why did you bring me forth from the womb?
> Would that I had died before any eye had seen me,
> and were as though I had not been,
> carried from the womb to the grave.
> Are not the days of my life few?
> Let me alone that I may find a little comfort
> before I go, never to return,
> to the land of gloom and deep darkness,
> the land of gloom and chaos,
> where light is like darkness.
> (Job 10:18–22)

---

29. See above, 31–34, 35–57.
30. On this, see, e.g., Clines, *Job 1–20*, 244.

Before we move on from here, we should take note of a significant and new issue that has been brought into play in this speech of Job, friendship.[31] For although Job has Bildad, Eliphaz, and Zophar, they have failed to be friends because they have insisted on arguing with him theologically and preaching to him. Thus it is, perhaps, that Job is led to cry out for an "umpire" (*môkîaḥ*) between himself and God (9:33), one who would be a friend of his "at court," who would arbitrate between these so-unequal parties, God and Job.[32] The line of thought has yet some way to run within the book of Job, and should be taken seriously, as will be shown below. While here in Job 9:33 there is Job utterly sure that he does *not* have one who will "arbitrate" between God and himself, later in 16:19 there is more hopeful talk of a "witness in heaven," and even further, in 19:25, is Job's wish that he might have a "redeemer." These will be discussed in what follows.

The next speech of Job is 12:1—14:22, and is a lengthy one that stands between the end of the first cycle of speeches and the second. In 12:1—13:18 the address is to the friends, in 13:19—14:22 to the Lord. Job begins by coming back strongly against the friends and what he sees as their parade of wisdom. He points out that he—and a lot of others, including birds and animals—can come to the same conclusions as they have (12:1-12), so in such talk what is new that his friends are saying to him? This polemic gives way in 12:13-25 to a hymn of praise to God, in particular to the wisdom and the great powers of the Lord. Then with 13:1-18 the talk is of the various relationships between Job, the friends, and the Lord. It is all very well, says Job, that the friends "lecture" him as they do, when in fact Job knows as much as they do (13:1-2). What, rather, Job desires is that he may "speak to the Almighty, / and I desire to argue my case with God" (13:3). In fact, Job accuses the friends of having spoken falsely for God (13:4-12), so that as far as Job is concerned they are "worthless physicians" (13:4), their "maxims are proverbs of ashes" (13:12). Let them therefore leave Job in silence (13:13)!

---

31. The matter has been helpfully and thoughtfully probed by Norman Habel, "Only the Jackal Is My Friend."

32. Coverdale in his 1535 version translated the Hebrew *mokiah* as "daysman," that is, an arbitrator, a mediator, and the whole concept for some Christians came to be taken as a prophecy of the incarnation. For a full discussion of this see Gibson, *The Book of Job*, 49-50. The LXX translated the Hebrew *mokiah* by *mesites* "mediator," a word that is employed in the New Testament at Gal 3:19, 20; 1 Tim 2:5; Heb 8:6; 9:15; 12:24.

From 13:19 to 14:22 Job's address is to God: may the suffering be removed from his life and his dread of the Lord (13:21), and then let them speak to one another, Job and God (13:22). For at present Job is in a parlous situation: not only is he beset with sufferings (13:23–28), but also as a human being his life is so short (14:1–22), in fact being a mortal he is "few of days and full of trouble" (14:1). Whereas there may be hope for a tree which having been cut down may sprout again, mortals for their part die, they do not rise again (14:7–17). Rather, the mortals are washed away, not even having the satisfaction of rejoicing in the ongoing life of their offspring (14:18–22). Thus with his outspokenness to both friends and God, and his elegy on the brevity of human life, Job's long speech comes to an end.

Job's next speech is in 16:1—17:16, but as Whybray observes, "it cannot be said that he [Job] has any essentially new arguments to put forward," adding, "The friends are only occasionally mentioned after the first few verses. Only occasionally also is God addressed. The main impression is of a monologue; nevertheless the *effect* of the speech is that of a cry to God for pity."[33] Within this "cry to God for pity" we should take particular note of 16:18–22, which NRSV renders:

> 18 O earth, do not cover my blood;
> let my outcry find no resting place.
> 19 Even now, in fact, my witness is in heaven,
> and he that vouches for me is on high.
> 20 My friends scorn me;
> my eye pours out tears to God,
> 21 that he would maintain the right of a mortal with God,
> as one does for a neighbor.
> 22 For when a few years have come,
> I shall go the way from which I shall not return.
> (Job 16:18–22)

Verse 18 seems to be indicating that Job is alive, but that when he dies he hopes his blood, like that of Abel (Gen 4:10), will cry out to God; as Abel's blood cried out for vengeance, so may Job's cry out for redress for all his (undeserved) sufferings. Then v. 19 goes on to say that even now, already, Job has his witness (ʿēd) in heaven, one who will testify to Job's innocence, making sure that innocence is recognized. The thought is given some explication in the second line of v. 19, namely

---

33. Whybray, *Job*, 84; his italics.

that Job has one who vouches for him, one who is on high, that is, in the heavenly places.

But who is this "witness," this "vouching one"? There are a number of possibilities: it could be none other than God himself, or it could be the "umpire" of 9:33, or it could be the "redeemer" (or "vindicator") of 19:25. It has to be said that different commentators come to different conclusions, yet what however is clear is that Job feels that he does have *someone* there in heaven who is "on his side," one who will seek to work for him, either God himself or else another. Nevertheless, the fact that this one is "in heaven," "on high," affords the strong suggestion that what is intended is that it is God himself. If this is what is intended then surely here is hope for Job!

There is still Job 16:20 to consider, the first line of which is translated in NRSV, "My friends scorn me." Now what is translated "scorn me" is in fact a participle, "my scorners," but the Hebrew verb can also mean "interpreter, spokesman, mediator" and this seems to be the meaning that it has in 33:23. Thus has arisen a considerable question as to how we are to translate the word here: either as "my scorners" or as (admittedly with a small change in vowel) "my mediator." Perhaps we should be cautious and plump for the "scorners," as NRSV renders it. Further, what follows does not come over as being particularly hopeful, hardly speaking of God as being positively on the side of Job. Maybe we have to say with Whybray that we are faced here with Job's ambivalent attitude towards God;[34] can Job trust God to give him a favorable hearing or not? Perhaps the Job of these verses still remains a truly tortured person, still in the pain and turmoil of deep suffering, and still feeling unsure about God. Further, Job feels that his death is not far away; within a few years, "I shall go the way from which I shall not return" (16:22).[35] Let Peake have the last word on this passage which in spite of its difficulties with translation and understanding is at the same time, he says,

> deeply moving. Mocked and betrayed by his friends, he [Job] lifts his face, all bathed in tears, to God. But he has only just complained of God as his bitter enemy, the implacable foe who has brought him to the gates of death. Yet to whom can the baffled

---

34. Whybray, *Job*, 86.

35. See also the treatment of Clines, *Job 1–20*, 388–92, of these verses. He thinks the "witness" of 16:19 must be God, and translates the first line of v. 20, "It is my cry that is my spokesman" (368).

one turn, when all human help fails him and his burden is too hard to bear, but to God? The native instinct, crushed by God's cruelty, still springs irrepressibly to seek its satisfaction in Him. In its uttermost extremity the soul flies from man to God.[36]

Job's next speech is in 19:1–29, and it is taken up with three brief addresses to the friends (vv. 2–6, 21–22, 28–29), an extended complaint about God, the state that God has caused Job to be in vis-à-vis his family, guests, servants and others (vv. 7–20), and the expression of his deep longing (vv. 23–27). It is to this last named that we must pay particular attention, to this great wish that Job harbors. We begin with the translation of these verses that NRSV offers.

> 23 O that my words were written down!
> O that they were inscribed in a book!
> 24 O that with an iron pen and with lead
> they were engraved on a rock forever!
> 25 For I know that my Redeemer lives,
> and that at the last he will stand upon the earth;
> 26 and after my skin has been thus destroyed,
> then in my flesh I shall see God,
> 27 whom I shall see on my side,
> and my eyes shall behold, and not another.
> My heart faints within me!
>
> (Job 19:23–27)

This, of course, is a passage both well-known and also well-loved by Christians, but two cautions need to be entered: first, there are considerable difficulties with the translation of the Hebrew and thus with deciding just what is being said, and second, what then is the meaning of the words?

The passage opens with Job expressing the very strong wish that his words may be clearly recorded and preserved for posterity (vv. 23–24). What he wishes to be indelibly recorded is presumably all that he has been saying both to his friends and to God in his self-defense. Job follows that—not, it has to be admitted, altogether logically—with what he *is* sure about (vv. 25–27). And here *our* problems begin.

First, who is the "redeemer" (Hebrew *gō 'ēl*)? Now we do hear elsewhere of a "redeemer" in the Old Testament, one being spoken about

---

36. Peake, *Job*, 169. Also quoted by Rowley, *Job*, 121.

in Lev 25:25, one having the responsibility of coming to the assistance of a relative, or a family, who had fallen on hard times. Thus there is the response that Boaz makes to the plight of Naomi and Ruth (Ruth 4:1–12). The word comes to be used in Isa 40–55 to speak of the God who comes to "redeem," "rescue" his people (Isa 41:14; 43:14; 44:6).[37] But who is the "redeemer" that Job is so sure that he has? What Job is saying here bears a marked similarity to what he says in 16:19 about his "witness" in heaven, the one who "vouches" for him on high, that it seems most likely that it is this "witness" who is being spoken about here. That is, the "redeemer" is none other than God himself—thus we note that NRSV renders it "Redeemer." While some come to different conclusions, nevertheless Clines, Whybray, Rowley and others conclude that the "redeemer" is God himself.[38]

Then, what about the second part of v. 25 with its, "and that at the last he will stand upon the earth"? As NRSV indicates in its marginal note, the Hebrew here can be construed to read, "and that he the last will stand upon the earth [lit. 'dust']." Perhaps we have to say that this apparently means that before the end, the end of his earthly life, his "redeemer," who appears to be God, will appear for Job on earth.[39] Verse 26 is also difficult, and perhaps we have to take "and after my skin has been thus destroyed"[40] as referring to Job's skin disease we heard about at the beginning of the book (2:7–8).[41] For if alternatively we understand the "destroying" of Job's flesh as taking place *after* his death, then it is hard to understand the following words, "then in my flesh I shall see God." Those words might possibly be translated "then without (*min*) my flesh I shall see God," but are more likely intended to read "then from (*min*) my flesh I shall see God."[42] And more, in v. 27a we have: Job will see God

---

37. For more details on *gōʾēl* see *TDOT* 2: 350–55.

38. See Clines, *Job 1–20*, 459; Whybray, *Job*, 95–96; Rowley, *Job*, 138. See also Rowley, "The Book of Job and its Meaning," 179–82.

39. This is to say that the "redeemer" is not being understood as eschatalogical, that is, as belonging to the "end times."

40. The phrase "and after my skin has been thus destroyed" is a particularly difficult bit of Hebrew, one that clearly seems to have undergone corruption; certainly the Hebrew has nothing about the "worms" that make their appearance in KJV.

41. Peake, *Job*, 194, suggests, "'this skin of mine,' Job illustrating his words by a gesture pointing to his diseased skin."

42. Whybray, *Job*, 96, says that, "'*without* my flesh' [his italics] is almost certainly a mistranslation."

on his side (literally "for me"). Presumably this is God no longer appearing to Job to be the divine antagonist who with his almighty wisdom and strength Job has been so sure was causing his sufferings. Rather, now he sees this same God, but now "on his side"—literally, says Job, "for me." This understanding of these words of v. 27a would seem to be confirmed by those that follow, "and my eyes shall behold and not another," which Clines renders, "to see him with my own eyes, not as a stranger."[43]

Job, in these words, is portrayed as experiencing something remarkable. It is nothing less than his coming to a new vision of God, coming to understand that God may after all be one who is present with him, not merely far away from him. It is as if he has come to know for himself that the almighty and illimitable God, the transcendent One, as well as being transcendent can also be for his people immanent and immediate to them in their deep needs and sufferings. Further, the book of Job, and in particular in the portrayed progression of these speeches of Job, has shown him, Job, longing for something different in God, and about God. Job here has come to make an affirmation of hope, thus at last being able to draw some significant conclusions for his on-going sufferings. For in 9:33 he was bewailing the fact that there was no "umpire" between himself and God; yet in 16:19 he was coming to some assurance that his "witness is in heaven, and he that vouches for me is on high." Thus it is perhaps now that Job can give voice to the assurance expressed in 19:25–27, in words that suggest that he now has grounds for real hope in his life. In the light of the foregoing discussion we may offer the following translation of those words, a translation that is intended to be literal rather than either elevated or artistic.

> 25 For I know that my redeemer lives,
> and that at last he will stand upon the earth;
> 26 and after my skin has been thus destroyed,
> then from my fleshly body I shall see God,
> 27 whom I shall see on my side,
> and my eyes shall see, and not another.
> My heart faints within me!
>
> (Job 19:25–27)

We hardly need to doubt the force and significance of the last words of v. 27, "My heart faints within me!" We can understand that this is

43. Clines, *Job 1–20*, 428.

Job's feeling in his moment of revelation, either that "he is emotionally exhausted, psychically drained, by the intensity of his feelings,"[44] or else that he is experiencing "the profound dejection that follows the exaltation of the mystic experience."[45] Whichever it is, we understand something of the reality.

We next hear from Job in 21:1–34, when supposedly he is responding to Zophar (20:1–29), a speech marking the end of the second cycle of the dialogue between Job and his friends. Thus Job's speech now before us (21:1–34) both closes the second cycle and also opens the third, and last, of them. But there is nothing new that is contributed here. Rather, Job opens in vv. 2–5 with an introductory address (exordium) to the friends, pointing to the sad and pitiful situation in which he, Job, finds himself; surely that is enough to silence them (21:5). Then the theme is the happiness of the wicked and the fact that their lives appear to be free of calamity (21:6–33). Thus apparently do the wicked live their lives, reach old age, and ever grow mighty in power (v. 7), and so Job asks why the almighty's faithful ones should serve him; in fact, "what profit do we get if we pray to him?" (v. 15). So then finally, says Job to his friends,

> How then will you comfort me with empty nothings?
> There is nothing left of your answers but falsehood.
> (Job 21:34)

Job's next contribution is a long speech in 23:1—24:25, but it does not respond to the preceding offering of Eliphaz (22:1–30). Job, rather, here expresses a most moving longing that he may be granted the opportunity to come before God and to present his case to him.

> Oh, that I knew where I might find him,
> that I might come even to his dwelling!
> I would lay my case before him,
> and fill my mouth with arguments.
> (Job 23:3–4)

Job wonders whether God "in the greatness of his power" would contend with him: perhaps not, but then would he (God) give heed to him (Job)? (23:6). In fact Job is obsessed here with two matters in his approach to

---

44. So Clines, *Job 1-20*, 462.

45. Gordis, *Job*, 207, which is quoted with approval by Janzen, *Job*, 145. Whybray, *Job*, 96, says these words "probably refer to Job's emotional exhaustion."

God: on the one hand he cannot perceive, behold, see God (23:8–9), and yet on the other he is sure that were he to see God he would be "terrified at his presence," and thus when he comes to think about it Job *is* terrified and in dread of God (23:15). In chapter 24 Job goes on to speak of the successful lives of wickedness that the unrighteous, who cause such sufferings to those who are innocent, live. Yet the cries and prayers of these sufferers appear to receive no response from the Lord (24:12).[46]

So we come to the speech of Job in 26:1—27:6.[47] In 26:2–4 Job does respond to what Bildad is portrayed as just having said, and speaks with heavy irony about what a help (Job does not think!) Bildad has been to him. "How you have helped one who has no power! . . . How you have counseled one who has no wisdom" (26:2, 3). Then Job expatiates upon the greatness of God, and about how he is Lord of the realms of the dead and the living, of light and darkness, of heaven and earth (26:4–13), and ends with the statement that while we can witness him in his greatness, if only he (Job) might hear his voice.

> These are indeed but the outskirts of his ways;
> and how small a whisper do we hear of him!
> But the thunder of his power who can understand?
> (Job 26:14)

In the meantime, in the bitterness that Job feels at the way he has been treated by God, nevertheless he will seek not to utter lies about God—

---

46. A considerable question mark must hang over Job 24:18–24/25. The view presented in these verses is not easy to reconcile with all else that Job has to say, reading much more like material that comes from the friends of Job. One way of understanding them may be to regard them as being in the nature of an inset quotation by Job or the sort of thing that his friends have been saying, which appears to be the way that NRSV with its quotation marks handles them. For more details see the discussion in Whybray, *Job*, 111; Rowley, *Job*, 167. Clines transfers 24:17–24 to Zophar's third speech, after 27:17. As these verses are not presenting anything new I am not considering them further in this particular work.

47. Once again, there is evidence here of a certain disarrangement in the text: 27:7–23 reads as if it is a contribution of one of the friends, setting forth their characteristic themes; and as in the text as it stands a final speech of Zophar is lacking, these verses are frequently regarded as being that speech. See, e.g., Whybray, *Job*, 119. Also see Rowley, *Job*, 175–76, who regards 27:7–12; 24:18–24; 27:13–23 as making up the missing speech of Zophar. In the context of this present work 27:7–23 has already been spoken of as likely making up the otherwise-missing third speech of Zophar. See above, 106, 117.

although he continues to be sure about his righteousness, and apparently is determined not to be convinced otherwise (27:2–6).

Where Shall Wisdom Be Found? (28:1–28)

At chapter 28 of the book of Job something different from all that precedes is found; indeed, *so* different that many have concluded that it was not originally part of the work.[48] Yet at the same time this chapter can be understood as making its own particular contribution to the issues with which the book is dealing. We have seen how in the preceding material a range of views has been offered to explain Job's sufferings. Those involved have offered their views on the subject, but in truth very little progress has been made in the attempt to explain the "why?" of apparently innocent suffering in the world.

Now a new approach is presented, and it is not expressed in frenetic or impassioned argumentation, but it is in fine and elevated Hebrew poetry, and its theme is the finding of wisdom and knowledge for the living of life in the world. J. C. L. Gibson, helpfully I believe, introduces this contribution in the following way.

> Let us imagine a pause after the petering out of the long and fractious disputation between Job and his three friends . . . A figure steps forward from the surrounding audience and recites this magnificent poem whose single thought is that true wisdom belongs to God alone and cannot be found by men.[49]

It is a magnificent poem, and it begins in vv. 1–11 by speaking about the remarkable cleverness and skill that human beings display in their lives in the world, such as their ability to mine precious metals and stones from the depths of the earth. How remarkable it is what those who do these things achieve; how developed are their skills and abilities! The writer goes into a series of fascinating details about the miners' underground activities. But—for so the writer appears, rhetorically, to interject—but, "where shall wisdom be found? And where is the place of understanding?" (28:12).

---

48. For a full discussion of these matters see e.g. Rowley, *Job*, 178–79; Habel, *Job*, 391–4. See Fyall, *Now My Eyes Have Seen You*, 65–73, for a positive assessment of the place of ch. 28 in the context of the whole book of Job.

49. Gibson, *Job*, 196.

What is being indicated and intended by this word "wisdom"? "Wisdom" in biblical studies is notoriously difficult to define, and perhaps in the context of this particular work we can accept the offering of J. L. Crenshaw, who says that, "wisdom is the reasoned search for specific ways to assure well-being and the implementation of those discoveries in daily existence."[50] That is apparently the question being posed by the one (whoever that was) who was responsible for the poem that has come down to us as the twenty-eighth chapter of the book of Job. Where is this real and authentic life of wellbeing in God's world to be found? This poem appears to be saying that in spite of all the remarkable skills and ingenuity that, for instance, the miners for earth's precious metals and stones display, yet even they—even they!—have not penetrated "deeply" enough to "get wisdom . . . get insight" (Prov 4:7).

Rather, the writer goes on to say the search for wisdom and knowledge will only be rewarded when these matters are sought in God. They are not to be found on the land or in the seas; they cannot be bought, weighed or valued; they cannot be equaled, and are beyond all human comparisons (28:13–19). Do perhaps those who approach those realms beyond earthly life, the realms of the dead, "Abaddon" (that is, Sheol), do they know of these things? And the poet answers, not completely, for, "Abaddon and Death say, / 'We have heard a rumor of it with our ears'" (Job 28:22).

Alas, only a rumor! Where then is this vital and yet elusive wisdom to be found? And the answer comes back that it is God alone who understands it, and that the nearest any human being can get to finding it is in God, through their "fear" of God, that is, through their reverence for him, through their seeking of him and their shunning of all and everything that is contrary to his purposes (evil). The whole of this response more than deserves to be quoted.

> God understands the way to it,
> and he knows its place.
> For he looks to the ends of the earth,
> and sees everything under the heavens.
> When he gave to the wind its weight,
> and apportioned out the waters by measure;
> when he made a decree for the rain,

---

50. Crenshaw, *Old Testament Wisdom*, 24.

>   and a way for the thunderbolt;
>   then he saw it and declared it;
>   he established it, and searched it out.
>   And he said to humankind,
>   "Truly, the fear of the Lord, that is wisdom;
>   and to depart from evil is understanding."
>   (Job 28:23–28)

What little is to be revealed to us on earth about the meaning of life, and the mysteries of suffering, are to be found—so it is being averred here—not through our theological arguments, however thorough, however sophisticated they may be, but rather in what we find in our worship and reverence of God, and in what God chooses to reveal to us. Which is perhaps to say that theology must give way to religion, or—at least—that theology without religion while it may be interesting, and even informative, will be neither life-giving nor appealing to the very depths of our being. This remarkable insight to which the Poem on Wisdom of Job 28 has led us will be given to us again, and perhaps with even greater force and depth, in the Speeches of the Lord in chapters 38–41, but before we can go to them there is Job himself to be heard again, and also the contribution of one we have not yet listened to, namely Elihu the son of Barachel the Buzite.

Job Speaks Yet Again (29:1—31:40)

Job's final speech runs from 29:1 to 31:40, following on from the passage about wisdom in chapter 28. Once again, we have a speech that does not answer the one that precedes it. Nor, further, does Job, in this his last speech, make any mention of his friends. In fact, God is only briefly addressed here (30:20–23). Rather, says Whybray, "Job's purpose in chs. 29–31 is to make use of every possible rhetorical device to elicit sympathy for his case and to persuade God—who, being in a position of absolute power, is in a sense judge as well as litigant—that his case is a convincing one."[51]

In the first part of this speech, in chapter 29, Job looks back to the good times of his past life, "when the friendship of God was upon my tent; / when the Almighty was still with me, / when my children were

---

51. Whybray, *Job*, 125. Rodd, *Job*, 55, says about this speech, "When he [Job] speaks again he will be calmer, but no less confident of his integrity."

around me" (29:4–5), when he was a respected person in his community who did good things for those who needed help. And thus he expected his life would go on (29:7–25). "But now" (30:1) how very different is his life makes the theme of chapter 30, and Job speaks sadly of the changes that have come to him. Where once he was a respected elder (29:7–17, 21–25), now he is mocked and afflicted, one who cries out but lacks those who will respond to him, without either light in life, or true friends, or any sense of joy (ch. 30). Finally, in chapter 31 Job, by singling out a series of situations in his earlier life, affirms his goodness and concern for justice and righteousness in his worldly dealings. But if, just if . . .

> If my land has cried out against me,
> and its furrows have wept together;
> if I have eaten its yield without payment,
> and caused the death of its owners;
> let thorns grow instead of wheat,
> and foul weeds instead of barley.
> (Job 31:38–40a)

And the chapter ends, "The words of Job are ended" (31:40b), and so in a sense they are. He will have a few words yet to say, but how different they will be, how weighty and heart-felt, charged with religious and spiritual reality (40:3–5; 42:1–6). Those will be after the speeches of the Lord. But first we must hear Elihu.

Elihu and His Speeches (32:1—37:24)

These four speeches of Elihu (32:1—33:33; 34:1–37; 35:1–16; 36:1—37:24), then, draw forth no response from Job, nor is Elihu mentioned in the book outside of his speeches. Thus, questions have been asked as to whether they were originally a part of the work.[52] However, we should take note of the fact that the speeches of Elihu end by speaking of the wondrous works of God (37:14–24), in particular speaking of clouds and lightning, winds, skies, with words such as "Out of the north comes golden splendor; / around God is awesome majesty" (v. 22). Does this not prepare us for the whirlwind out of which the Lord answered Job (38:1)? And does not this therefore suggest that perhaps there has been some intended placing of the speeches of Elihu just before the first of the

---

52. See above, 107.

speeches of the Lord in 38:2—40:2?[53] Further, they do presuppose what has gone before in the debate between Job and his friends, continuing to make the point that sinfulness will inevitably bring in its train divine judgment. Moreover, it is frequently observed of the speeches of Elihu that, to use Marvin Pope's characterization, "Their style is diffuse and pretentious, nearly half of the content of the four discourses devoted to prolix and pompous prolegomena."[54] Rowley's comments about the first of Elihu's speeches are very much on the same lines when he says they are "repetitious and diffuse. No less than four times we are told that Elihu was angry. His professed modesty is belied by his self-importance and pomposity."[55]

Nevertheless, Elihu does have his own particular approach in coming at matters already well discussed in the book of Job, and having also some new things to contribute. Concerning the first of these, Elihu is in agreement with the friends in maintaining that Job must have sinned, yet he does strike something of an original note in taking up the language of the "umpire" (32:12, *môkîaḥ*) that Job longed to have alongside himself in his approach to the Lord (9:33). Elihu seems here to be, as it were, appointing himself as this "umpire," yet making clear that such are Job's apparent sins that he as Umpire Elihu must speak for the Lord rather than for Job! This comes out in his first speech (32:1—33:33) in which he also stresses that his youth displays more wisdom than do the years of the friends (32:6–14), that it is now the silence of the friends that leads him to make his contribution (32:15–22). Thus he calls for Job's attention to what he will say (33:1–7), emphasizing that Job cannot have been innocent of sin against God (33:14–28), calling on Job to speak to him if he has something to say, but if not to remain silent (33:29–33).

Then the new matter that Elihu has to contribute to the great debate: this is divine disciplining, or perhaps better expressed, divine education. This is, however, "almost new" because it has already been, albeit briefly, presented by Eliphaz in his first speech (4:1—5:27):

---

53. On this point see McKay, "Elihu—A Proto-Charismatic?" a contribution that I think makes some helpful points about the Elihu speeches, though I might wish to demurr from McKay's major conclusion at the end of his article. On the place of the speeches of Elihu in the book of Job see also Habel, "The Role of Elihu in the Design of the Book of Job."

54. Pope, *Job*, xxvi.

55. Rowley, *Job*, 207.

> How happy is the one whom God reproves;
> therefore do not despise the discipline of the Almighty.
> For he wounds, but he binds up;
> he strikes, but his hands heal.
> (Job 5:17–18)

Now it makes a further appearance, for example in 33:15–33, where Elihu tells of God speaking to a person through dreams, warning them to turn away from their deeds and so "spare their souls from the Pit, / their lives from traversing the River" (33:15–18). Here Elihu is suggesting that through the medium of dreams God warns a person about their deeds, that through this warning that person may turn away from their sins, and so avoid destruction. The thrust of v. 18 is that otherwise that (sinful) person will have to confront death. The thought is advanced in the following verses, where the emphasis is on suffering being a *warning* that a person is on a slippery slope. The suffering one is envisaged as being in a desperate situation (vv. 19–22):

> [T]hen he prays to God, and is accepted by him,
> he comes into his presence with joy,
> and God repays him for his righteousness.
> That person sings to others and says,
> "I sinned, and perverted what was right,
> and it was not paid back to me.
> He has redeemed my soul from going down to the Pit,
> and my life shall see the light."
> (Job 33:26–28)

And there is the presentation of suffering as a divine discipline, as a divine education if you will. The thought that lies behind it is that God in his care and concern for such a person—not, that is, necessarily in anger—allows suffering to afflict a person so that they may reflect upon what is wrong and amiss in their lives, and thus turn back to God. This approach to the matter of human suffering is spoken of again by Elihu in 34:31–37, and also in 36:7–13 and 15–16.

This is not an explanation or rationale for suffering that finds a prominent place in the Old Testament, though it does appear in Amos 4:6–11—yet according to the text it did not work, for we are told more than once "yet you did not return to me, says the Lord" (vv. 6, 8, 9, 10, 11). Further, some commentators are somewhat harsh about this emphasis of Elihu. Thus E. W. Nicholson speaks of Elihu's depiction of the "chastening" as bringing the sufferer virtually to destruction to achieve its desired goal (33:19–33). "The 'chastening' is monstrously out of proportion to the 'error' it is intended to correct."[56] But the scale of the "chastening," in one particular example in a work that sets out a wide range of options for understanding suffering, may not be germane. The book of Job does not seem to be intended to present a record, a history, of the suffering of Job, but rather to debate the matter of why it is that religious people are afflicted with suffering. In such a work the viewpoints are no doubt exaggerated in order to make their particular contributions. Hence we do not need to reject the viewpoint of Elihu on the grounds of the relative proportions of the "error" and the "chastening." At any rate, others have found more hope and help in this approach to the religious problems of suffering, as we shall see later.[57]

Perhaps more significant is what Elihu is portrayed as doing in preparing Job for meeting God. Thus some parts of the speeches of Elihu are intensely theocentric, seeking to point Job to the Lord. This is to be seen, for example, in 34:21–30, and maybe even more so towards the close of all his words, in this way,

> Hear this, O Job;
> stop and consider the wondrous works of God.
> Do you know how God lays his command upon them,
> and causes the lightning of his cloud to shine?
> Do you know the balancings of the clouds,
> the wondrous works of the one who whose knowledge is perfect,
> you whose garments are hot
> when the earth is still because of the south wind?
> Can you, like him, spread out the skies,
> Hard as a molten mirror?
> Teach us what we shall say to him;
> we cannot draw up our case because of darkness.
> (Job 37:14–19)

Thus, says Edgar Jones, with a quotation from Samuel Terrien, "In many ways the speeches of Elihu can be regarded 'as a kind of "gradual" to the divine theophany.'"[58]

---

56. Nicholson, "The Limits of Theodicy as a Theme of the Book of Job," 78.
57. See below, 153–54, 182–84.
58. Jones, *The Triumph of Job*, 73; Terrien, "The Book of Job." In *IB* 3:1128.

The Lord Speaks (38:1—40:2)

At last, the Lord speaks! The last thing that we heard from Job was of him exclaiming, "O that I had one to hear me! . . . I would give him an account of all my steps; / like a prince I would approach him" (31:35, 37). Yet now the Lord speaks to him, but it is hardly the response that Job was expecting. All those matters that have made up the intense debate of Job, his friends—and also Elihu—are not so much as mentioned in this speech of the Lord. Far from there being any opportunity for the suffering man to be listened to, and for him to render to the Lord an account of all his troubled steps and experiences, it is rather the Lord who does the speaking. Further, the Lord does not speak about Job's particular problems, and certainly does not give to him any explanation as to why he, Job, has gone through all these things. Rather, in a vigorous speech the Lord proclaims that he knows what he is doing in his creation and governance of the world. Moreover, his speech is clearly intended to make Job aware of the fact that while he, God, and he alone, knows what he is doing in his creation and sustaining of the world, Job has neither knowledge nor skills in these matters.

Yet the Lord does speak to Job and his speaking is in a setting and manner different from those of the earlier speeches in the book. Rather, here "the Lord answered Job out of the whirlwind" (38:1). That is, what is being spoken of is what might be termed a mighty appearance of the Lord, the sort of divine appearance spoken about in Ezek 1:4 and Zech 9:14.[59] This is what in biblical studies is referred to as a "theophany," an act in which God makes a personal appearance to an individual. This is not what Job is portrayed as having expected. For the fact is that what Job—and the reader of the book of Job—expects is an explanation of the painful reality of suffering of the devout in the world. Rather, no theological explanation is given, and the divine appearance is in a highly dramatic form. Thus we may say that at this point in the book theology (literally, "God talk") gives way to theophany (the appearance of God). Further, any speaking on the part of the Lord is all of a piece with the Lord's dramatic (theophanic) appearance to Job; far from it being about Job's problems it is about the wonders of the creation, about the earth and the sky, about light and morning, about seas and rivers, and much else.[60]

---

59. Other places in the Old Testament where such dramatic divine appearances are spoken about are Exod 19:16–25; Judg 5:4–5; Pss 18:7–15; 29; 68:7–10; Hab 3.

60. Robinson, *The Cross in the Old Testament*, 43, speaks of our being given in this

Rather than God giving explanations for the justice of his ways with the likes of Job, instead he addresses to Job a series of rhetorical questions, all of which are answerable on the lines of "only you, Lord can know this/do this." Thus there is in these two chapters a phalanx of questions from the Lord to Job: Where was Job when God laid the foundations of the earth? (38:4–7); when God contained the sea? (38:8–11); has Job commanded the morning to appear? (38:12–15); entered the springs of the sea? (38:16–18); found the way to the source of light? (38:19–21); entered the storehouses of the snow? (38:22–24) and so on and so forth right up to the end of chapter 39. And at the end of this—shall we call it?—interrogation, there is one final question accompanied by a demanding statement from God to Job:

> Shall a faultfinder contend with the Almighty?
> Anyone who argues with God must respond.
> (Job 40:2)

Before we move on, we should be clear what it is that this first speech of the Lord is about. Rather than hearing any *words* from God, Job has in fact *seen God* himself. Thus Otto in his *The Idea of the Holy* said about this part of the book of Job,

> If you start from rational ideas and concepts, you absolutely *thirst* for such a conclusion to the discourse. But nothing of the kind follows; nor does the chapter intend at all to suggest such teleological reflections or solutions. In the last resort it relies on something quite different from anything that can be exhaustively rendered in rational concepts, namely, on the sheer absolute wondrousness that transcends thought, on the *mysterium*, presented in its pure, non-rational form.[61]

And Job Speaks Again (40:3–5)

So what is Job's response? Far from it being anything along the lines of God having failed to answer all, or even any, of Job's question, rather it is in terms of Job's humble submission to God.

---

speech of the Lord, "a brilliant description of natural phenomena—the subject-matter of the modern sciences of geology, physiography, meteorology, and astronomy—of course from the ancient point of view, and with the ancient limitations of knowledge."

61. Otto, *The Idea of the Holy*, 81.

> Then Job answered the Lord:
> "See, I am of small account; what shall I answer you?
> I lay my hand on my mouth.
> I have spoken once, and I will not answer;
> twice, but will proceed no further."
> (Job 40:3–5)

What for Job has happened here? Is it that Job has become convicted of all that there is in the Lord's creation and maintenance of the world that he is silenced? Or is it perhaps that as he wanted to speak to the Almighty (13:3), as he was sure that somewhere in heaven there was his "witness," one on high who would vouch for him (16:19), that in his flesh he might see God, whom he would see on his side (19:26b–27a), so something of that *has* happened so that he has been made content—even if at the same time, humbled? Perhaps it is in fact something of both of these.

As far as the first is concerned, Job was made fully aware that God has his own work to do in the world, both in its creation and in its preservation, and that Job is not the only person in the world who has a place of some possible significance. Job has been made aware of the mighty works with which the Lord, to speak in earthly language, is busily occupied. But further, and alongside this, God has appeared to Job and spoken to him, and in that something quite tremendous has taken place, for the holy and great God has spoken to a person of earth, and here we are surely not far from those sorts of experiences about which we read elsewhere in the Old Testament, as for example in the book of Isaiah, "In the year that King Uzziah died, I saw the Lord sitting on a throne, high and lofty; and the hem of his robe filled the temple" (Isa 6:1).

This is the moment that Job has longed for and, speaking from a literary point of view, we have had to wait until chapter 40 of the book to reach it. And when we get to it, after all the words that have been uttered and all the speeches that have been made, how remarkably few are the words of response that come from Job. There is surely a sense in which Job is completely overcome by the mightiness of the awe-inspiring appearance and speech of God. How important did Job in the past think that *he* was, and, perhaps with some degree of self-importance, how necessary it was that the full tale of his problems should be heard by God. Yet when it came to the moment of revelation, this moment of theophany, how silenced was Job, how few were his words, how deep, apparently, was his sense of unworthiness: "I am of small account; what shall I answer you?" (40:4a).

What are we to understand Job's mood and feeling is at this point? Perhaps Habel is correct when he understands the expression "I am of small account" as meaning, "I am reduced to smallness, I am humbled," and that "Job's reply is a reluctant admission that Yahweh is the greater power and that he will press his case no further against such a formidable opponent. For Job the case may as well be closed."[62] In fact there is more to happen, for the Lord has a further, and if anything even more vigorous, speech to make.[63]

The Lord Speaks Again (40:6—41:34)

Now the Lord speaks again, making another long speech. At first sight this seems repetitious, and after Job's submission and confession in 40:3-5 the divine words in 40:6-14 seem harsh, so earning the comment of A. S. Peake, "When Job has confessed his error, such rebuke comes perilously near nagging."[64] The language *is* outspoken here, and in 40:8 God takes up Job's talk of courts and trials, and accuses Job of putting him, God, on trial, and in v. 9 goes on—apparently mockingly—to ask if Job has divine powers and abilities.

> Will you even put me in the wrong?
> Will you condemn me that you may be justified?
> Have you an arm like God,
> and can you thunder with a voice like his?
> (Job 40:8-9)

So, "Would Job like to have a go at being God?" seems to be the theme of 40:10-14, expressed in a tone that is clearly ironic, if not downright sarcastic. We do not hear of any reply of Job, in no small measure, no doubt, because our writer is anxious to portray God as not giving

---

62. Habel, *Job*, 549.

63. Thus Gibson, *Job*, 241, counsels the reader of the book at this stage not to be hasty in making judgments: "What are we to say? I suggest at this juncture, the less the better. For, whatever he [God] thinks of the partially deflated, but still sulking, man on the ash heap in front of him, God does condescend to speak to him again. Caution dictates that, until we have carefully listened to the second speech out of the whirlwind, we do not rush either to condemn or to excuse."

64. Peake, *Job*, 332.

him a chance to get a word in edgeways, but plowing on with his speech, which is now dominated by one theme: what does Job know about two creatures, Behemoth and Leviathan.

The first of these, Behemoth (40:15–24), is clearly a large land creature that has great strength (40:16–18), was one of the first of the Lord's creative acts and only God as Maker can approach it—and at that with a sword (40:19). It is apparently beyond human ability and strength to capture it (40:24). This is sometimes understood, and thus translated, hippopotamus, and we may also be intended to see a relationship between the Hebrew *bĕhēmôt* (Behemoth) and *bĕhēmāh* (beast), the former being the plural of the latter, and maybe therefore intended to indicate "great beast." The second, Leviathan (41:1–34 [Hebrew 40:25—41:26]), is clearly a sea creature, monster, such being its size that it cannot be caught or tamed by human beings (41:1–11), and is most frightening (41:12–34). Leviathan is also spoken about in Isa 27:1; Pss 74:14; 104:26; Job 3:8, and it is generally felt that the crocodile is intended.

But what is the significance of the talk of these two creatures here? How is it that one whole chapter of the book of Job can be taken up with descriptions of them? Are they cited merely as examples of the largest known land and sea creatures, who owe their creation to God, and who are tamable and controllable only by the Lord, and are thus intended to magnify the strength and authority of God, and thereby put the (mere) man Job "in his place"? I have to say that does not convince me; it would be suggesting that many words are employed to make a comparatively straightforward, even mundane, point. Further it means that the second speech of the Lord (40:6—41:34) is doing hardly more than repeating the matters set forth in his first speech (38:1—40:2), and in that case Peake would have correctly observed that here the Lord comes "dangerously near nagging." Moreover there are certain details given about these creatures, such as Leviathan breathing out fire and smoke (41:18–21), suggesting that these descriptions are intended to indicate mythical creatures rather than creatures of the natural world. That is to say, they are intended to represent, and speak to us of, religious matters.

Thus it is likely that Behemoth and Leviathan represent those great forces that are at work in the world, that do not act in accord with the will and purpose of God, and that yet are subject—mysteriously, wonderfully—only to the control and authority of God. Certainly, in Isa 27:1 Leviathan is a portrayal of those evil powers that will be defeated on the day of the Lord by the Lord himself. In Ps 74:14 we have God's battle with Leviathan in his creation of the world, while in Ps 104:26 Leviathan is portrayed as having been tamed, and thus become the harmless creature that splashes around in the sea.[65] Further, while there are no references in the Old Testament to Behemoth being a portrayal of an evil force, in certain of the extra-biblical apocalyptic writings Leviathan and Behemoth are linked together as mythical beasts of the End Time.[66]

It seems reasonable then that we should understand the talk about Behemoth and Leviathan in the Lord's second speech in Job 40:6—41:34 in these terms.[67] That is, we should understand that our author is accepting that there are malign, even evil, forces in the world that are liable to exert themselves against God and his purposes. This is perhaps our author's way of grappling with the baffling and uncomfortable reality that there is evil in the world. Yet if this is the world that God has created, and of which he is the sole Lord, how then can there be these forces of evil? If God is the sole Lord there cannot be other gods. We may suggest that through this language of myth[68] the author is accepting that there are malign, even evil, forces in the world, but that they are kept under control by God, being in fact subject to him.[69]

This then further allows us to understand that the second speech of the Lord is not merely repeating what has been said in the first, but has itself something vitally important to say, which may be expressed

---

65. For further details, and for parallels in other ancient Near Eastern traditions see Lepinsky in *TDOT* 7: 504–9. See also the entry "Leviathan," in *ABD* 4: 295–96; Day, *God's Conflict with the Dragon and the Sea*; Fyall, *Now My Eyes Have Seen You*, 157–74.

66. See *1 En.* 60:7–9; *4 Esd.* 6:49–52; *Apoc. Bar.* 29:4. On Apocalyptic Literature, see below 157–73.

67. This is argued by Gibson in his, "On evil in the Book of Job." See also Gibson, *Job*, 246–56; Day, *God's Conflict with the Dragon and the Sea*, 62–88.

68. My usage of the word "myth" here, it hardly needs saying, is not intended to indicate what should be regarded as fictional, but rather in the characteristic technical usage of the word "myth" in biblical studies as an expression in story form that is intended to convey a religious truth, to present to us some significant religious facts. See Rogerson, "Myth."

69. It is surely significant, in view of the Hebrew Bible's general emphasis that the sea is a place of chaos and evil, that Leviathan is a *sea* creature, and as such represents that chaos and evil. The good news, however, is that Leviathan has been tamed and brought under the Lord's control. Even more cause for rejoicing and hope is to read in the book of Revelation that in the new heaven and the new earth, "the sea was no more" (Rev 21:1).

in the following way: While the first speech sets forth the greatness of God and his rule on earth, the second speech speaks of his ultimate rule over, and control of, those forces in the world that threaten the stability of the creation and the well-being of its inhabitants. What this second speech then means for the suffering man Job is that in spite of those conclusions that he, Job, may have been drawing from the experience of his apparently unjust and uncontrolled sufferings, the Lord of creation does have control over those forces whose operations are apparently contrary to his will. It may be that Job is unable to see and understand that there is justice in some of the more dreadful happenings in the world, but he has at least come to appreciate that there are dimensions to the divine activity in the world of which he was clearly unaware. And thus concerning some of his earlier outspokenness, he now must needs approach the Lord with a new, or renewed, sense of humility and confession.

Job Speaks, One Last Time (42:1–6)

Thus we come to what are the last words of Job in the book that bears his name.[70] These are words uttered by the Job who is no longer angry with either human friends or God. Further, these are not the words of the "patient" Job encountered in the first two chapters of the book. This, rather, is the Job to whom God has spoken: in the style of a theophany, God has come to him, and through his speaking to him Job has come to understand that God can do all things and that nothing and none can stop or hinder him in his divine purposes (42:2). Job has further come to understand that earlier he had spoken seriously incorrect things about God, that he had sought to speak of things that are wonderful in their depth and reality, so deep and wonderful that Job's words were in fact not far short of being sheer travesty (42:3). And thus he concludes,

> I had heard of you by the hearing of the ear,
> but now my eye sees you;
> therefore I despise myself,
> and repent in dust and ashes.
> (Job 42:5–6)

---

70. Not all of these words are in fact from Job, but some of them take up what the Lord had earlier said to him. Thus in 42:3a we have some of the Lord's words uttered in 38:2, and in 42:4 those from 38:3b.

Strahan at this point in his commentary on the book of Job says of Job, "having said many things as a sufferer, he speaks his last words as a sinner whose heart is full of penitential sorrow,"[71] and finely quotes from John Henry Newman's *The Dream of Gerontius*,

> And these two pains, so counter and so keen,—
> The longing for Him, when thou seest Him not;
> The shame of self at the thought of seeing Him, –
> Will be thy veriest, sharpest purgatory.[72]

We heard at the beginning of the book about Job sitting in the ashes (2:8); now, near the end of the book we read of him repenting in dust and ashes (42:6). We are surely intended to hear, to observe in the text, this allusion in the latter reference to the former, and to appreciate the difference between sitting among ashes, and repenting in dust and ashes.[73] Sitting in ashes was a regular and customary sign of grief, such as displayed by Tamar (2 Sam 13:19), the mourning Jews in the book of Esther (Esth 4:3), the king of Nineveh in the book of Jonah (Jonah 3:6), and that was Job's condition at the beginning of his book (Job 2:8). However, Job at the end of the book is portrayed as having become aware of his personal unworthiness before the Lord, and thus there is talk in 42:6 of his despising himself and repenting in dust and ashes. We also read of Abraham in his humble approach to God praying on behalf of the few righteous people of Sodom and declaring himself to be "but dust and ashes" (Gen 18:27). The expression is also found in Job 30:19, the sense there being that Job has been reduced to this situation because God has humiliated him. All this is to say that we are surely intended to understand that Job has moved from a state of grief to a sense of his personal unworthiness.

The Epilogue (42:7–17)

This, the last passage of the book, is in prose, and it falls into two parts. It tells how, first, the Lord expresses his anger at what Eliphaz and his

---

71. Strahan, *The Book of Job*, 348.

72. Newman, *The Dream of Gerontius*, 43. The words are uttered by the Angel of the Agony, and come late in the *Dream*, shortly before, in the Angel's words, "We have gained the stairs / Which rise towards the Presence-chamber [of the Lord]."

73. For this phenomenon, "intertextuality", as found in the book of Job see notes 14 and 28 above.

friends have been saying to Job, for they have "not spoken of me what is right, as my servant Job has" (42:7, and compare v. 8). Therefore let them offer a burnt offering to God and thereby seek God's forgiveness, and let Job pray for them. We are told that they did this, and that the Lord accepted Job's prayer (42:9).

Here is clear condemnation of the three friends of Job (Elihu not being mentioned), especially that they have exhibited "folly" (*nĕbālâ*, 42:8), that they have spoken foolishly, and have not spoken of God "what is right, as my [God's] servant Job has" (vv. 7 and 8). Thus is clearly stated that what Job has been saying all along (presumably, that he was innocent) was correct, while what the friends were saying (presumably referring to their consistent viewpoint that Job must have sinned) was nothing less than foolishness (*nĕbālâ*). This is surely tantamount to a refutation both of the theological position of the friends that the sufferings of Job must be due to his sinfulness, and also an affirmation of Job's viewpoint that his sins cannot possibly have brought all the calamities he experienced upon himself. What these verses do not offer is any alternative theodicy to explain why it is that Job, who has spoken and done what is right, should have had to experience such suffering. Nevertheless, what they do is to reject the notion that Job "deserved" his sufferings, and this is surely a most significant point that is being made as the book comes to a close.

Then second, in 42:10–17 we read about the Lord restoring the fortunes of Job, and that "the Lord gave Job twice as much as he had before" (v. 10). Thus was Job's family reconstructed, along with all who had known him before the time of all his sufferings, showing him comfort and offering sympathy, bringing him gifts (v. 11). Finally, we have the concluding note that the last days of Job became even better and more blessed than the earlier ones had been, not only through his coming to have vast numbers of sheep, camels, oxen and donkeys, but yet more in that he became the father of seven sons and three daughters. We are not told what were the names of these sons, but those of the daughters were Jemimah, Keziah, and Keren-happuch—they being, we are told, the most beautiful women in the land, who received from their father an inheritance along with their brothers. As for Job himself, he lived for 140 years and saw his children and his children's children, and thus did he die like Isaac of old (Gen 35:29), "old and full of days" (Job 42:17).

What are we to say about the remarkable transformation of the life and fortunes of Job spoken about here? For this is something more than Job's fortunes being restored (v. 10): in the end he has more than he had at the beginning of the story. This reads rather like an "and they all lived happily ever after" ending to a story, and does not that rather trivialize what this remarkable work has been all about?

One answer, and a reasonable one, is to say that this is a continuation of the folk tale with which the book began (Job 1–2). In the very nature of such stories perhaps there is an inevitability about there being a "happy ending," and in that literary genre, as Whybray observes, "The doubling of the hero's wealth at the conclusion of the story is . . . a common motif."[74] And in the context of the completed book of Job, there in that ending to the tale of all Job's suffering is indeed a theodicy, namely that in the fullness of time things will come right, the justice of God in his dealings with the people of the world will be made manifest in the ways in which they come, eventually, to peace and happiness. Whether we feel able to accept such a view as a way of dealing with the problem of suffering is another matter, and that will make up the subject of what now follows.

Theodicy in the Book of Job

Job does not ask, in so many words, "Where is the God of justice?," yet many of his own words, in speech after speech, echo them. The agonized theme is there, for example, in Job's second speech in the second cycle,

> God gives me up to the ungodly,
> and casts me into the hands of the wicked.
> I was at ease and he broke me in two;
> he seized me by the neck and dashed me to pieces;
> he set me up as his target;
> his archers surround me.
> (Job 16:11–13a)

What help is there in this long and remarkable book for those who, like Job of old, experience suffering? In particular, what is there in the various speeches and contributions that may give hope to religious people, to those who put their trust in God, for their earthly lives? There are a number of theodicies presented to us in this book, and this, so I have

---

74. Whybray, *Job*, 173.

argued, is what this work is intended to do; it sets before us a number of ways of thinking about the reality of suffering in the world. Some of the theodicies presented to us in the book are in fact to be rejected as inadequate. But we need to begin at the beginning.

As we have seen the book of Job begins with what has commonly been called The Prologue (1:1—2:13), which sets the scene for what is to come in the rest of the book. It has to be said that it presents us with a picture of a rather capricious God, who is portrayed as allowing the sufferings of Job to proceed so that he (God) can be shown to be correct in his assessment of the goodness and faithfulness of Job. Now it is generally felt that this Prologue takes up what has been called a folk story, and there are two ways of regarding this part of the book. The first is to say that this story is used purely and simply to set the scene for the debate about suffering that will then ensue, and that it is not intended to set forth a theodicy. I have to say that this is my own view.

An alternative view understands that here there is a possible theodicy, but it has to be said that it is one in which God is portrayed as acting in a somewhat capricious sort of way. Can we be intended to accept that God would act in such a monstrous way merely so that he could win his wager with the satan? Here, I would say, is the presentation of one particular theodicy that the book of Job intends that we should reject, and this for the reason that it is not faithful to the portrayal of God set forth in the Scriptures.

Then there are the responses in the immediacy of the situation of great suffering of Job and his wife. Strictly speaking they are not theodicies, because they do not seek to give any explanation for the fact of suffering. Job for his part says piously and in a spirit of worship, "Naked I came from my mother's womb, and naked shall I return there; the Lord gave, and the Lord has taken away; blessed be the name of the Lord" (1:21). Later, when Job's sufferings increased and the going was getting even tougher, his wife said, "Do you still persist in your integrity? Curse God, and die" (2:9). These, as has been observed, are not theodicies, for they explain nothing. They are rather what may be called the existential reactions of Job and his wife to the crises that have befallen him, and also them. Of Job's wife we do not hear any more in the book, but about Job himself we can read how he became the more outspoken and radical, not remaining patient with his "blessed be the name of the Lord." Yet in all that will follow, Job's feelings and words will be portrayed as increasingly occupying various parts of the middle ground between his "blessed be the name of the Lord" and his wife's "curse God, and die."

The friends of Job, Eliphaz, Bildad, and Zophar, do however present a theodicy. They adhere strongly, consistently, and unitedly to the doctrine that the cause of suffering in the world is human sinfulness, and for them Job *must have* sinned. In speech after speech they ram their message home, and yet in speech after speech their views are not accepted by Job. It is not so much that Job continues to confute them and their arguments, but he certainly does not accept them, continuing with his own themes about his sufferings and in speaking to both them and God about his increasingly dark and dreadful situation. It has to be said that it is a bold and consistently maintained presentation of the friends' theodicy—yet it is a theodicy that the book of Job decisively rejects. This is shown in the first place by the consistent way in which the friends' arguments and viewpoints are not accepted by Job, but also in the fact that in the closing of the book, in the Epilogue, the friends are condemned by the Lord himself as having spoken incorrectly, whereas Job *has* spoken correctly. Thus, "The Lord said to Eliphaz the Temanite: 'My wrath is kindled against you and against your two friends; for you have not spoken of me what is right, as my servant Job has'" (Job 42:7). This indicates surely that the author of the book of Job was rejecting the "deserved calamity" type of theodicy.

Then there is a theodicy presented in the poem on wisdom of Job 28, where the emphasis is markedly on reverence for God, and that any understanding of the mystery of earthly suffering is to be found in worship and in the associated reverence for God. That is to say, any understanding of suffering will come within the realm of worship and religion, rather than in that of thought and theology.

So to the contribution of Elihu in chapters 32–37 of the book, for in reality Elihu does have a new point to make, that suffering may serve as a divine discipline, to bring about the religious development, education of a human being. The theme had already been broached by Eliphaz in his words,

> How happy is the one whom God reproves;
> therefore do not despise the discipline of the Almighty.
> For he wounds, but he binds up;
> he strikes, but his hands heal.
> (Job 5:17–18)

But as far as the Old Testament is concerned the matter is developed in its most major way by Elihu, and as Edgar Jones says of it, "Here he [Elihu] enunciates a truth that is greater than his exposition of it. God can use the suffering of man to teach and educate the spirit of an innocent man as well as a sinful one."[75]

Yet we are moving towards the heart of the matter, and we may recall that Samuel Terrien has suggested that we should see these speeches of Elihu as being "a kind of 'gradual' to the divine theophany."[76] Perhaps we may develop that piece of liturgical imagery a little by adding to it the suggestion that by the same token the poem on wisdom of chapter 28 is some sort of "preparation" on the way to the "gradual"—and so (shall we say?) on to the "gospel" (in the divine speeches)? Here in Job 28 is surely "preparation," for the Poem on Wisdom is fully centered on the themes of the adoration of, the approach to, and the praise of the Lord God Almighty.

So we come, once again, to the speeches of the Lord, the first being in 38:1—40:2, and the second in 40:6—41:34, the climax of this remarkable book. As we have already seen there are no immediate answers given in either of these speeches to humanity's urgent questions as to the reasons for suffering in a world created and sustained by a God of power and love. Yet what these great speeches are about is the fact that God does come to his people, and that he is aware of them. The challenge of these divine speeches to us is: Are we aware of who and what God is, what he has made, and what are his concerns? Are we aware of the fact that while there may be evil in the world, yet at the same time he, the Lord, does in the mystery of his being keep that evil, and its associated tendencies to chaos, firmly under control? It is hardly what theologians would call a theodicy that is set forth in these speeches, for perhaps we have met here what are the inevitable earthly "limits of theodicy." Yet something much more important and valuable than theodicy talk has been presented, for theology (God talk) has given way

---

75. Jones, *The Triumph of Job*, 72. Jones goes on to say that "Elihu limits the effectiveness of this instrument of God's dealing with men to one class only, the guilty. But as we know from the Prologue, God is dealing with an innocent man and Elihu's use of the disciplinary view of suffering becomes irrelevant when applied to Job." This may be so in the particular portrayed circumstances of the man Job, but that hardly applies if the book is intended to be dealing with issues of suffering and theodicy in a more general way.

76. See above, 141.

to theophany (the appearance of God); theodicy and its questions about "where is the God of justice?" have given way to the religion of revelation. Thus Job speaks for the last time—and how appropriate it is that now he speaks with such brevity:

> I had heard of you by the hearing of the ear,
> but now my eye sees you;
> therefore I despise myself,
> and repent in dust and ashes.
> (Job 42:5–6)

We must not forget the Epilogue (42:7–17), which inevitably after what has preceded must seem anti-climactic. It records the divine judgment upon Job's friends, and thereby presumably the author's judgment upon their theodicy (42:7–9). It looks as if we are back in the world of the "folk tale" with which the book began (1:1—2:13), and many a critic has argued that in a religious world lacking a belief in a life after death there had to be this sort of "happy ending." Yet it does seem like anticlimax after the great speeches of the Lord and those few but deeply religiously laden words of the Lord's now humble and submissive servant Job. Surely, the book of Job had plumbed deeper depths than this final tally of Job's even greater possessions and blessings than he ever knew in those days before all seemed to go so wrong for him.[77] I therefore close with quotations from two scholars who each in their own way offer what they see as the real insight and contribution of the book of Job.

H. H. Rowley said about the book of Job, "It falls far short of an intellectual solution of the problem of suffering. But it achieves the spiritual miracle of the wresting of profit from the suffering through the enrichment of the fellowship of God. It was in this that the author of the book of Job was interested and to this that he leads the reader."[78] And Robert Gordis said, speaking of the poet/author of Job,

---

77. I am conscious of the fact that once when speaking to a church group about this part of the book of Job, a member of the group came to me at the end of the session to say that a similar experience to Job's had been his earlier in his life. In a time of great suffering he had lost much, not only his business but also his wife. However, by the time I met him, things had changed for the good in remarkable ways, both as regards his business and his family life. I thanked him for sharing his experience with me. There is a stimulating and helpful discussion of the Epilogue to the book of Job by John Job in his *Where is my Father?* 115–23.

78. Rowley, "The Book of Job and its Meaning," 183.

The poet's ultimate message is clear: Not only *Ignoramus*, "we do not know," but *Ignorabimus*, "we may never know." But the poet goes further. He calls upon us *Gaudeamus*, "let us rejoice," in the beauty of the world, though its pattern is only partially revealed to us. It is enough to know that the dark mystery encloses and in part discloses a bright and shining miracle.[79]

---

79. Gordis, *The Book of God and Man*, 134.

7

The Long View

The Apocalyptic Hope

In common parlance the word *apocalyptic* is used—that is, if it is used at all—to indicate what is fantastic, dark, and menacing; what is foreboding, gloomy, and presaging disaster. Concerning its specialized usage in biblical studies Christopher Rowland offers the following explanation.

> About the time of the rise of Christianity there were produced by unknown Jews texts which purported to offer revelations from God by means of either visions or auditions concerning some of the most intractable problems of human existence, e.g. the reasons for human suffering and the character of God's purposes for the world. The particular concern of these texts to offer divine wisdom by means of revelation is known as apocalyptic or apocalypticism.[1]

This explanation helpfully introduces us to this biblical genre of writing and in its reference to suffering conveniently points us to its importance in this particular study. The phenomenon of apocalypticism can be seen to have taken its rise in the Old Testament period, and a few apocalyptic writings are to be found among the contents of the Hebrew Bible. The only fully developed piece of apocalyptic in the Hebrew Bible is in the second part of the book of Daniel (chs. 7–12), but there are

1. Rowland, "Apocalyptic," 34.

evidences of the genre in its developmental stages—generally known as proto-apocalyptic—in the book of Isaiah, in chapters 24–27 and 34, in the book of Joel, in Zech 12–14, and elsewhere. The word *apocalyptic* is connected with a Greek word meaning, "unveil, reveal," and the biblical apocalyptic literature comes from between about 300 BCE and 100 CE. The main features of this literature include numerical symbolism, obscure language, a doctrine of angels, talk of a coming time of salvation, and a division of history into periods.

We cannot be sure as to the antecedents to the apocalyptic literature. Did it develop from the prophetic or wisdom traditions?[2] Perhaps it owed something to both of these. What is clearer is that it took its rise in conditions when the people of Israel were not free to order their own national life, when they were dominated by far superior political and military powers, and when at times they suffered persecution. It would be generally agreed that the book of Daniel came from the period of the Seleucid empire (c.201–142 BCE), in particular from the time of oppression and persecution of Jewish people and their leaders by Antiochus IV Epiphanes (175–164 BCE).[3] It is not surprising that just such a time as this should raise the question in the hearts of religiously faithful Jewish people, "Where is the God of justice?"

The book of Daniel comes to us with a clutch of critical problems of which we must take some notice. In the first place the book is made up of two parts, the first part (chs. 1–6) comprising a series of well known stories about Daniel and his friends, replete with a burning, fiery furnace, a lion's den, Belshazzar's feast, and an image that must be bowed down to at the sound of musical instruments. These stories are not in apocalyptic language and are portrayed as taking place in the time of the Babylonian exile early in the sixth century. Yet the historical details given do not correspond accurately with what we otherwise know of this era, and it is generally felt that these stories are intended to relate to the second century BCE. Thus, we may say that in Dan 1–6 we have two horizons, the earlier portrayed one in the sixth century BCE, and what appears to be the later and intended one in the second century BCE. The second part of the book of Daniel is in chapters 7–12 and is in the language of apocalyptic. In these chapters there are revealed to Daniel

---

2. For a recent study of apocalyptic and apocalypticism see Rowland, *The Open Heaven*; Collins, "Apocalyptic Themes in Biblical Literature," 117–30.

3. For full details see, e.g., Davies, *Daniel*, 20–34.

divine secrets, heavenly knowledge, about the troubled times through which he and his fellow Jews are living.[4]

Thus it appears that the historical setting for the book of Daniel is the reign of the Seleucid ruler, Antiochus IV Epiphanes. This was a time of great crisis in Jerusalem in which Jewish people were under considerable pressure to renounce their faith; certainly what we read in the biblical sources sounds serious and shocking. In Dan 11:31 and 12:11 we read of the regular burnt offerings in the temple being taken away and the setting up of an "abomination of desolation" (NRSV "the abomination that makes desolate"), though just what was intended by these words we are not sure, much the same going for what we read about concerning these times in the books of Maccabees.[5] Further, while the historical details of this period are not as clear to us as we might wish,[6] it does seem that there was some religious persecution in Jerusalem, that Antiochus Epiphanes "banned Jewish practices, desecrated the temple, and provoked a war of resistance under the leadership of the Maccabees which, after his death, succeeded in restoring the temple and traditional Jewish religious practices."[7] Here surely was rampant evil at large and at work in the world, whose worst effects were apparently directed towards those who sought to continue in the faithful worship and practice of their ancient faith. Where indeed was the God of justice in this serious situation?

As regards its contents then, the book of Daniel is made up of these two parts, chapters 1–6 and 7–12, yet the work makes up a satisfying

---

4. For full details of the two historical eras in Daniel, see Davies, *Daniel*, 20–34. Just to complete this tale of the "pairs" in the book of Daniel it may be mentioned also—though it does not immediately impinge upon this particular study—that as well as there being two parts to the book, and the two historical eras, there are also two languages in the book: it begins in Hebrew (1:1—2:4a), is then in Aramaic (2:4b—7:28), and goes back to Hebrew from 8:1 to the end. No satisfactory explanation has yet been given for this fact, in particular that the Aramaic part is neither wholly in the first part of the book (chs. 1–6) nor wholly in the second (chs. 7–12), but straddles them both. Further there are two forms of the book: the LXX text is longer than the Hebrew, the extra being "Song of the Three Children," "Susannah," and "Bel and the Dragon," which are more often than not in our English versions printed in the Apocrypha. See Davies, *Daniel*, 35–39, for full details of the bilingual nature of the book.

5. See 1 Macc 1:54, 59; 4:43–47; 2 Macc 6:2, 7.

6. See Grabbe, *Judaism from Cyrus to Hadrian*, 221–311; Jagersma, *A History of Israel to Bar Kochba*, Part 2, 44–67.

7. Davies, "Daniel," 564.

whole. Chapters 1–6 speak of the situation on earth, while chapters 7–12 take us into the heavenly realms and enable us to see things in the world as being in the care of and even under the control of God. Further, both parts of the book make reference to the matter of evil in the world that brings great suffering upon faithful Jewish people, and each part has its own contribution to make in answering questions about the presence of God with his people in these situations, and thus to presenting a theodicy. It should be noted that any theodicy presented in the book of Daniel is specifically concerned with what has been called a moral evil, that is "evil that we human beings originate: cruel, unjust, vicious, and perverse thoughts and deeds," as distinct from natural evil, "the evil that originates independently of human actions: in disease bacilli, earthquakes, storms, droughts, tornadoes, etc."[8] In the book of Daniel the issue of suffering and the justice of God is caused by the use of excessive and oppressive authority and power by an empire that is perceived to be evil.

In the various stories of the young men in chapters 1–6 the consistent theme is that continually they are being put into settings where the dominant political power in the land puts the faith and practice of these Jewish youths into a difficult situation, yet where each time the young men retain the integrity of their faith. Further, despite the severity of the inevitable punishment meted out to them, they are, by the power of God, delivered from their affliction, with the result that their enemies, their captors, are amazed at the power and devotion of the God of these young men. Thus are affirmed the wisdom of the ways of these young men who remain faithful to the ways and demands of their Lord God, both as regards diet (Dan 1), and also skill in the interpretation of dreams (Dan 2, 4). The same is true concerning the worship of the Lord God, that he alone is worthy of such worship (Dan 3), and about the future of the evil earthly kingdom (Dan 5, 6).

A word needs to be said at this point about what may be perceived to be the somewhat fantastical nature of these stories. In fact, we need to be aware of, and at the same time willing to enter into, the world of the story, to engage in the world of the storyteller's art. There has to be what has been called a "willing suspension of disbelief,"[9] the aware-

---

8. The quotations above are from Hick, *Evil and the God of Love*, 18.

9. The expression "willing suspension of disbelief" comes from Coleridge, and according to Michael Parkinson, "Belief," 21, "implies a contract between author and reader: the reader is encouraged to imagine that what is portrayed is real or possible rather

ness of the fact that the story teller exaggerates and perhaps embellishes their story, in order that their point may be made with all force and clarity. Thus we are well aware of the intense danger that faces human beings who may be so unfortunate as to be thrown into a burning, fiery furnace—and indeed we hardly do expect them to come out alive! Thus too we understand that the storywriter in the book of Daniel is seeking to make a very serious point about the deep devotion of those young men to their God, and at the same time of the devotion and power of their God for them.

The other point that needs to be made about these stories is that, in the words of Goldingay, they have been turned "into children's stories (the young men in the fiery furnace/Daniel in the lion's den), when the stories are of such deadly seriousness about problems facing adult believers living their lives in a strange land—like ourselves—that they almost require protecting from use in a children's context because of the trivializing this leads to."[10] In fact, these stories do have serious and vital things to say to adult religious believers, and not least about issues of theodicy, the age-old question in times of suffering, "Where is the God of justice?"[11]

Consistently these powerful stories bring out the fact that the Lord God of Israel is the one who has the real power while the earthly and oppressive rulers are at the end of the day no more than paper tigers. Nevertheless, while their pseudo-powers last they succeed in making life remarkably difficult for those who would remain faithful to the Yahwistic tradition of faith. But neither dens of lions (Dan 6) nor burning, fiery furnaces (Dan 3) can stand in the way of the triumph of those who maintain their faith and the practice of that faith. Moreover, there comes over in these stories the assurance of the presence of God with his people in their afflictions, a matter that is brought out especially clearly in Dan 3:24–25 where the evil King Nebuchadnezzar was astonished to witness that the three men who at his command had been

---

than remain querulously aware of its fictionality and impossibility, and hopes thereby to attain satisfactions and discoveries for which involvement, not distance, is required."

10. Goldingay, *Daniel*, ix–x.

11. A certain sense of regret at this point may be registered at the lack of any readings from Dan 1–6 in the widely and commonly used *Revised Common Lectionary* by many churches these days. See Consultation on Common Texts, *The Revised Common Lectionary*, esp. 112–28, the Scripture Readings Index II: Listed According to the Books of the Bible.

thrown into the furnace, securely bound, were seen to have become four men unbound, the fourth having the appearance of a divine being, that is one who was an attendant upon God, a member of his court.[12] As Jeremiah in some of his worst experiences of being a prophet of the Lord was assured that the Lord would be with him (Jer 15:20–21), so here through this "story" is the same sort of assurance being given to suffering Jewish people in the second century BCE that God was with them in their afflictions at the hands of their enemies.

Further, there occur among these stories in Dan 1–6 various expressions of confidence in God. The first of these is in 2:20–22 and comes within Daniel's explanation of the meaning of Nebuchadnezzar's dream.

> 20 Daniel said:
> "Blessed be the name of God from age to age,
> for wisdom and power are his.
> 21 He changes times and seasons,
> deposes kings and sets up kings;
> he gives wisdom to the wise
> and knowledge to those who have understanding.
> 22 He reveals deep and hidden things;
> he knows what is in the darkness,
> and light dwells with him.
> (Dan 2:20–22)

Particularly to be noted here is the assurance in v. 21 that the Lord of history is God, and that tyrants of the ilk of Nebuchadnezzar may only be around for a season. Let those who suffer at the hands of such tyrants take notice, and even more take heart. For this God knows all and everything, even "what is in the darkness" (v. 22); as Porteous says, "There is nothing so hidden or mysterious that it is inaccessible to God's knowledge."[13]

---

12. The Aramaic is *bar ʾĕlāhîn*, a being that in Hebrew was called *ben ʾĕlōhîm*, undoubtedly a subordinate being to God. NRSV translates "a god," but that is what is purported to be the word of Nebuchadnezzar (Dan 3:25). This is the storyteller's art, and we are surely meant to understand that to the supreme representative of the evil power this did look like "a god." This indeed is tantamount to the Hebrew Bible saying that God was "with" these men in the affliction brought upon them through their religious faithfulness.

13. Porteous, *Daniel*, 42.

The second of these expressions of confidence in God is in the nature of a confession of faith and it is portrayed as coming from none other than Nebuchadnezzar. This again comes after a revelation from God has been given to the tyrant through a dream (Dan 4:1–34). Nebuchadnezzar said,

> 34b I blessed the Most High,
> and praised and honored the one who lives forever.
> For his sovereignty is an everlasting sovereignty,
> and his kingdom endures from generation to generation.
> 35 All the inhabitants of the earth are accounted as nothing,
> and he does what he wills with the host of heaven
> and the inhabitants of the earth.
> There is no one who can stay his hand
> or say to him, "What are you doing?". . .
> 37b For all his works are truth,
> and his ways are justice;
> and he is able to bring low
> those who walk in pride.
> (Dan 4:34b–35, 37b)

What is set forth here is intended to witness to the supreme being and authority of the God of the Jews. Here is portrayed the (humanly) mighty king Nebuchadnezzar coming to his (religious) senses, and confessing both the power (vv. 34–35) and the wisdom (v. 37) of the Lord Most High. For those who could, and who today will, "suspend disbelief" in the fantastical notion of this great change coming upon the evil king, there is hope indeed in God for a good life on earth and for the triumph of justice in the world.

The third of these expressions of confidence in God is in Dan 6:26b–27, and once again is put into the mouth of an evil king, this time Darius, he who in the book of Daniel is infamously spoken of as having sent Daniel to the den of lions for the crime of having prayed to his own God (Dan 6:1–18). Daniel, of course, *did* pray to his God and thus *was* cast to the lions, yet was not harmed (6:19–24). Thus Darius made his own confession of faith about the God of Daniel,

> 26b For he is the living God,
> enduring forever.
> His kingdom shall never be destroyed,
> and his dominion has no end.

> 27 He delivers and rescues,
> he works signs and wonders in heaven and on earth;
> for he has saved Daniel
> from the power of the lions.
> (Dan 6:26b–27)

This surely is to be understood as the witness of the author of the book of Daniel to his belief in the justice of the ways of God which in the fullness of time would be made manifest in the world. That is, here in these stories of Daniel and his three friends in their clashes and contretemps with what are portrayed as various Babylonian rulers—but which modern scholarship is convinced are in fact Greek, in particular Seleucid, rulers—is his statement of belief that there is a justice in the life of the world. Here in these stories in the first six chapters of the book of Daniel is presented the theodicy of this writer. It would appear that his answer to that agonized question of his age for his own people "Where is the God of justice?" was that the will and ways of the Lord God would be made plain in the world in the fullness of time, when the God who "delivers and rescues," who "works signs and wonders in heaven and on earth" (Dan 6:27) would be revealed in the working of his works. But then, how convinced would those who were suffering in the Holocaust/Shoah have been by the stories of Daniel and his three friends, of Nebuchadnezzar and Darius?[14]

As yet we have considered only the first part of what our writer has to offer on this most serious theme, and it is to the second part that we must now turn. This second part of the book of Daniel comprises chapters 7–12 and is presented in the style of apocalyptic, inviting us to see things in the world from the heavenly point of view.

Here with chapter 7 it is now Daniel who is the dreamer, no longer the interpreter of others' dreams. Rather Daniel himself will require an interpreter, and thereby he will be given knowledge of divine mysteries, for indeed, "there is a God in heaven who reveals mysteries" (Dan 2:28). Daniel 7 comprises four main parts, and we consider each of these in turn.

Daniel 7:1–8 tells how Daniel had a vision, given to him in a nighttime dream. This is dated in the days of Belshazzar, king of Babylon but as will become clear it is much more likely that the political scene being

---

14. See Sweeney, *Reading the Hebrew Bible After the Shoah*, 222–26.

brought into focus is that of the Seleucid kingdom of the second century BCE (v. 1). In this vision winds were causing great disturbance in the seas, and four great beasts came up out of the sea (vv. 2–3), the first being like a lion but having the wings of eagles, but when it was *sans* wings it stood up like a human being (v. 4). The second beast was like a bear having three tusks in its mouth and was being told, "Arise, devour many bodies!" (v. 5). Then there was a leopard with four wings and four heads, "and dominion was given to it" (v. 6), and finally a fourth beast, "terrifying and dreadful and exceedingly strong," with great iron teeth and ten horns, and we are told that, "It was different from all the beasts that preceded it" (v. 7). And then a little horn appeared which had "a mouth speaking arrogantly," room having been made for it by plucking up three of the earlier horns (v. 8).

What is this strange language all about? This is the language of apocalyptic and it is widely agreed among critics that what are being spoken about here are four world empires, in fact those same four world empires that we believe are being spoken about in Dan 2, in Nebuchadnezzar's vision of the statue made up of different metals. These four kingdoms are first, the Babylonian, second, the Median, third, the Persian, and, last of all—and the most frightening—the Greek. The horns are generally considered to be Greek rulers, though how many of these are intended to be Ptolemies or Seleucids is much debated. However, the last of them would seem to be a clear reference to Antiochus Epiphanes, who according to 1 Macc 1:24 spoke arrogantly, and who according to Dan 11:36 spoke "horrendous things against the God of gods." All told then, these verses would seem to be speaking about that series of rulers from Nebuchadnezzar to Antiochus Epiphanes under whom the Jewish people had perforce to live during the centuries that led up the days when the book of Daniel was written.

Daniel 7:9–14 gives us a picture that is in marked contrast with all this. We are taken, in vision, into the world of heaven, where there is the Ancient of Days (Ancient One) and the scene is reminiscent of that portrayed in Ezek 1. Many beings were serving the Ancient of Days, a court sat in judgment, and books were opened (v. 10). Once again, there were the arrogant words of the horn, but then the beast (presumably the beast who had borne those horns) was put to death, and its body was destroyed and given over to be burned with fire (v. 11). As for the rest of the beasts, although their dominion was taken away their lives were prolonged "for a season and a time" (v. 12). That is, while the evil kingdoms may yet go on for some time, they have no abiding authority. Rather, "their doom is writ;" their time is severely limited.

In their place authority was given to one "like a human being," according to the translation of NRSV (7:13). This is more commonly translated "one like a son of man," and the expression has generated enormous discussion. Further, the expression was taken up later, either by Jesus or by the Gospel writers, as a self-designation for Jesus, but in the earlier context of the book of Daniel what are we to understand by this expression, "son of man"—in Aramaic *bar ʾĕnāš*, in Hebrew *ben ʾādām*? In particular, are we to understand this phrase as indicating a human being or alternatively a divine figure? That is, is this a person who comes from the nation of Israel and, as its leader, defeats the evil tyrant, or is he one who comes from the divine side of things, such as those figures spoken about in Dan 8:15; 10:5? Or, as some have argued, is he to be identified with Michael of Dan 12:1?[15] Perhaps we have to accept that as far as the reference in Dan 7:13 is concerned we cannot be sure about just what was intended, but what nevertheless is clear about this "Son of Man" figure is that he is appointed by none other than the Lord (the Ancient One, the Ancient of Days) to receive the kingdom and all its glory, and to assume the place spuriously occupied by that arrogantly speaking horn.

> To him was given dominion
> and glory and kingship,
> that all people, nations, and languages
> should serve him.
> His dominion is an everlasting dominion
> that shall not pass away,
> and his kingship is one
> that shall never be destroyed.
> (Dan 7:14)

For Daniel, famed though he may be portrayed in the book that bears his name as being a skilled interpreter of dreams, was unable to understand this one. Yet what Daniel cannot do, an attendant, presumably a divine attendant (Dan 7:16), does for him (7:17–28), and assures

---

15. See, e.g., amidst much literature on the subject, the articles "Son of Man," in *EDB*, 1242 (Senior); *ABD*:6, 137 (Nickelsburg); *IDB Sup*, 833–36 (Perrin); Casey, *Son of Man*.

him that all this is about the evil tyrant losing his power and authority, while that authority and power will be given by God (the Ancient of Days, the Ancient One) to "the holy ones of the Most High" (7:18, 22), who would appear to be, in the words of Porteous, "the faithful among the Jews, with emphasis upon the power of God which was to operate through them when they would represent his triumphant rule."[16]

We may pause at this stage in our consideration of the book of Daniel and allow ourselves to understand what this rather strange apocalyptic language in Dan 7 is intended to say, not only to those who in the days when it was written were suffering under the rule of an arrogant tyrant, but also to sufferers in similar situations in all subsequent ages. There is surely a theodicy here, the message that the sufferings of such people will not go on for ever, but that in such situations—which appear to be far beyond human and earthly powers to do anything about—there is hope in God, who both knows what his people are suffering and also has the power, authority, and will to act so as to change their situations and fortunes. There is an assurance for those who suffer in these sorts of situations being given by these apocalyptic thinkers and writers, which in the words of Rowley goes like this. "They [the apocalyptists] believed that evil is evil, and that of itself it could beget nothing but evil. But they did not believe that evil could not give place to good. On the contrary, they affirmed with confidence that the best was yet to be, and that it would be a best surpassing all that the mind of man could conceive. It would not arise of itself, however. It would have its source in God, and when evil gave place to good it would be because God swept evil away and established good."[17]

This sort of assurance for people suffering at the hands of an evil power is also given in the following chapter of Daniel, where it is expressed once again through the medium of a dream scene (Dan 8:1–14). Here the hostile foreign powers are pictured as animals, and in 8:15–27 help was given to Daniel to understand what these things meant, in particular that the evil power of the last of these was the horn that acted arrogantly, among other things causing the cessation of the sacrifices in the temple and the overthrowing of that sanctuary (8:9–12). Nevertheless these terrible events will last for only a limited time, "For

---

16. Porteous, *Daniel*, 112.
17. Rowley, *The Relevance of Apocalyptic*, 178.

two thousand three hundred evenings and mornings; then the sanctuary shall be restored to its rightful state" (8:14): a source of hope for suffering people that eventually there will be a satisfactory answer to the question "Where is the God of justice?"

There is yet a further vision in the book of Daniel that must be spoken about, and it has extensive coverage in chapters 10–12, chapters that present something of a world history, understanding it in terms of a great conflict between worldly and divine powers.[18] It makes a distinctive contribution to our theme of theodicy in the Old Testament. The three chapters, Dan 10–12, are generally felt to belong together as one single composition. They tell of a revelation that Daniel was given in the third year of Cyrus and set forth in varying amounts of detail the history of the Persian period, the subsequent reign of Alexander the Great, the history of the Seleucid rule up to and including that of Antiochus Epiphanes, and what will happen after that. At the end of this revelation there is a further word about the expression "a time, two times, and half a time" (12:7; see also 7:25; 9:27) which is understood and interpreted in two ways, as indicating one thousand two hundred and ninety days in 12:11, and one thousand three hundred and thirty-five days in 12:12.[19] Once again, the theodicy is that the evil and injustice manifest in the world through the tyrants has but a limited time to run. Yet again the message is that the doom of the tyrants is writ.

There is another aspect of the theodicy issue raised in Dan 12; in fact here a new theodicy is being presented. Daniel 12:1 speaks about the time dawning when Michael, "the great prince, the protector of your people, shall arise. There shall be a time of anguish, such as has never occurred since nations first came into existence."

---

18. It will be noticed that I am omitting here any consideration of Dan 9. This is because that chapter is dominated by a long prayer of confession that has at its heart the Deuteronomistic approach to theodicy, that "our sins" have caused this suffering to come upon us (noted above, 17, n. 16). On the prayer of Dan 9 see Thompson, *I Have Heard Your Prayer*, ch. 3, esp. 79–82.

19. Why might these two figures be given? Were they due to different calendars being employed, or reference being made to different events (see Goldingay, *Daniel*, 309–10), or were they both glosses on the expiry of the one thousand one hundred and fifty days of 8:14 (see Heaton, *Daniel*, 250), or to a recalculation (see Davies, "Daniel," 570). However, much more significant, surely, is "to believe that behind these mysterious calculations an unquenchable faith was active which kindled and maintained a like faith in many who were living through dark and calamitous days" (so Porteous, *Daniel*, 172).

And then: "But at that time your people shall be delivered, everyone who is found written in the book. Many of those who sleep in the dust of the earth shall awake, some to everlasting life, and some to shame and everlasting contempt. Those who are wise shall shine like the brightness of the sky, and those who lead many to righteousness, like the stars forever and ever" (Dan 12:1b–3). This clearly speaks of personal resurrection from the dead, although it is a text very much on its own and coming, as far as the Hebrew Bible is concerned, very late in time. It utters, with a marked note of confidence, the belief about a relationship between God and a faithful believer that can transcend death, a belief towards which, as we have already seen, the psalmists of Pss 49 and 73 were possibly pointing, hinting, hoping.[20] Further, spoken about here is a division of people at death; the talk is of the faithful going to everlasting life and others to shame and everlasting contempt. This may indeed seem harsh and so it has been labeled, for example, by Heaton: "If we owe a debt of gratitude to the writer for breaking the silence of the grave and affirming the communion of saints as part of the purpose of God, we must at the same time regret that he did not rise above the crude demand for strict retribution, which runs through the OT like an acrid stream."[21] But we would perhaps do better to consider these words of Dan 12 in their context, and understand them as coming out of, and making their distinctive contribution to, what was maybe the greatest political crisis that the people of ancient Israel ever had to face. Here was the assurance that those who had on earth stood firm in the name of the Lord would in a future age receive their great reward. That is, here was a conviction that came out of a particular moment of political and religious crisis, but further consequences of that new conviction would need time, space, and opportunity, maybe the very things that the author(s) of the book of Daniel did not have.[22] It is these religiously

---

20. See above 81–84, 100–104. On Dan 12:2 see Johnston, *Shades of Sheol*, 225–27; Martin-Achard, *From Death to Life*, 138–46.

21. Heaton, *Daniel*, 247, quoted by Porteous, *Daniel*, 171.

22. The helpful words of Goldingay, *Daniel*, 306, about Dan 12:2 should be noted, where he says, "Its exegesis must be approached via what precedes it, not via the formulated doctrine of resurrection later developed by groups such as the Pharisees and adopted by Christians. Indeed, we must avoid treating it as a piece of theological 'teaching': it is a vision or a flight of the imagination, not a 'fully developed' belief in resurrection." Brueggemann has, again I believe helpfully, associated the thought and formulation of Dan 12:2 with other Old Testament passages that speak of profound reversals when the

faithful ones, these "wise" ones, who will apparently be given places of honor in the universe. Such would appear to be the meaning of the expression in 12:3: "Those who are wise shall shine like the brightness of the sky, and those who lead many to righteousness, like the stars forever and ever." Have these faithful ones, the "wise," become in the nature of celestial beings, such as are spoken about in Dan 8:10; Judg 5:20; Job 38:7; *1 En.* 104; *T. Mos.* 10:9? Or are they being envisaged in more human, albeit glorious and exalted, mode in such language as used of—or to flatter—an Israelite king of old in Num 24:17; 1 Sam 29:9; 2 Sam 14:17, 20? We cannot be sure, but what seems clear is that their honor and worth are envisaged as having been divinely bestowed.

There is one other Old Testament passage that in this regard we should consider, Isa 26:19, which reads,

> Your dead shall live, their corpses shall rise.
> O dwellers in the dust, awake and sing for joy!
> For your dew is a radiant dew,
> and the earth will give birth to those long dead.
> (Isa 26:19)

This is part of Isa 24–27, chapters that are frequently called the Large Apocalypse (as distinct to the Small Apocalypse of Isa 34) of the book of Isaiah. It is generally agreed that here we have what has been called proto-apocalyptic literature,[23] material that is in the developmental stage of what will result in the sort of apocalyptic writings we have in the second part of the book of Daniel. Isaiah 26:7–21 is called by Clements "The life of the final age,"[24] and it speaks about new life, this being made clear at v. 19. The preceding verses, in particular vv. 17–18, have spoken about the present futility of life, likening it in vv. 17–18a to a woman's labor pains but which bring forth nothing more than wind. Thus, "We have won no victories on earth, / and no one is born to inhabit the world" (26:18b). Then comes v. 19, what Wildberger calls "the great 'however,' over against vv. 17f."[25] Here is a real expression of hope with its words about "your dead shall live."

---

powerful are put down and the powerless are exalted. See Brueggemann, "From Dust to Kingship," 11–12. See also Brueggemann, *Theology of the Old Testament*, 483–85.

23. For introduction to this part of the Isaiah book see, for example, Clements, *Isaiah 1–39*, 196–200; Barton, *Isaiah 1–39*, 90–92.

24. Clements, *Isaiah 1–39*, 213.

25. Wildberger, *Isaiah 13–27*, 567.

But about what is it an expression of hope? Although a number of commentators make a vigorous case for it being about the revival of the nation,[26] a larger number regard it as indicating individual resurrection, seeing it along with Dan 12:2 as being an expression of a belief in a life after death. In particular, some of the words here used would seem to indicate that the most likely reference is to individuals who have died, namely "your dead," and also "your corpses"—the last of which though in the Hebrew is in the singular, should be read, it is generally agreed, in the plural as the verb "shall rise" is in the plural. Further, the word "corpse" (*nĕbēlâ*) is in the Hebrew Bible used of human corpses, of animal carcasses, and (ironically) in Jer 16:18 of carcasses of idols, but never of the "corpse" of the nation.[27] Then there is the word *rĕpā'îm*, translated in NRSV at Isa 26:14 by "shades," and at Isa 26:19 by "those long dead." These are the inhabitants of the world of the dead, and again are individual people.[28] This is not to say that these words could *not* be used in a collective and metaphorical sense to indicate a "nation," but in view of their usage in the Hebrew Bible there is at least a certain probability that the reference is to individual resurrection from the dead.[29]

Thus in this word of salvation in Isa 26:19 is a real expression of hope for people who were in distress. Although there may not be the assurance of an immediate deliverance from their present evils and setbacks of life, there is the promise of a good future for them after death. Brevard Childs says of Isa 26:19, "The sign of the new [age] is not that pain and misery cease, but that the promised life in God's kingdom extends even beyond the grave . . . It is not by chance that in both Judaism and Christianity the belief in God's ultimate victory has incorporated as a cornerstone of faith a confession in the resurrection of the dead, which sustains the faithful who await the consummation of the age."[30]

What can we say then, by way of summary, about the contribution of the Old Testament's apocalyptic literature to questions about

---

26. So, for example, Clements, *Isaiah 1–39*, 216–17; Wildberger, *Isaiah 13–27*, 567–70; Goldingay, *Isaiah*, 146.

27. For the Hebrew word *nĕbēlâ* see *TDOT* :9, 151–57.

28. For the Hebrew word *rĕpā'îm* see *TDOT* :13, 602–14; Johnston, *Shades of Sheol*, 128–42.

29. Apart from these considerations, see the vigorous defence of Isa 26:19 being about individual resurrection in Blenkinsopp, *Isaiah 1–39*, 370–71.

30. Childs, *Isaiah*, 192.

suffering, and in particular to those who in their worldly settings and experiences may find themselves asking urgent questions about their sufferings and where for them is the God of justice? We have seen that there are three things in particular that the Old Testament's apocalyptic literature has for us as regards these matters.

In the first place the stories in Dan 1–6 not only present us with examples of faithful discipleship in times of great suffering and political pressure, but also carry within them the assurance of a corresponding commitment on the part of God for his people of earth. The theme in these stories is the wisdom and rightness of Daniel and his three friends, and at the same time the delivering strength given to them for their moments of crisis by the Lord, and the talk of their success in the worldly sphere through their faithful trusting in their Lord. The theme of these stories is very much that difficult though the worldly path of religious faithfulness may be in days when there is an evil empire, greater still will be the strength given by God to his servants that they may prevail. Thus, a representative of an evil empire, one Darius, can be portrayed as being led through his experiences to confess about the God of the Jewish people:

> For he is the living God,
> enduring forever.
> His kingdom shall never be destroyed,
> and his dominion has no end.
> He delivers and rescues,
> he works signs and wonders in heaven and on earth;
> for he has saved Daniel
> from the power of the lions.
> (Dan 6:26b–27)

In the second place there is the message for suffering people in the second part of the book of Daniel (chs. 7–12) assuring them that it is just a matter of time before there will come about a real change in the situation for the people of earth. The days of the evil empire, and the days when power can be stolen by one evil leader from another evil leader, are severely limited. The day will come when none other than God will give the power to a person of his own choosing, who will exercise that power and responsibility in good and beneficial ways. Whether in the book of Daniel that individual—that "Son of Man" individual—is intended to be understood as indicating a human or alternatively a divine personality remains a matter of debate. What is clearly portrayed is that the time for his appointment in the world is surely coming, and that his coming presages a much-changed situation, one for the better, in the world.

Third, there is in the second part of the book of Daniel (Dan 7–12) the assurance for faithful people that there will be a life after death. This belief is also spoken about in Isa 24–27. Both Dan 12:2 and Isa 26:19 set forth the belief that under God there can be a life after death for faithful people, a new life the other side of death. While this is not a hope that can be realized in the present worldly life, which may include in its make-up a large degree of suffering, it does present real hope for the future.

All told, it has to be said that there is no immediate-solution theodicy presented in the Hebrew Bible's apocalyptic literature. Even so, the message is clearly there in these documents that the faithful are called to hang on, to continue in their faithfulness and good works, in the assurance that God will truly bring about radical changes in the situation on earth, and in the lives of his faithful individual followers in future times.

8

Retrospect and Reflection

We have seen that in the Hebrew Bible there are clear and honest statements of the experiences of difficulties and sufferings that certain individuals and communities endured, and also, at times, their sense of the absence of God in those desperate times. Thus for example, "My God, my God, why have you forsaken me? Why are you so far from helping me, from the words of my groaning?" (Ps 22:1). Or again, "Why do you hide your face? Why do you forget our affliction and oppression?" (Ps 44:24). Further, "Truly, you are a God who hides himself, O God of Israel, the Savior" (Isa 45:15), and yet a prophet of an earlier time could say about this God in a spirit of trust, "I will wait for the Lord, who is hiding his face from the house of Jacob, and I will hope in him" (Isa 8:17).

It has been my purpose in this work to present a study of those parts of the Old Testament that speak of the sufferings of individuals and communities and, though I do not claim to have made an exhaustive examination of all the Old Testament material in this regard, I hope that by the end of the task I have considered most of it, certainly the most important parts.[1] I have also been concerned to ask whether alongside

---

1. I am conscious of gaps in my treatment. I am aware that I have not said anything about Gen 22, but it seems that chapter is about something more than a divine call to suffer, but about what that "something" is I am less sure. On Gen 22 see Crenshaw, *A Whirlpool of Torment*, 9–29, Crenshaw, "A Monstrous Test: Genesis 22"; Moberly, *Genesis 12–50*, 39–56; Moberly, *The Bible, Theology, and Faith*. On violence in the texts about Moses see Sweeney, *Reading the Hebrew Bible after the Shoah*, 42–63. On the subject of war in the Old Testament, including extermination of enemies see Niditch,

these accounts of suffering there is presented a theodicy, some attempt by way of explanation for the presence of that suffering.

As we have seen, the most prevalent explanation given within the Old Testament for the experience of suffering is that which links it with sinfulness. It affirms that righteous living leads to success and prosperity, while sinfulness leads to suffering and disaster. I borrowed the language of Father Paneloux in Albert Camus's novel *The Plague*, calling this the "deserved calamity" theodicy. It is deeply embedded in the Hebrew Bible, in the book of Deuteronomy, and in a particularly thoroughgoing way in the so-called Deuteronomistic History (Josh–2 Kgs), where it is used to explain the twin catastrophes of the 722 BCE exile of Israel and the 587 BCE exile of Judah. It is also there in the books of the prophets, in Lamentations, in Chronicles, and in some of the wisdom writings, in particular Proverbs.

While there is a certain appeal to reason in the thesis that sin brings in its train disaster, it is clear that this explanation is not adequate as a catchall solution to the problem of suffering. While we can sometimes see evidence of sin leading to disaster, we may observe that it is not always the sinners themselves who suffer, but sometimes others, sometimes even those of later generations. Further, many a time we appear to be witnessing suffering in the lives of individuals or communities and we are honestly not able to see or understand where there was sin, or what might be supposed to be the sin causing this.[2] The Old Testament itself has objections to this theory: in lament psalms; in what we read of the experiences Jeremiah; in psalms that specifically ask questions about suffering (Pss 37, 49, 73). It is there too in the experience of religious faithfulness in the days of the Greek kingdoms, as we read in the book of Daniel, and above all in the book of Job. For the man Job does not accept the doctrine, and nor does the writer of the book, and the book itself surely presents the theory as threadbare. In fact, it may be said that

---

War in the Hebrew Bibles; Davies, *The Immoral Bible*. On Esther see Korpel, "Theodicy in the Book of Esther." On what are indeed "texts of terror" in the Old Testament see, among many works, Trible, *Texts of Terror*; Davies, *The Dissenting Reader*; Seibert, *Disturbing Divine Behaviour*.

2. Bowker, *Problems of Suffering*, 12, says this "understanding of suffering which Deuteronomy and the Deuteronomistic historians applied to history . . . and to individual experiences of suffering . . . was open to an important objection: it was not true. Even the most casual observation of life makes it apparent that the wicked do not get cut off, and that the ruthless frequently prosper."

most of the material in the foregoing work after chapter 1 makes up a great chorus of questions about the "deserved calamity" doctrine, no small amount of this material being couched in language that exudes almost the spirit of protest, thus presenting urgent questions to God, like "Why?" and "How long?"[3]

With Qoheleth some questions about the ways of God in the world are asked, albeit gently. Thus in this brief book there is no great theological "rocking of the boat." Rather, as Samuel Terrien characterized it, taking up an expression of Hector in Shakespeare's *Troilus and Cressida*, it is "modest doubt" that is being aired here; Robert Davidson characterized Qoheleth "The Radical Conservative."[4] Qoheleth seems not to doubt the reality of God but does not speak as if there is any meaningful relationship between himself and the Deity. Rather, perhaps, that God is a Deity far away, humans being left somewhat on their own to make their own sense of life in the world. The counsel of Qoheleth seems to be, "Fear God, and keep his commandments; for that is the whole duty of everyone" (Eccl 12:13). Yet he has aired his doubts, but he has hardly developed them into a theodicy.

Whereas Qoheleth does not speak *with*—as distinct from speaking *about*—God, with at least some of the psalmists there is a remarkable outpouring to God of their burdens caused by sufferings. This lament tradition is widespread and plentiful in the psalter, especially in the earlier part of it, and within this tradition three psalms in particular witness a grappling with issues of suffering. As we have seen there is no theological solution to the problem of the suffering of the apparently innocent, no theodicy, presented in these so-called "wisdom psalms." Yet what there is here is, on the one hand, great openness and courage manifested in the bold presentation to God of the matter of apparent

---

3. In this regard see Burrell with Johns, *Deconstructing Theodicy*, 125–26, who says that the primary function of the book of Job in the Hebrew canon "may well be to correct 'mechanical' readings of Deuteronomy that remain heedless of the graceful divine initiative the covenant embodies. Here, of course, the target is not theologians so much as religious leaders, epitomized in Job's companions, who invariably attempt to channel God's generous initiative into manageable patterns."

4. See Terrien, *The Elusive Presence*, 373–80. The words "modest doubt" occur in *Troilus and Cressida* at ii.2.15. Terrien also includes an allusion to Qoheleth's book in Melville's *Moby Dick*: "The truest of all men was the Man of Sorrows, and the truest of all books is Solomon's, and Ecclesiastes is the fine hammered steel of woe. 'All is vanity.' ALL." See Terrien, *Elusive Presence*, 379; Melville, *Moby Dick*, 535. The reference to Davidson is from *The Courage to Doubt*, 184.

injustice and, on the other, true religion being revealed. For without explanation being given the psalmist clearly and sufficiently finds satisfaction, courage, cause for thanksgiving, apparently in God. Perhaps there is a clue given by the psalmist of Ps 73, for we are told in v. 17 that it was when he "went into the sanctuary of God" that he became convicted about the preciousness of his relationship with God, and the abiding nature of his portion in God (Ps 73:25–26), that in comparison his life-problems apparently sank into insignificance. Thus as Samuel Terrien observed, the poet of Ps 73 "began a song on the issue of theodicy and ended it as a credo on the eternal presence."[5]

This lament tradition in fact makes up one of the Hebrew Bible's most significant contributions to the Christian theodicy debate. In spite of the fact that it does not offer explanations nor present theodicies, yet it tells us about those who directly address the Lord with their sufferings and distresses, with their hurts and anger, and thereby at length find the presence of God—almost as if he had been there all the time. We should surely take this lament tradition seriously and, particularly in the Western European Christian tradition, encourage one another to use it in prayer. That is, we should accept that there are times when our prayers need to have a real "edge," making them prayers in which we address God in a profound sense of urgency, without the more usual politeness towards God many of us are accustomed to employ.

The prayers of lament are also to be observed in those so-called "confessions" of Jeremiah (Jer 11:18–23; 12:1–6; 15:15–21; 17:14–18; 18:19–23; 20:7–18) where it appears that the speaker is the prophet himself crying out to God about the dreadful difficulties that have come to him as he has been faithful in his prophetic calling. Even if the historical Jeremiah did not actually say such things as these, then at least those who mediated to us what we know today as the book of Jeremiah vividly portray their prophet as being remarkably outspoken to the Lord.

It is not in any way that the prophet is enabled to take an easier course in his ministry as a result of his outspoken prayers to God. Far from it: the prophetic work continues unabated with all the accompanying pressures and sufferings. What however Jeremiah is vouchsafed is the assurance of the Lord's presence with him: "for I am with you to save you and deliver you, says the Lord" (Jer 15:20); "But the Lord is with me like a dread warrior" (Jer 20:11). We are reminded of the harrowing

---

5. Terrien, *Elusive Presence*, 316.

scene that Elie Wiesel paints for us of the execution of three prisoners in one of the Holocaust camps in the Second World War. One of those prisoners was a child, who took an excruciatingly long time to die:

> But the third rope was still moving: the child, too light, was still breathing . . .
> And so he remained for more than half an hour, lingering between life and death, writhing before our eyes. And we were forced to look at him at close range. He was still alive when I passed him. His tongue was still red, his eyes not yet extinguished.
> Behind me, I heard the . . . man asking:
> "For God's sake, where is God?"
> And from within me, I heard a voice answer:
> "Where He is? This is where—hanging here from this gallows."[6]

We shall return to the lament tradition when we consider the book of Job, for many of the so-called speeches of Job are "laments." In the meantime we need to turn back to that explanation of suffering which understands sin as being its cause. For clearly at least a part of the purpose of the prophecy of Habakkuk was to challenge this understanding. The particular problem that this prophet had was with understanding how the Chaldeans can have been sent as a divine judgment upon the people of Judah when in fact those Chaldeans were appearing to be more evil than those whose evils they were being sent to sort out. Thus Habakkuk questions the Lord, "why do you look on the treacherous, and are silent when the wicked swallow those more righteous than they?" (Hab 1:13). The answer that Habakkuk receives from the Lord is that he must be patient, and further wait patiently in faith. He is assured that in the appointed time things will be made clear to him. For this he is to wait: "If it seems to tarry, wait for it; it will surely come, it will not delay" (Hab 2:3).

In fact, the resolution to the book of Habakkuk, coming in the third chapter, is both a strong expression of hope for suffering people on earth and also an equally strong condemnation of those whose way of

---

6. Wiesel, *Night*, 65. Wiesel in *The Town Beyond the Wall*, reminds us of the danger in such situations of the victim becoming a spectator, and, given a chance, even something of an executioner, in fact of becoming all three at the same time, victim, spectator, executioner. With some of the harsher words that Jeremiah uttered about his enemies, and what he expressed as wishing that might happen to them (e.g., Jer 20:12), we cannot altogether acquit the prophet of this.

life is characterized by out-and-out evil. It is perhaps not going too far to say that what we have here is an affirmative expression for the life of faithfulness to God and trust in his purposes, and at the same time an assurance of the ultimate defeat of the forces of evil and all that stands opposed to the Lord God. This is particularly brought out in Hab 3:8 with the wrath/anger/rage of the Lord against the rivers and the sea, "rivers" and "sea" apparently being parallel concepts which in parts of the Old Testament, borrowing from Ugaritic mythical language, stand for chaos, even the chaos monster which certain of the biblical psalms speak about as having been conquered by the Lord (Pss 77:16; 78:13; 93:2–4).[7] Here then, in the prophecy of Habakkuk, is the strong assurance that the present sufferings of the people of earth are by no means the end of the matter, but that under God there will be victory. Thus can Habakkuk exult in the God of his salvation (Hab 3:18)—even in the midst of and beset by present sufferings. But the drama has ended in terms of theophany: theological talk has not afforded help, but the mighty appearance of God has.

We have observed too how in the climax of the Joseph Story (Gen 37–50) there is the assurance of meaning after the sufferings endured by the various characters in the story. Above all—and mysteriously, for this story does not seek to probe into how this was done—at the end it is seen how the purposes of God have triumphed, that through various human decisions and experiences God was in fact at work. The point is made a number of times by Joseph to his brothers, first in chapter 45: "And now do not be distressed, or angry with yourselves, because you sold me here; for God sent me before you to preserve life" (Gen 45:5). Then again, "So it was not you who sent me here, but God; he has made me a father to Pharaoh, and lord of all his house and ruler over all the land of Egypt" (Gen 45:8), and also later, "Even though you intended to do harm to me, God intended it for good, in order to preserve a numerous people, as he is doing today" (Gen 50:20). The passage of time is a crucial factor here; there is no rapid answer to the meanings of those sufferings endured by the various participants in what we call the

---

7. See the article *nāhār* (river) in *TDOT*:9, 261–70, esp. 269–70. Note also that this mythological imagery is to be found in Song of Songs, at what appears to be the climax of the Song: in Song 8:7 love is said to be even stronger than "waters" or "rivers." The first part of the verse could be translated, "Mighty waters cannot quench love, no river can sweep it away." See e.g. Munro, *Spikenard and Saffron*, 112–14.

Joseph Story. Yet by the end of this story there is indeed the deliverance of the Lord—in this instance from the depredations of famine—and the making clear those crucial roles that various human beings, some of them markedly human and fallible, had played in this drama, at the time doing so all unwittingly. Most amazingly, the purposes of God, especially as they had been renewed with Abraham (Gen 12:1–3), went on. We might perhaps say that here in this story the matter of waiting is taken seriously; it is only in the fullness of time that it becomes clear why there were those earlier sufferings.

I now turn to the book of Job, a book that I understand as offering its readers a series of approaches to the problem of suffering. That is, it sets before us a series of theodicies that we are invited to "take and read," to consider them with a view to either rejecting or accepting one or more of them. The first of these is what appears in the Prologue to the book (Job 1:1—2:13), explaining the suffering that has come upon Job as being due to a "wager" having taken place between God and a member of the divine entourage, the satan. I have already suggested that we cannot accept this as a viable theodicy for it presents such a monstrous understanding of the Lord's actions. Rather, the Prologue appears to be a story that the author of the book of Job had to hand, so to speak, and which he used to set the scene of Job's great sufferings. Thus can the debate as to the meaning of suffering take place.

After Job has made his opening speech in which he speaks of his deep distress and agony that spring from his losses of animals, workers, family, livelihood and health (Job 3:1–26), his three friends, Eliphaz, Bildad, and Zophar, set forth their doctrine: human goodness brings about divine blessing, while human sinfulness inevitably leads to divine judgment and suffering. In the purposes of the author of the book of Job, the role of the friends of Job seems to be to set forth this understanding of the cause of suffering, and through their exceedingly repetitious and undeveloping speeches to demonstrate the somewhat threadbare nature of this explanation.

For it has to be said that so much else in the book of Job tells against the acceptance of this explanation for the reality of suffering, in particular in an individual life. The book clearly portrays the man Job as unable to accept this: Job denies that he has sinned, at least to the extent of having brought all this suffering upon himself. Further, what we know about the man Job also tells against this explanation, for we are told that he was blameless and upright, a man who feared God and turned away from evil (Job 1:1). Moreover, at the end of the book the Lord is portrayed as roundly condemning the friends because they have spoken folly and not what is right (Job 42:8). Thus the author of the book of Job does not present the friends as having spoken the truth, or even a modicum of sense, about the reality of suffering, and we are irresistibly drawn to the conclusion that the author of the book wishes to argue and thus persuade his readers into abandoning the "deserved calamity" explanation of suffering.

Our author clearly had here a Sisyphean task in directing his readers away from adhering to this understanding. For as well as being deeply rooted in the Old Testament, and in other religious traditions, this explanation for suffering is also recorded in the New Testament, as we have already seen in John 9:1–2, but also in, for example, the story of the falling of the tower of Siloam and the killing thereby of eighteen people, accompanied as it is by the warning "unless you repent, you will all perish just as they did" (Luke 13:1–5). Thus has this theory gone on in strength, having become known in the history of Christian theology as the Augustinian view, so-labeled by John Hick in his helpful study, *Evil and the God of Love*.[8] Augustine's contribution to this comes in a number of his works, one of them being *Enchiridion*, where, making reference to Gen 2:17, he says, "God had indeed threatened man with death as penalty if he should sin. He endowed him with freedom of the will in order that he might rule him by rational command and deter him by the threat of death."[9] It is there also in Augustine's *On Christian Teaching* where he says, "If a person's soul does not die to the present world and begin to be conformed to the truth, it is drawn by the death of the body into a worse death and reborn not to experience a new heavenly state but to suffer the retribution of punishment."[10]

Yet there are serious problems with this theodicy, in particular if it is employed as an explanation for all manner of sufferings. Certain sins do indeed bring in their train sufferings, either for the sinner or sinners concerned, and also maybe for those around them, or maybe for their successors. We are well aware that in the twentieth century hideous sins were committed in warfare and ethnic conflicts, bringing about untold

---

8. Hick, *Evil and the God of Love*, 43–75.
9. Augustine, *Enchiridion* VIII, 25 (see Augustine, *Confessions and Enchiridion*, 354).
10. Augustine, *On Christian Teaching*, 16.

and horrendous sufferings for so many people. That having been said, in the instance of Job's sufferings, the book portrays powerfully the limitations of this theodicy.[11] We have already noted the objection to it in Albert Camus's novel *The Plague*, where a young child dies of the plague and the doctor said fiercely to Father Paneloux (who had earlier proclaimed that the plague was a calamity that had come to the deserving sinners of the town), "That child, anyhow, was innocent—and you know it as well as I do!"[12] It may also be added that coming from the vantage point of the New Testament the fundamental criticism of John Hick to what he called the Augustinian theodicy lies in "the impersonal or subpersonal way in which God's relationship to His creation is prevailingly conceived."[13] His point is pertinent also as far as the Lord God of the Old Testament is concerned in his relationship with his creation and with his people.

The young man Elihu, as we have seen, takes an independent line from Eliphaz, Bildad, and Zophar as regards Job's sufferings. He does not deny that Job has sinned, but the particular angle that he takes is that suffering may serve as a divine discipline so as to bring about religious development, the education of a person. Thus does God, says Elihu, seek to open the ears of sinners, terrifying them with warnings, so that they may be turned aside from what they are doing (Job 33:16–17). Although this point has already been made briefly by Eliphaz (Job 5:17–18), and while it is to be found, for example, in Amos 4:6–11 (and also in Wis 3:1–9), it is by no means a common explanation in the Old Testament for suffering. It is, however, what Hick has characterized the Irenaean type of theodicy,[14] saying, "Irenaeus sees our world of mingled good and evil as a divinely appointed environment for man's development towards the perfection that represents the fulfillment of God's good purpose for him."[15] As Hick has pointed out, Austin Farrer seems

---

11. See the remarks of Soelle, *Suffering*, 114, about this doctrine in the hands of Job's friends: "Actually the doctrine about the punitive nature of suffering . . . needs to be silenced forever. It is almost incomprehensible that it has survived and been renewed again and again through the centuries within the framework of the same culture which produced the poem about Job. Job's friends don't die out!" See further Adams, *Horrendous Evils and the Goodness of God*, 39–43.

12. Camus, *The Plague*, 177.

13. Hick, *Evil and the God of Love*, 199.

14. Ibid., 205–76.

15. Ibid., 221.

to suggest that this makes for a comprehensible way for us to accept some aspects of the enigmas and sufferings as we live our lives in the world. Farrer says, "But suppose he creates a whole physical world, and places creaturely minds in it; suppose he so attaches them to it, that they are initially turned towards it, and find in it their natural concern. May he not then have strong animal minds, aspiring to know him in spite of their native physicality, instead of feeble spirits, whose obstacle lies in the mere poverty of their spirituality?"[16]

At any rate this "vale of soul-making"[17] theodicy makes the starting-point for the proposal entitled "A Theodicy for Today" that Hick presents in the final part of his work.[18] Yet though it does make a definite contribution to the whole theodicy debate, both in times long past (and for that we must be grateful for the way in which the author of the book of Job courageously developed and presented it through the words of his character Elihu) and also in recent times, even so it only makes a limited answer to the problem, by no means a complete one. Its Achilles' heel may be in its asking us to believe that in certain settings a person may have to suffer greatly in order to be warned about a possible comparatively minor lapse.[19] Nevertheless, it does have a contribution

---

16. Farrer, *Love Almighty and Ills Unlimited*, 66.

17. The phrase "vale of soul-making" comes from the poet John Keats, and occurs in a letter to his brother and sister of April 1819: "The common cognomen of this world among the misguided and superstitious is 'a vale of tears' from which we are to be redeemed by a certain arbitrary interposition of God and taken to Heaven—What a little circumscribed straightened notion! Call the world if you Please 'The vale of Soul-making.'" He goes on to say, "Do you not see how necessary a World of Pains and troubles is to school an Intelligence and make it a Soul?" See Keats, *The Letters*, 335–36.

18. Hick, *Evil and the God of Love*, 277–400. Is it with this sort of thought, which has come to be expressed in the "vale of soul-making" theodicy, that George Eliot's character Mr Gascoigne, the Rector, says to his niece, Gwendolen, in her time of loss and crisis, "This trouble has come on you young, but that makes it in some respects easier, and there is benefit in all chastisement if we adjust our minds to it"? See Eliot, *Daniel Deronda*, 289. The Reverend Peter Green has pointed out to me the words of Abbot John Chapman in a letter of Good Friday, March 22, 1913, to a certain Jesuit scholastic, "I hope you are having much suffering, and you have my best wishes and prayers for more of it." We do not have the earlier letter of the Jesuit scholastic to Chapman that drew forth this remark, but might the response have been in the terms of the "vale of soul-making" theodicy? See Chapman, *Spiritual Letters*, 247.

19. See above, 140–41 and the references there to the contribution of Nicholson, "The limits of theodicy as a theme of the book of Job." See also Adams, *Horrendous Evils and the Goodness of God*, 53, where she says, "To give this life, or any career

to make and, for that reason, we may wish to pay heed to the word of Elihu the son of Barachel the Buzite: "Listen to me; let me also declare my opinion" (Job 32:10).

However, while the insights of Elihu may not take us to the heart of the matter, with Job 28 we are surely being pointed in the direction where real help for our suffering is to be found. Certainly in the overall architecture of the book Job 28, far from having a questionable place as many have argued, can be seen to function as something akin to a signpost for humanity's search for God. It is, so the matter is portrayed here, as one makes a reverential approach to the holy and awesome God that one begins to find a way to understanding the deeper mysteries of life, among which must be counted problems of suffering. Even those who in the Joban author's day were venturing into hitherto uncharted territories, such as the miners seeking their precious metals and stones, even they in their explorations had not yet hit upon "the place of understanding."

For in this wonderful chapter the question is asked not once, but, with a small change in wording, twice: "But where shall wisdom be found? And where is the place of understanding?" (Job 28:12, cf. v. 20). It is not to be found by intrepid searchers in the depths of the earth, nor by other beings on earth, or in heights or depths. Rather it is to be found in God alone, as expressed in v. 28:

> And he [God] said to humankind,
> "Truly, the fear of the Lord, that is wisdom;
> and to depart from evil is understanding."
> (Job 28:28)

How are we intended to understand this chapter? Is it merely talking about a search being conducted in the wrong place, that is down in the depths of the earth instead of looking (up?) to God, or is it perhaps concerned that there is a search for riches and the precious things of earthly life rather than with reaching out to God? Perhaps the former interpretation is the safer one, yet maybe if I opt for the latter I am not merely speaking out of my western twenty-first-century experience of feeling surrounded by a "secular age," for does not the book of Deuteronomy

---

involving participation in horrors, positive significance, some parameter of positive meaning for horrors other than 'educational' benefit must be found!" See the remarks of Surin, *Theology and the Problem of Evil*, 92–96, on the "soul-making" theodicy.

warn those who come into the good land of the grave danger of forgetting God when surrounded by plenty and abundance? "When you have eaten your fill and have built fine houses and live in them, and when your herds and flocks have multiplied, and your silver and gold is multiplied, and all that you have is multiplied, then do not exalt yourself, forgetting the Lord your God, who brought you out of the land of Egypt, out of the house of slavery" (Deut 8:12–14). For the argument of the friends of Job, our old friends Eliphaz, Bildad, and Zophar, and all those for whom in the thought and architecture of the book of Job they stand, are looking at possessions, wealth, and prosperity as the essential hallmark of the favor and presence of God. Perhaps part of the burden of the Job 28 poem on wisdom is that the real search must be for God and in God, in particular that in the fear of God—or as we might say, in reverence for the Lord, in a sense of awe before God—is wisdom and understanding to be found.

Which does indeed lead us on to what must be regarded as the denouement, the climax of the book of Job. This comes in the two speeches of the Lord, neither of which provide any answers to the questions that Job was so urgently laying before those around him—both his earthly friends and also God. Further, Job's avowed intention of seeking to present the whole matter of his grievous sufferings before God appears to go completely by the board. What however Job does have is God speaking to him, not once but twice, each time we are told, "out of the whirlwind" (Job 38:1; 40:6). The first speech of God (Job 38:2—40:2) is all about the great wonders of the creation, all that is attributable to the almighty intelligence and power of God, and with the clear suggestion that there are all manner of things in the universe that Job has no *idea* of, much less any *knowledge* of. There is further, perhaps, an implicit suggestion that there are yet more things that are to be learned about the created world and all its wonders.

The second of the divine speeches runs from Job 40:6 to 41:34, and is taken up with descriptions of the two great monsters Behemoth and Leviathan, the first in 40:15–24 and the second in a longer and markedly more expansive passage, 41:1–34. As I have argued, there must surely be something new that the author has to say to us, something further than has already been expressed in the first divine speech.[20] What is new here

---

20. See above, 146–48.

is the triumph of God over the forces of evil in the world, represented in his hold over those monstrous creatures Behemoth and Leviathan. It is accepted that there are forces of evil at work in the world, but yet that they are held in check by the Lord God. And that perhaps is part of the theodicy that the author of the book of Job presents to us. There is only one God, and while it is clear that there are forces of evil in the world which cause individuals, groups, and nations to go astray, and at the same time to cause all manner of terrible things in the world, even so their sway is limited. Here we are assured that contrary to what we may feel about the state of things in the world, God does have things under his divine control.

Further, the fact that God has appeared—and moreover has spoken to Job—seems to be sufficient for Job. For Job is affirmed, at the same time being called to offer a burnt offering for, and to pray for, his friends who have been seriously misguided (Job 42:7–9)—this being perhaps in the nature of a parting shot at what is for the Joban author the unsatisfactory argument that human righteousness brings about prosperity while sinfulness causes suffering. And perhaps the tailpiece to the book telling of Job's restoration and of his new family and possessions is to be understood as our author's way of speaking of quiet and peace after the storms of life, that in the end we are surely led into ways of peace.

I used once again in the last-but-one paragraph the word "theodicy," but in truth when we come to the denouement of the book of Job, with the two lengthy and powerful speeches of the Lord, we are no longer in the realm of theodicy talk, for in fact *theodicy* has given way to *theophany*. Overall the book of Job, it may be said, endeavors to administer the last rites (alas, as things turned out, rather too soon) to the "deserved calamity" theory as a catchall theodicy; it has given considerable space to the "divine discipline" explanation; and it has further presented two rather difficult pictures of the matter of worldly suffering in the Prologue and the Epilogue. Yet the predominant message the book seeks to convey is that Job is given no answer to his questions about why he has been and is still suffering. Yet God has made his appearance! That is, theodicy has given place to theophany. And this *is* theophany: it is no gentle, but rather a mighty appearance of God "out of the whirlwind" (*sĕʿārâ*), a word that makes its appearance in a number of theophanies and other mighty happenings portrayed in the Hebrew Bible as having been initiated directly by God.[21] Here is a mighty manifestation of the Lord to Job which stops him in his tracks, drawing from him the spirit of repentance, the confession of his new awareness of his smallness and of having spoken too much (Job 40:4–5)—of having spoken of what he had heard only second hand but which now he had experienced at first hand, as a result of which he despised himself and repented in dust and ashes (Job 42:5–6).

With Isaiah chapter 53, as we have seen, there is something new in the Old Testament's contribution to questions about suffering. Here is a faithful servant of the Lord who willingly accepts suffering in the faithful discharge of his ministry. Suffering is not portrayed here as an anomaly, but as the very way in which the servant's ministry is worked out. In fact, as has been pointed out, there is in this passage (Isa 52:13—53:12) and in the other "servant passages" in Isa 40–55 (42:1–4; 49:1–6; 50:4–9) a perceptible movement away from privilege and favor towards a vision of a religious life that has suffering and rejection as hallmarks. In such ways the work of God is envisaged as going on. Opinion has long been divided over whether the prophet of these passages envisaged an individual servant or a corporate one. My own view, which I set out above, is that in all probability it is the corporate one that should be understood, and that here is given a vision of how the work of God will be done in future days. Rather than in a way of triumphal success and apparent progress, it will be through suffering, and even rejection. Yet, so we are told in these passages, and especially in the fourth of them, it will be in such ways that the work of God will be done. Here is the vision that in future days there may be suffering at the heart of faithful religious life.

Further, while this servant's suffering-work is completed in his death, there is talk of a life *after* death, though no details are given as to any condition or setting of that post-mortem existence. What *is* spoken of is the assurance that beyond ignominious death there will a life of honor: "Out of his anguish he shall see light" (Isa 53:11), his days will be prolonged, he will see his offspring (v. 10). Here we are in the thought and belief world of some of the apocalyptic writers who could envisage a life for faithful followers after death. Both of these aspects give a very different and significant aspect to the reality of earthly suffering, and as

---

21. For examples see, 2 Kgs 2:1, 11; Ps 107:25, 29; Isa 29:6; 40:24; 41:16; Jer 23:19; 30:23; Ezek 1:4; 13:11, 13; Zech 9:14. Further, see Fabry *sāʿar* in *TDOT*:10, 291–96.

we know, these twin aspects are clearly reflected in the further revelation given in Christ Jesus.

In the book of Daniel there is serious emphasis on God's people remaining faithful to him in deeply troubled times, both politically and religiously. In such unfavorable outward conditions faithfulness in religion will almost inevitably bring about suffering, for here is the conflict of religion and an evil empire. This must be endured for the time that the evil empire lasts, but the book of Daniel proclaims that that time is limited: it is until the earthly power is put into the safe hands of the person of the Lord's choosing. Then will come about a new era, infinitely for the better. Thus here is suffering that is presented as being part and parcel of the life of faith—as it is portrayed as being for the servant of the Lord in Isa 52:13—53:12. There is also here in the book of Daniel—expressed in Dan 12:2 and also there in the so-called Large Apocalypse in the book of Isaiah (Isa 26:19)—the assurance of life after death for those who have remained faithful to God. While this does not furnish an answer to questions about why there is evil in the world, it does offer to those caught up in it the assurance of something far better in a post-mortem existence. This particular promise of a better future should not, I suggest, be regarded as something of a fob off to distract attention from earthly sufferings and the associated urgent theological questions, but should be seen as coming out of a dire earthly situation which is far beyond human power to change, and in which sufferers can only wait for the future that God has graciously prepared for them.

What, then, can be said about the Hebrew Bible and suffering? Is it possible to perceive within its varied documents some leading ideas, some abiding themes in its responses to suffering? Have its stories and accounts, its expressions of bewilderment and outrage over the experience of suffering, anything in common, and what can we say by way of summary about how those various suffering individuals and communities found peace—while perhaps at the same time continuing to suffer?

There is to be observed one great commonality held by most, but not quite all, of those whose stories we have considered, and that is their relationship with God, which they have found, sometimes *at the eleventh hour*, to be of enormous sustaining worth. I purposely lay emphasis on my expression *at the eleventh hour*, for sometimes the true reality of the sufferer's precious relationship with God only comes to be appreciated at a late hour. Until the time of resolution of their problem, or at least of their coming to some accommodation with it, frequently they shout and rail at God, complain of their lot—yet, of course, that may only be possible as they see and understand themselves as being held in a relationship with the Lord! For it is indeed only the fools who in their hearts say, "There is no God" (Ps 14:1).

The people whose stories we have been considering were either aware from the beginning, or else became aware at a later stage, that they were in a deeply supportive relationship with God. Thus could Jeremiah declare, "But the Lord is with me like a dread warrior" (Jer 20:11); a suffering psalmist could affirm, "Whom have I in heaven but you? And there is nothing on earth that I desire other than you" (Ps 73:25; cf. Pss 13:6; 37:39–40; 49:15); in a spirit of faithful trust in God Habakkuk could wait for the divine answer of God to the conundrum that he and his people were grappling with (Hab 2:1); Joseph demonstrated his closeness to and relationship with God through his ability in the interpretation of dreams (Gen 40:8–15, 16–19; 41:1–36; cf. Gen 39:23).[22] The fourth of the passages about a/the servant in Isa 52:13—53:12 is redolent with expressions of the relationship that the servant has with the Lord; Job, although above all shouting and railing at God, is sure that the Lord is there. Further, this Lord ultimately speaks to him, and Job is reassured in his relationship with him (Job 42:2, 3b, 5). Daniel is portrayed as faithful above all else in his following of, and his relationship with, God (Dan 1:8; 6:10).

This is the great matter possessed in common by those whose words and stories we have been studying. All these people exemplify the reality famously expressed by St Augustine, "for thou hast made us for thyself and restless is our heart until it comes to rest in thee."[23] This is what Marilyn McCord Adams speaks about when she says, "participation in horrors can be integrated into the participants' relation to God, where God is understood to be the incommensurate Good, and the relation to God is one that is overall incommensurately good *for the participant.*"[24] The matter of this relationship between God and his people in which God's goodness is so overwhelmingly great and good, is also emphasized by David Burrell, who writes about "expressing the

---

22. On dreams and the interpretation of them see Smith-Christopher "Dreams." In *EDB*, 356–57.

23. Augustine, *Confessions and Enchiridion*, 31.

24. Adams, *Horrendous Evils and the Goodness of God*, 155, her italics.

inexpressible" covenant relationship that human beings can have with God, saying that while there is a distinction between creatures and their creator, there is at the same time a relation between them. "Both prove," says Burrell, "to be foundational to any attempt to grasp our transcendent origins as gift." And he goes on to say, "Job offers a poignant poetic rendition of the inexpressible relation, personally executed in the heart of affliction."[25] This is, of course, what in parts of the Old Testament is indicated by the word "covenant" (*běrît*), "God's choice of his people and their 'choice' of him, that is, their free decision to be obedient and faithful to him. Thus understood, 'covenant' is the central expression of the distinctive faith of Israel as 'the people of Yahweh', the children of God by adoption and free decision rather than by nature or necessity."[26] It is within this relationship that there were those in Ancient Israel who in their sufferings felt the reality of their relationship with the Lord—even if the full implications of that relationship only became real to them in the eleventh hour of their sufferings.

However, the marked exception among those we have studied in this work is Qoheleth. He is different in that he does *not* speak of his relationship with God; while he has a good deal to say *about* God and about his experience of life in the world, what he does not do is to speak *to* God. As was said just over one hundred years ago, "Though a skeptic, he [Qoheleth] has not abandoned his belief in God. It is true that God is for him no longer a warm personality or a being intimately interested in human welfare. The ancestral faith of Israel in Yahweh has been outgrown; Qoheleth never uses the name. God is an inscrutable being."[27] Is it this apparent inability—or lack of willingness?—to speak to God, Yahweh, that leaves Qoheleth so singularly adrift in his observations of life, with little hope, and with that almost inevitable refrain to what he writes, "Vanity of vanities . . . all is vanity" (Eccl 1:2 etc.)?

I noted above John Hick's criticism of the "deserved calamity" theodicy: "Perhaps the most fundamental criticism to be made of the Augustinian type of theodicy . . . is the impersonal or subpersonal way

---

25. Burrell with Johns, *Deconstructing Theodicy*, 137–38. Elsewhere in Job Burrell says, 119, "Moreover, is not the entire book [of Job] cast in the covenantal mode, so portraying God as interacting with creatures? And does not God answer Job, thereby showing that he is a person?"

26. Nicholson, *God and his People*, 216.

27. Barton, *Ecclesiastes*, 49–50.

in which God's relationship to His creation is prevailingly conceived."[28] While it would have to be admitted, further, that there is a certain harshness in much of the recorded proclamation of Israel's prophets about their people's sins,[29] it is also true that there is another aspect to their preaching. For example, while in the book of Hosea there are stinging rebukes of Israel's leaders (for example Hos 5:1–15), there is also portrayed in this book a much more tender side to God and depths of emotion that the Lord feels for his people in their failings. Thus, whereas God is portrayed first as giving warning of coming judgment upon his sinful people (Hos 11:1–7), there is then portrayed his deep and emotional concern for them, such that he finds himself unable to bring the (deserved) judgment upon them. These are his own people for whom his heart recoils within him; he is the Lord whose compassion grows warm and tender, and who will not execute his fierce anger (Hos 11:8–9).

We may perhaps regard these words in the prophecy of Hosea as representing a more sympathetic approach on the part of at least some of the leaders of Israel than that, perhaps more general approach, which instead of merely excoriating the people and their leaders, felt for them in their sinfulness and failings, perhaps even associating themselves with them as also being sinful. Might one perhaps feel that the prophecy of Hosea has within it something of that prophet's awareness of his own sin and failure—maybe as regarding his marriage, maybe in connection with sexual matters? Was the prophet maybe standing with his people in their sinfulness and suffering, associating himself with them? One is reminded of Albert Camus's later depiction of Father Paneloux, the Jesuit priest, in his novel *The Plague* who, while at first proclaiming to the people *their* sinfulness as the cause of the plague, is later challenged by Dr Rieux about the death of the—surely not sinful!—young child, and thus about how the priest came to address the people differently: "And it was in a cold, silent church, surrounded by a congregation of men exclusively, that Rieux watched the Father climb into the pulpit. He spoke in a gentler, more thoughtful tone than on the previous occasion, and

---

28. Hick, *Evil and the God of Love*, 199. See above, 182.

29. What Burrell with Johns, *Deconstructing Theodicy*, 132, refer to as "the prophets' consistent excoriation of Israel's leaders for their failure to heed God's promises and activity in the life of the people."

several times was noticed to be stumbling over his words. A yet more noteworthy change was that instead of saying 'You' he now said 'We.'"[30]

Another place where the Old Testament presents us with a gentler, less judgmental understanding of God is in the prophecy of Ezekiel, in particular in the part that speaks of hope for Israel then in exile (Ezek 33–37). Within these chapters is Ezek 34:1–16, which speaks of the failure of the human shepherds who were supposed to have been looking after the people, but who have failed to do so. The burden of these words is that Israel's national leaders have failed in the exercise of their responsibilities, and as a result now God himself will come and seek out his people and will rescue them (Ezek 34:11–16).[31] This presents us with the picture of God as the shepherd of his people, a picture that occurs not infrequently in the Old Testament, particularly well-known to us above all in Ps 23, but also in Gen 49:24 and elsewhere.

Terence Fretheim, in a study of some years ago entitled *The Suffering of God*, maintained that, "The prophet's life was reflective of the divine life." He went on to say, "To hear and see the prophet was to hear and see God, a God who was suffering on behalf of the people."[32] That is surely begging quite a number of questions: how can we know whether or not God suffers? Is it really true that the "prophet's life was reflective of the divine life," and that to "hear and see the prophet was to hear and see God"? In fact, was not the matter of true and false prophecy something of the Achilles' heel of the Israelite prophetic movement, namely was this or that prophet speaking *truly* of the things of God? When we ask, "Does God suffer?" I suggest that as far as the Old Testament is concerned we have to say that we do not know. If, however, we read on from the Old into the New Testament, then I think that the answer is different. For the New Testament *does* appear to some of us to portray God suffering, in Christ, and above all on the cross.[33] And that surely

---

30. Camus, *The Plague*, 182. For my earlier references to and comments about Camus's work see above, 7–8 and 20–21.

31. The question may be raised whether or not this and the surrounding chapters come from the same prophet whose prophecies are recorded in the book of Ezekiel. See the vigorous case for the prophet of these hopeful words being Ezekiel in Joyce, *Ezekiel*, 195–96.

32. Fretheim, *The Suffering of God*, 149.

33. The matter is disputed. See, e.g., Adams, *Horrendous Evils and the Goodness of God*, 173–74; Moltmann, *The Crucified God*; Soelle, *Suffering*, 145–50; von Hügel, "Suffering and God."

adds a whole new dimension to the picture of suffering as the Christian Bible speaks about it.

We shall return to the New Testament, but in the meantime we need to draw together what results we can from our study of what the Old Testament has to say to, and about, those individuals and communities whose lives involve suffering. Further, what help might there be here in the Old Testament for us in our sufferings today?

It has become abundantly clear that the Hebrew Bible is more than open about the fact that people *do* suffer in the world, whether they be righteous and devout or whether they be sinful and unrighteous. Their stories are presented in many parts of the Hebrew Bible, and the mere presence of those stories, coming as they do from varieties of settings and ages, constitute profound help and encouragement to those who read them in age after age, or hear them read. These Scriptures are well aware of the fact of evil in the world, but nowhere explain it, clinging tenaciously to the belief that there is only one God who can be taken with any seriousness. Thus all things in the creation are owing to Yahweh, who—so it seems we are being assured in the book of Job in its talk of Leviathan, that mythical creature of the deep seas—does keep those forces of evil in check and under his control.[34]

Further, the Old Testament does have a number of theodicies. Most extensive among these is what in this study I have labeled the "deserved calamity" theodicy, which explains suffering as being due to human sinfulness. This theodicy makes its appearance in wide swathes of the Old Testament, and while it should not be dismissed, its teachings should be pondered with care. We might say that in *certain* situations it has something to say to us that we should hear, but that at the same time it is clearly inadequate as an explanation for the occurrence of a large number of life's sufferings. So it seems the book of Job seeks to proclaim the inadequacy of the "deserved calamity" approach as a catchall explanation for *all* experiences of suffering.

Then there is what has come, long after the times from which the Old Testament documents date, to be labeled the "vale of soul-making" theodicy, which is not given over-much treatment in the Old Testament but whose staunchest defender is the young man Elihu in the book of Job. It is variously assessed by philosophers, positively by

---

34. Surin, *Theology and the Problem of Evil*, 162 says, "Evil, and its root and essence, is a mystery." See also Levenson, *Creation and the Persistence of Evil*.

John Hick in his helpful study of suffering, much more negatively by Marilyn McCord Adams. Perhaps it does have something to contribute, yet perhaps not too much.

With the book of Daniel there is the realization and acceptance that evil in the world may be due to the ambitions and activities of an evil political regime. In such a situation maybe all that the faithful can do is to remain faithful to their God, being given the assurance, or experience, that the Lord is with them in their suffering. There is also in this book the assurance of a future redressing of fortunes, both on earth and also, for those who have remained faithful, in a yet-to-come post-mortem life. Further, in the second part of the book of Isaiah is the new insight that suffering may be a part and parcel accompaniment of faithful service: faithful service of God may in fact be taking place in and through that suffering. Also here, in Isa 53, is the talk of a life after death: once again the redressing of what has been suffered on earth.

Other approaches and responses to suffering found in the Old Testament cannot really be designated theodicies in that they do not seek to explain *why* there is suffering taking place. Yet what the Old Testament does present us with is a series of what we might call *strategies* to deal with the reality of suffering. There are all those parts of the Old Testament where an individual cries out to God for his help and/or his presence. This we read of psalmists doing, of the prophet Jeremiah doing, above all, and on a scale and in a class all of its own, of the suffering man Job doing. And in each case there is at least some satisfaction, sometimes sooner sometimes later, granted to the one who cries out to the Lord: at times, as in the case of Job, satisfaction on a grand scale; at other times, as for example in the case of Jeremiah, just sufficient assurance for the courage to continue the journey. But here is surely one of the Hebrew Bible's most noteworthy and significant contributions to the questions that religious people ask as to why there is suffering in the world. The questions may not be answered as to why there is suffering, yet here is the way to finding the presence of the all-sufficient God for the time of and the enduring of that suffering. Alas, that Qoheleth could only speak *about* God, and—as far as we are told—did not feel able to try speaking *to* him! Perhaps we may also say that neither did Qoheleth appear to have the patient trust in the face of life's disappointments that Joseph, Habakkuk and the psalmist of Ps 37 showed, Luther's "the patience of the saints."

What we have above all in the Old Testament in its abundant stories of suffering individuals and communities is, in the main, the realization that the sufferers are in a covenant relationship with the Lord, and come to the discovery, or rediscovery, of their ineffable relationship with God, so that—in the language of Marilyn McCord Adams—as well as there being horrendous evils there is most surely also the goodness of God.

How then, it will be asked, are Christian people to "read" these Old Testament stories about horrendous evils and the goodness of God? Now that they have the New Testament can the Old be left on one side—as is so common in parts of the Christian church today? "By no means!" For the Old Testament represents, shall we say, so much "experience" of suffering, not only of individuals and groups but also within a wide range of settings and historical circumstances, both in peace and prosperity, and also in war and strife. There is surely here in the Hebrew Bible too much "lived experience" of the life of faith in God that mysteriously is attended by setbacks, disappointments, tragedy, illness, evil, and disaster, for this remarkable witness and record to be set on one side, left as it were unused. Yet, for Christians these stories in the Old must surely be read alongside the New Testament, and be interpreted within that aura of the further light shed by the New.[35] Within that aura of further light must be reckoned above all the message of the cross: God in Christ suffering *with* us, suffering surely *for* us, warning his followers that *their* discipleship must take into account the possibility of its having its own share of suffering (Mark 8:34 etc.), that maybe in suffering there will be a (necessary?) sharing in what Christ endured (Col 1:24?). There is also here in the New Testament the message of the ultimate defeat of the powers of evil in the death and resurrection of Christ,[36] and the promise of resurrection and new life the other side of death. Here are new dimensions and assurances about the ineffable relationship that God offers his faithful people, what Marilyn McCord Adams speaks of as the "incommensurate" goodness of God.

---

35. This, I am well aware, is a highly compressed statement, maybe inexcusably compressed. I can only plead that the whole subject of hermeneutics is of such importance that it needs a study all of its own. I have found the following to be helpful: Schneiders, *The Revelatory Text*; Ferguson, *Biblical Hermeneutics*; Jeanrond, *Theological Hermeneutics*; Thiselton, *The Two Horizons*; and also Thiselton *New Horizons in Hermeneutics*. See also Watson, *Text, Church and World*.

36. See the classic study of Aulen, *Christus Victor*.

Yet we must remain grateful for the record in the Hebrew Bible of those theological speculations of Qoheleth, of Job and his friends, of Deuteronomists and others, and thankful too for the witness of prophets, sages, psalmists, and apocalyptists. Yet, as Job learned so dramatically, all too often what we say we do not understand, and that at the heart of it all are "things too wonderful for me, which I did not know" (Job 42:3), realities perhaps never more sublimely expressed than by one of the psalmists:

> Whom have I in heaven but you?
> And there is nothing on earth that I desire other than you.
> My flesh and my heart may fail,
> but God is the strength of my heart and my portion forever.
> (Ps 73:25–26)

Thus many years later Austin Farrer, towards the conclusion of his *Love Almighty and Ills Unlimited*, would say about divine love and earthly ills, "the value of speculative answers, however judicious, is limited. They clear the way for an apprehension of truth, which speculation alone is powerless to reach," going on to say that, "the substance of truth is grasped not by argument, but by faith. The leading of God through evil out of evil and into a promised good is acknowledged by those who trust in his mercy."[37] And to that, as we have seen, the Old Testament bears its own particular witness.

---

37. Farrer, *Love Almighty and Ills Unlimited*, 164.

Bibliography

Achtemeier, Elizabeth. *Nahum–Malachi*. Interpretation. Atlanta: John Knox, 1986.
Adams, Marilyn McCord. *Horrendous Evils and the Goodness of God*. Ithaca, NY: Cornell University Press, 1999.
Allen, Leslie C. *Jeremiah: A Commentary*. Old Testament Library. Louisville: Westminster John Knox, 2008.
Amos, Clare. *The Book of Genesis*. Epworth Commentaries. Peterborough, UK: Epworth, 2004.
Andersen, Francis I. *Habakkuk*. Anchor Bible. New York: Doubleday, 2001.
———. *Job*. Tyndale Old Testament Commentaries. Nottingham, UK: InterVarsity, 1976.
Anderson, Arnold A. *The Book of Psalms*. New Century Bible Commentary. London: Marshall, Morgan and Scott, 1972.
Astell, Ann W. "Reading the Bible with Holocaust Survivors and Rescuers: A New Biblical Spirituality." *Int* 56 (2002) 181–91.
Augustine, Saint. *Confessions and Enchiridion*. Translated by Albert C. Outler. Library of Christian Classics 7. London: SCM, 1955.
———. *On Christian Teaching*. Translated by Roger P. H. Green. Oxford: Oxford University Press, 1997.
Aulen, Gustaf. *Christus Victor*. Translated by S. G. Hebert. London: SPCK, 1965.
Balentine, Samuel E. *The Hidden God: The Hiding of the Face of God in the Old Testament*. Oxford: Oxford University Press, 1983.
Barton, George A. *A Critical and Exegetical Commentary on the Book of Ecclesiastes*. International Critical Commentary. Edinburgh: T. & T. Clark, 1908.
Barton, John. *Isaiah 1–39*. Old Testament Guides. Sheffield, UK: Sheffield Academic, 1995.
Barton, John and John Muddiman. *The Oxford Bible Commentary*. Oxford: Oxford University Press, 2001.
Baumgartner, Walter. *Jeremiah's Poems of Lament*. Translated by D. E. Orton. Historic Texts and Interpreters in Biblical Scholarship 7. Sheffield, UK: Almond, 1988.
Becking, Bob and Dirk Human. *Exile and Suffering: A Selection of Papers Read at the 50th Anniversary Meeting of the Old Testament Society of South Africa OTWSA/OTSSA Pretoria August 2007*. Old Testament Studies, 50. Leiden: Brill, 2009.
Bellinger, William H. and William R. Farmer. *Jesus and the Suffering Servant: Isaiah 53 and Christian Origins*. Harrisburg, PA: Trinity, 1998.
Blenkinsopp, Joseph. *Isaiah 1–39*. Anchor Bible 19. New York: Doubleday, 2000.

———. *Isaiah 40–55*. Anchor Bible 19A. New York: Doubleday, 2000.
Bowker, John. *Problems of Suffering in Religions of the World*. Cambridge: Cambridge University Press, 1970.
Boys, Mary C. "Holocaust." In *The New SCM Dictionary of Christian Spirituality*, edited by Philip Sheldrake, 343–44. London: SCM, 2005.
Briggs, Charles A. and Emilie G. Briggs. *A Critical and Exegetical Commentary on the Book of Psalms*. International Critical Commentary. Edinburgh: T. & T. Clark, 1906.
Broyles, Craig C. *The Conflict of Faith and Experience: A Form-Critical and Theological Study*. JSOTSup 52. Sheffield, UK: JSOT Press, 1989.
Brueggemann, Walter. "The Costly Loss of Lament." *JSOT* 36 (1986) 57–71.
———. "From Dust to Kingship." *ZAW* 84 (1972) 1–18.
———. *A Pathway of Interpretation: The Old Testament for Pastors and Students*. Eugene, OR: Cascade, 2008.
———. "Psalm 37: Conflict of Interpretation." In *Of Prophets' Visions and the Wisdom of Sages*, edited by Heather A. McKay and D. J. A. Clines, 229–56. JSOTSup 162. Sheffield, UK: JSOT Press, 1993.
———. "Some Aspects of Theodicy in Old Testament Faith." *Perspectives in Religious Studies* 26 (1999) 253–68.
———. *The Theology of the Book of Jeremiah*. Old Testament Theology Series. Cambridge: Cambridge University Press, 2007.
———. *Theology of the Old Testament: Testimony, Dispute, Advocacy*. Minneapolis: Fortress, 1997.
Buber, Martin. "The Heart Determines: Psalm 73." In *Theodicy in the Old Testament*, edited by James L. Crenshaw, 109–18. Issues in Religion and Theology 4. Philadelphia: Fortress, 1983.
Burnett, Joel S. *Where Is God?: Divine Absence in the Hebrew Bible*. Minneapolis: Fortress, 2010.
Burrell, David B. with A. H. Johns, *Deconstructing Theodicy: Why Job Has Nothing to Say to the Puzzled Suffering*. Grand Rapids: Brazos, 2008.
Calvin, John. *Genesis*. Translated by John King. London: Banner of Truth, 1965.
———. *Sermons from Job*. Selected and translated by L. Nixon. Grand Rapids: Baker, 1952.
Camus, Albert. *The Plague*. Translated by Stuart Gilbert. Harmondsworth, UK: Penguin, 1960.
Carlyle, Thomas. *On Heroes, Hero Worship and the Heroic in History*. 1841. Reprinted, London: Chapman and Hall, 1898.
Carroll, Robert P. *Jeremiah*. Old Testament Library. London: SCM, 1986.
Casey, Maurice. *Son of Man: The Interpretation and Influence of Daniel 7*. London: SPCK, 1979.
Chapman, John. *Spiritual Letters*. London: Burns & Oates, 2003.
Childs, Brevard S. *Isaiah*. Old Testament Library. Louisville: Westminster John Knox, 2001.
Clements, Ronald E. *Isaiah 1–39*. New Century Bible Commentary. London: Marshall, Morgan and Scott, 1980.
———. *Jeremiah*. Interpretation. Atlanta: John Knox, 1988.
Clines, David J. A. *Job 1–20*. Word Biblical Commentary 17. Dallas: Word, 1989.
———. *Job 21–37*. Word Biblical Commentary 18A. Nashville: Nelson, 2006.
———. *Job 38–42*. Word Biblical Commentary. Forthcoming.

Coats, George W. *From Canaan to Egypt: Structural and Theological Context for the Joseph Story*. CBQMS 4. Washington, DC: Catholic Biblical Association, 1976.
Collins, Adela Y. "Apocalyptic Themes in Biblical Literature." *Int* 53 (1999) 117–30.
Collins, John J. "Daniel and His Social World." *Int* 39 (1985) 131–43.
Consultation on Common Texts. *The Revised Common Lectionary*. Norwich, UK: Canterbury, 1992.
Cooper, Alan. "Reading and Misreading the Prologue of Job." *JSOT* 46 (1990) 67–79.
Craigie, Peter C. *Psalms 1–50*. Word Biblical Commentary 19. Waco, TX: Word, 1983.
Crenshaw, James L. *Defending God: Biblical Responses to the Problem of Evil*. New York: Oxford University Press, 2005.
———. *Ecclesiastes*. Old Testament Library. London: SCM, 1988.
———. "Job." In *The Oxford Bible Commentary*, edited by John Barton and John Muddiman, 331–55. Oxford: Oxford University Press, 2001.
———. *Old Testament Wisdom: An Introduction*. Atlanta: John Knox, 1981.
———. "Suffering." In *Oxford Companion to the Bible*, edited by Bruce Metzger and M. D. Coogan, 718–19. Oxford: Oxford University Press, 1993.
———. "Theodicy." In *ABD* 6:444–47.
———. "Theodicy and Prophetic Literature." In *Theodicy in the World of the Bible*, edited by Antti Laato and J. C. de Moor, 236–55. Leiden: Brill, 2003.
———. "Theodicy in the Book of the Twelve." In *Thematic Threads in the Book of the Twelve*, edited by Paul L. Redditt and A. Schart, 183–91. BZAW 325. Berlin: de Gruyter, 2003.
———, ed. *Theodicy in the Old Testament*. Issues in Religion and Theology 4. Philadelphia: Fortress, 1983.
———. *Urgent Advice and Probing Questions: Collected Writings on Old Testament Wisdom*. Macon, GA: Mercer University Press, 1995.
———. *A Whirlpool of Torment: Israelite Traditions of God as an Oppressive Presence*. Overtures to Biblical Theology. Philadelphia: Fortress, 1984.
Croft, Steven J. L. *The Identity of the Individual in the Psalms*. JSOTSup 44. Sheffield, UK: JSOT Press, 1987.
Curtis, Adrian. *Psalms*. Epworth Commentaries. Peterborough, UK: Epworth, 2004.
Danby, Herbert, trans. *The Mishnah*. London: Oxford University Press, 1933.
Davidson, Robert. *The Courage to Doubt: Exploring an Old Testament Theme*. London: SCM, 1983.
———. *Wisdom and Worship*. London: SCM, 1990.
Davies, Eryl W. *The Dissenting Reader: Feminist Approaches to the Hebrew Bible*. Aldershot, UK: Ashgate, 2003.
———. *The Immoral Bible: Approaches to Biblical Ethics*. London: T. & T. Clark, 2010.
Davies, Philip R. *Daniel*. Old Testament Guides. Sheffield, UK: JSOT Press, 1985.
———. "Daniel." In *The Oxford Bible Commentary*, edited by John Barton and John Muddiman, 563–71. Oxford: Oxford University Press, 1993.
Day, John. *God's Conflict with the Dragon and the Sea: Echoes of a Canaanite Myth in the Old Testament*. Cambridge: Cambridge University Press, 1985.
———. *Psalms*. Old Testament Guides. Sheffield, UK: JSOT Press, 1990.
Dell, Katharine. *Shaking a Fist at God: Struggling with the Mystery of Undeserved Suffering*. London: Fount, 1995.
———. *"Get Wisdom, Get Insight": An Introduction to Israel's Wisdom Literature*. London: Darton, Longman & Todd, 2000.
Dhorme, Edouard P. *A Commentary on the Book of Job*. Translated by Harold Knight. London: Nelson, 1967.

Diamond, A. R. Pete. *The Confessions of Jeremiah in Context: Scenes of Prophetic Drama*. JSOTSup 45. Sheffield, UK: Sheffield Academic, 1987.
Dostoevsky, Fyodor. *The Brothers Karamazov*. Translated by C. Garnett. Revised by R. E. Matlaw. Norton Critical Edition. New York: Norton, 1976.
Eaton, John. *The Psalms: A Historical and Spiritual Commentary with an Introduction and New Translation*. London: T. & T. Clark, 2003.
Eliot, George. *Daniel Deronda*. London: Penguin, 1995.
Emmerson, Grace I. *Isaiah 56–66*. Old Testament Guides. Sheffield, UK: JSOT Press, 1992.
Fabry, Heinz-Josef. "lēḇ." In *TDOT* 7:399–437.
———. "nāhār." In *TDOT* 9: 261–70.
———. "nᵉḇēlâ." In *TDOT* 9: 151–57.
———. "sāʿar." In *TDOT* 10: 291–96.
Farrer, Austin. *Love Almighty and Ills Unlimited: An Essay on Providence and Evil*. Garden City, NY: Doubleday, 1961.
Ferguson, Duncan S. *Biblical Hermeneutics: An Introduction*. Atlanta: John Knox, 1986.
Fisher, Loren R. *The Many Voices of Job*. Eugene, OR: Cascade, 2009.
Frazer, James G. *The Golden Bough: A Study in Magic and Religion*. Abridged edition. London: Macmillan, 1922.
Freedman, David R. and J. R. Lundbom, "ḥārâ." In *TDOT* 5:171–76.
Fretheim, Terence E. *The Suffering of God: An Old Testament Perspective*. Overtures to Biblical Theology. Philadelphia: Fortress, 1984.
Frost, Stanley B. "The Death of Josiah: A Conspiracy of Silence." *JBL* 87 (1968) 369–82.
Fyall, Robert S. *Now My Eyes Have Seen You: Images of Creation and Evil in the Book of Job*. New Studies in Biblical Theology. Leicester, UK: Apollos, 2002.
Garrison, Roman. *Why Are You Silent, Lord?* The Biblical Seminar 68. Sheffield, UK: Sheffield Academic, 2000.
Gaster, Theodor H. "Sacrifices and Offerings, OT." In *IDB* 4: 147–59.
Gese, Hartmut. "The Crisis of Wisdom in Koheleth." In *Theodicy in the Old Testament*, edited by James L. Crenshaw, 141–53. Issues in Religion and Theology 4. Philadelphia: Fortress, 1983.
Gibson, Edgar C. S. *The Book of Job*. Oxford Commentaries. London: Methuen, 1899.
Gibson, Jeffrey B. "Satan." In *EDB* 1169–70.
Gibson, John C. L. *Job*. Daily Study Bible. Louisville: Westminster John Knox, 1985.
———. "On Evil in the Book of Job." In *Ascribe to the Lord: Biblical and Other Studies in Memory of Peter C. Craigie*, edited by Lyle Eslinger and Glen Taylor, 399–419. JSOTSup 67. Sheffield, UK: JSOT Press, 1988.
Gillingham, Susan. *Psalms through the Centuries*, vol. 1. Blackwell Bible Commentaries. Oxford: Blackwell, 2008.
Goldingay, John E. *Daniel*. Word Biblical Commentary 30. Dallas: Word, 1989.
———. *Isaiah*. New International Biblical Commentary. Peabody, MA: Hendrickson, 2001.
———. *The Message of Isaiah 40–55: A Literary-Theological Commentary*. London: T. & T. Clark, 2005.
Goldingay, John, and David Payne. *Isaiah 40–55*. International Critical Commentary. 2 vols. London: T. & T. Clark, 2006.
Gordis, Robert. *Koheleth—The Man and His World: A Study of Ecclesiastes*. 2nd ed. New York: Schocken, 1968.
———. *The Book of God and Man: A Study of the Book of Job*. Chicago: University of Chicago Press, 1965.

———. *The Book of Job*. New York: Jewish Theological Seminary of America, 1978.
Gottwald, Norman K. *Studies in the Book of Lamentations*. Studies in Biblical Theology 14. London: SCM, 1954.
Gowan, Donald E. "Habakkuk." In *The Oxford Bible Commentary*, edited by John Barton and John Muddiman, 601–4. Oxford: Oxford University Press, 2001.
Grabbe, Lester L. *Judaism from Cyrus to Hadrian*. London: SCM, 1994.
Gutiérrez, Gustavo. *On Job: God-Talk and the Suffering of the Innocent*. Translated by M. J. O'Connell. Maryknoll, NY: Orbis, 1987.
Habel, Norman C. "'Only the Jackal Is My Friend': On Friends and Redeemers in Job." *Int* 31 (1977) 227–36.
———. *The Book of Job*. Old Testament Library. London: SCM, 1985.
———. "The Role of Elihu in the Design of the Book of Job." In *In the Shelter of Elyon: Essays on Ancient Palestinian Life and Literature in Honour of G. W. Ahlström*, edited by W. Boyd Barrick and John R. Spencer, 81–98. JSOTSup 31. Sheffield, UK: JSOT Press, 1984.
Hartley, John E. *The Book of Job*. New International Commentary on the Old Testament. Grand Rapids: Eerdmans, 1988.
Hayward, C. T. Robert. *The Jewish Temple: A Non-Biblical Sourcebook*. London: Routledge, 1996.
Heaton, Eric W. *The Book of Daniel*. Torch Bible Commentary. London: SCM, 1967.
Hebblethwaite, Brian. *Evil, Suffering and Religion*. Rev. ed. London: SPCK, 2000.
Heiler, Friedrich. *Prayer: A Study in the History and Psychology of Religion*. Translated by Samuel McComb. Oxford: Oxford University Press, 1932.
Hick, John. *Evil and the God of Love*. London: Fontana, 1968.
Holladay, William L. *Jeremiah*. Vol. 1. Hermeneia. Philadelphia: Fortress, 1986.
Houtman, Cornelis. "Theodicy in the Pentateuch." In *Theodicy in the World of the Bible*, edited by Antti Laato and Johannes C. de Moor, 151–82. Leiden: Brill, 2003.
Hügel, Friedrich von. "Suffering and God." In *Essays and Addresses on the Philosophy of Religion*, Second Series, 167–213. London: Dent, 1926.
Humphries, W. Lee. *The Tragic Vision and the Hebrew Tradition*. Overtures to Biblical Theology. Philadelphia: Fortress, 1985.
Illman, Karl-Johan. "Theodicy in Job." In *Theodicy in the World of the Bible*, edited by Antti Laato and Johannes C. de Moor, 304–33. Leiden: Brill, 2003.
Jagersma, H. *A History of Israel to Bar Kochba*. Part 1. Translated by John Bowden. London: SCM, 1982.
———. *A History of Israel to Bar Kochba*. Part 2. Translated by John Bowden. London: SCM, 1985.
Janowski, Bernd and Peter Stuhlmacher. *The Suffering Servant: Isaiah 53 in Jewish and Christian Sources*. Translated by D. P. Bailey. Grand Rapids: Eerdmans, 2004.
Janzen, J. Gerald. *At the Scent of Water: The Ground of Hope in the Book of Job*. Grand Rapids: Eerdmans, 2009.
———. *Job*. Interpretation. Atlanta: John Knox, 1985.
Japhet, Sara. "Theodicy in Ezra-Nehemiah and Chronicles." In *Theodicy in the World of the Bible*, edited by Antti Laato and Johannes C. de Moor, 429–69. Leiden: Brill, 2003.
Jeanrond, Werner G. *Theology and Hermeneutics: Development and Significance*. London: SCM, 1991.
Job, John B. *Jeremiah's Kings: A Study of the Monarchy in Jeremiah*. Aldershot, UK: Ashgate, 2006.
———. *Where Is My Father? Studies in the Book of Job*. London: Epworth, 1977.

John of Salisbury. *Metalogicon*. Edited by C. C. J. Webb. Oxford: Clarendon, 1929.
Johnson, Bo. "*mišpāṭ*." In *TDOT* 9:86-98.
Johnston, Philip S. *Shades of Sheol: Death and Afterlife in the Old Testament*. Leicester, UK: Apollos, 2002.
Johnstone, William. "Guilt and Atonement: The Theme of 1 & 2 Chronicles." In *A Word in Season*, edited by J. D. Martin and P. R. Davies, 113-38. JSOTSup 42. Sheffield, UK: JSOT Press, 1986.
Jones, Douglas R. *Jeremiah*. New Century Bible Commentary. London: Marshall Pickering, 1992.
Jones, Edgar. *The Triumph of Job*. London: SCM, 1966.
Jones, Gwilym H. *1 & 2 Chronicles*. Old Testament Guides. Sheffield, UK: JSOT Press, 1993.
Jones, Malcolm V. "Dostoevskii and Religion." In *The Cambridge Companion to Dostoevskii*, edited by W. J. Leatherbarrow, 148-74. Cambridge: Cambridge University Press, 2002.
Joyce, Paul M. *Ezekiel: A Commentary*. LHBOTS 482. London: T. & T. Clark, 2007.
Keats, John. *The Letters of John Keats*. Edited by M. B. Forman. 3rd ed. London: Oxford University Press, 1947.
Kellermann, Diether. "*ʾāšām*." In *TDOT* 1:429-37.
Kirkpatrick, A. F. *The Book of Psalms, Book I, Psalms I-XLV*. Cambridge Bible. Cambridge: Cambridge University Press, 1917.
Klein, Ralph W. *Israel in Exile: A Theological Interpretation*. Overtures to Biblical Theology. Philadelphia: Fortress, 1979.
Korpel, Marjo C. A. "Theodicy in the Book of Esther." In *Theodicy in the World of the Bible*, edited by Antti Laato and Johannes C. de Moor, 351-74. Leiden: Brill, 2003.
Kraus, Hans-Joachim. *Psalms 1-59*. Translated by Hilton C. Oswald. Continental Commentary. Minneapolis: Augsburg, 1988.
———. *Psalms 60-150*. Translated by Hilton C. Oswald. Continental Commentary. Minneapolis: Augsburg, 1989.
———. *Theology of the Psalms*. Translated by K. Crim. Continental Commentary. Minneapolis: Augsburg, 1986.
Laato, Antti. "Theodicy in the Deuteronomistic History." In *Theodicy in the World of the Bible*, edited by Antti Laato and J. C. de Moor, 183-235. Leiden: Brill, 2003.
Laato, Antti, and Johannes C. de Moor, eds. *Theodicy in the World of the Bible*. Leiden: Brill, 2003.
Leibniz, Gottfried W. F. *Theodicy: Essays on the Goodness of God, the Freedom of Man, and the Origin of Evil*. Translated by E. M. Huggard. New Haven: Yale University Press, 2003.
Lepinsky, E. "*liwyātān*." In *TDOT* 7: 504-9.
Levenson, Jon D. *Creation and the Persistence of Evil*. Princeton: Princeton University Press, 1988.
Linafelt, Tod. *Surviving Lamentations: Catastrophe, Lament, and Protest in the Afterlife of a Biblical Book*. Chicago: University of Chicago, 2000.
———. *Strange Fire: Reading the Bible after the Holocaust*. New York: New York University Press, 2000.
Lindström, Fredrik. *Suffering and Sin: Interpretations of Illness in the Individual Complaint Psalms*. Coniectanea Biblica: Old Testament Series 37. Stockholm: Almqvist & Wiksell, 1994.
———. "Theodicy in the Psalms." In *Theodicy in the World of the Bible*, edited by Antti Laato and Johannes C. de Moor, 256-303. Leiden: Brill, 2003.

Liwak, R. "*rᵉpāʾîm*." In *TDOT* 13: 602–14.
Martin-Achard, Robert. *From Death to Life: A Study of the Development of the Doctrine of the Resurrection in the Old Testament*. Translated by J. P. Smith. Edinburgh: Oliver and Boyd, 1960.
Mays, James L. *Psalms*. Interpretation. Louisville: Westminster John Knox, 1994.
McKane, William. *A Critical, and Exegetical Commentary on Jeremiah*. Vol. 1. International Critical Commentary. Edinburgh: T. & T. Clark, 1986.
McKay, John W. "Elihu—A Proto-Charismatic?" *ExpT* 90 (1978–9) 167–71.
McKeating, Henry. *The Book of Jeremiah*. Epworth Commentaries. Peterborough, UK: Epworth, 1999.
Melville, Herman. *Moby Dick*. London: Penguin, 1986.
Mettinger, Tryggve N. D. "Intertextuality: Allusion and Vertical Context Systems in Some Job Passages." In *Of Prophets' Visions and the Wisdom of Sages: Essays in Honour of R. Norman Whybray on His Seventieth Birthday*, edited by Heather A. McKay and D. J. A. Clines, 257–80. JSOTSup 162. Sheffield, UK: JSOT Press, 1993.
Miller, J. Maxwell and John H. Hayes. *A History of Ancient Israel and Judah*. London: SCM, 1986.
Mills, Mary E. *Alterity, Pain and Suffering in Isaiah, Jeremiah and Ezekiel*. LHBOTS 479. London: T. & T. Clark, 2007.
Milton, John. *John Milton: The Complete Poems*. Edited by B. A. Wright. London: Dent and Dutton, 1980.
Moberly, R. Walter L. *Genesis 12–50*. Old Testament Guides. Sheffield, UK: JSOT Press, 1992.
———. *The Bible, Theology, and Faith: A Study of Abraham and Jesus*. Cambridge: Cambridge University Press, 2000.
Moltmann, Jürgen. *The Crucified God*. Translated by R. A. Wilson and J. Bowden. London: SCM, 1974.
Morrow, William S. *Protest against God: The Eclipse of a Biblical Tradition*. Sheffield, UK: Phoenix, 2006.
Munro, Jill M. *Spikenard and Saffron: A Study in the Poetic Language of the Song of Songs*. JSOTSup 203. Sheffield, UK: Sheffield Academic, 1995.
Murphy, Roland E. *Ecclesiastes*. Word Biblical Commentary 23A. Dallas: Word, 1992.
Mursell, Gordon. "Suffering." In *The New SCM Dictionary of Christian Spirituality*, edited by Philip Sheldrake, 602–3. London: SCM, 2005.
Newman, John Henry, *The Dream of Gerontius*. Oxford: Mowbray, 1986.
Newsom, Carol A. "Job." In *NIB* 4: 317–637
———. *The Book of Job: A Contest of Moral Imagination*. Oxford: Oxford University Press, 2002.
Nickelsburg, George W. E. "Son of Man." In *ABD* 6:137–50.
Nicholson, Ernest W. *God and His People: Covenant and Theology in the Old Testament*. Oxford: Clarendon, 1986.
———. "The Limits of Theodicy as a Theme of the Book of Job." In *Wisdom in Ancient Israel: Essays in Honour of J. A. Emerton*, edited by John Day, R. P. Gordon, and H. G. M. Williamson, 71–82. Cambridge: Cambridge University Press, 1995.
Niditch, Susan. *War in the Hebrew Bible: A Study in the Ethics of Violence*. Oxford: Oxford University Press, 1993.
North, Christopher R. *The Second Isaiah*. Oxford: Oxford University Press, 1964.
———. *The Suffering Servant in Deutero-Isaiah: An Historical and Critical Study*. 2nd ed. Oxford: Oxford University Press, 1956.

O'Connor, Kathleen M. *Lamentations and the Tears of the World*. Maryknoll, NY: Orbis, 2002.
———. "Lamenting Back to Life." *Int* 62 (2008) 34–47.
Orlinsky, Harry M. *Studies on the Second Part of the Book of Isaiah*. VTSup 14. Leiden: Brill, 1977.
Otto, Rudolf. *The Idea of the Holy: An Inquiry into the Non-Rational Factor in the Idea of the Divine and its Relation to the Rational*. Translated by J. W. Harvey. London: Oxford University Press, 1936.
Parkinson, Michael. "Belief." In *A Dictionary of Modern Critical Terms*, edited by Roger Fowler, 21–22. London: Routledge & Kegan Paul, 1973.
Parry, Robin A. *Lamentations*. Two Horizons Old Testament Commentary. Grand Rapids: Eerdmans, 2010.
Peake, Arthur S. *Job*. Century Bible. Edinburgh: Jack, 1905.
Perrin, Norman. "Son of man." In *IDBSup* 833–36.
Phillips, Catherine. *Gerard Manley Hopkins*. Oxford Poetry Library. Oxford: Oxford University Press, 1995.
Pope, Marvin H. *Job*. Anchor Bible 15. Garden City, NY: Doubleday, 1965.
Porteous, Norman W. *Daniel*. Old Testament Library. London: SCM, 1965.
Provan, Iain. W. *Lamentations*. New Century Bible Commentary. London: Marshall Pickering, 1991.
Rad, Gerhard von. *Genesis*. 2nd ed. Translated by J. H. Marks. Old Testament Library. London: SCM, 1963.
———. *Old Testament Theology*, vol. 1. Translated by D. M. Stalker. London: Oliver and Boyd, 1962.
Renkema, Johan. "Theodicy in Lamentations." In *Theodicy in the World of the Bible*, edited by Antti Laato and J.C. de Moor, 410–28. Leiden: Brill, 2003
Reventlow, Henning G. *Liturgie und prophetisches Ich bei Jeremia*. Gütersloh: Mohn, 1963.
Ringgren, Helmer. "gāʾal." In *TDOT* 2: 350–55.
Roberts, J. J. M. *Nahum, Habakkuk, Zephaniah*. Old Testament Library. Louisville: Westminster John Knox, 1991.
Robinson, H. Wheeler. *The Cross in the Old Testament*. London: SCM, 1955.
Rodd, Cyril S. *The Book of Job*. Epworth Commentaries. London: Epworth, 1990.
Rogerson, John W. "Myth." In *A Dictionary of Biblical Interpretation*, edited by Richard J. Coggins and J. L. Houlden, 479–82. London: SCM, 1990.
———. *A Theology of the Old Testament: Cultural Memory, Communication and Being Human*. London: SPCK, 2009.
Römer, Thomas C. *The So-called Deuteronomistic History: A Sociological, Historical and Literary Introduction*. London: T. & T. Clark, 2005.
Rowland, Christopher. "Apocalyptic." In *A Dictionary of Biblical Interpretation*, edited by Richard J. Coggins and J. L. Houlden, 34–36. London: SCM, 1990.
———. *The Open Heaven: A Study of Apocalyptic in Judaism and Early Christianity*. London: SPCK, 1982.
Rowley, Harold H. "The Book of Job and its Meaning." In *From Moses to Qumran: Studies in the Old Testament*, 141–83. London: Lutterworth, 1963.
———. *The Book of Job*. New Century Bible. London: Marshall, Morgan and Scott, 1976.
———. *The Relevance of Apocalyptic: A Study of Jewish and Christian Apocalypses from Daniel to the Revelation*. Rev. ed. London: Lutterworth, 1963.

Salters, Robert B. *Jonah and Lamentations*. Old Testament Guides. Sheffield, UK: JSOT Press, 1994.
Sanders, E. P. *Judaism: Practice and Belief 63 BCE–66 CE*. London: SCM, 1994.
Schneiders, Sandra M. *The Revelatory Text: Interpreting the New Testament as Sacred Scripture*. San Francisco: Harper, 1991.
Schoors, Antoon. "Theodicy in Qoheleth." In *Theodicy in the World of the Bible*, edited by Antti Laato and Johannes C. de Moor, 375–409. Leiden: Brill, 2003.
Seibert, Eric A. *Disturbing Divine Behaviour: Troubling Old Testament Images of God*. Minneapolis: Fortress, 2009.
Seitz, Christopher R. "The Book of Isaiah 40–66." In *NIB* 6: 307–522.
Senior, Donald. "Son of Man." In *EDB*, 1242.
Seybold, K. "*hebhel*." In *TDOT* 3:313–20.
Sheldrake, Philip. *The New SCM Dictionary of Christian Spirituality*. London: SCM, 2005.
Silberman, L. H. " 'You Cannot See My Face': Seeking to Understand Divine Justice." In *Shall Not the Judge of All the Earth Do What Is Right? Studies on the Nature of God in Tribute to James L. Crenshaw*, edited by David L. Penchansky and P. L. Redditt, 89–95. Winona Lake, IN: Eisenbrauns, 2000.
Skinner, John. *Prophecy and Religion: Studies in the Life of Jeremiah*. Cambridge: Cambridge University Press, 1930.
Smith, Ralph L. *Micah–Malachi*. Word Biblical Commentary 32. Waco, TX: Word, 1984.
Smith-Christopher, Daniel L. "Dreams." In *EDB*, 356–57.
Soelle, Dorothee. *Suffering*. Translated by E. R. Kalin. Philadelphia: Fortress, 1975.
Soggin, J. Alberto. "Notes on the Joseph Story." In *Understanding Poets and Prophets: Essays in Honour of George Wishart Anderson*, edited by A. Graeme Auld, 336-49. JSOTSup 152. Sheffield, UK: Sheffield Academic, 1993.
Strahan, James. *The Book of Job*. 2nd ed. Edinburgh: T. & T. Clark, 1914.
Surin, Kenneth. *Theology and the Problem of Evil*. Oxford: Blackwell, 1986.
Sweeney, Marvin A. *King Josiah of Judah: The Lost Messiah of Israel*. Oxford: Oxford University Press, 2001.
———. *Reading the Hebrew Bible after the Shoah: Engaging Holocaust Theology*. Minneapolis: Fortress, 2008.
Tate, Marvin A. *Psalms 51–100*. Word Biblical Commentary 20. Dallas: Word, 1990.
Terrien, Samuel. "The Book of Job." In *IB* 3: 875–1198.
———. *The Elusive Presence: Towards a New Biblical Theology*. New York: Harper & Row, 1978.
Thiselton, Anthony C. *The Two Horizons: New Testament Hermeneutics and Philosophical Description: With Special Reference to Heidegger, Bultmann, Gadamer, and Wittgenstein*. Exeter: Paternoster, 1980.
———. *New Horizons in Hermeneutics: The Theory and Practice of Transforming Biblical Reading*. London: HarperCollins, 1992.
Thomas, D. Winton. *Documents from Old Testament Times*. New York: Harper & Row, 1961.
Thompson, Michael E. W. *I Have Heard Your Prayer: The Old Testament and Prayer*. Peterborough, UK: Epworth, 1996.
———. "Prayer, Oracle and Theophany: The Book of Habakkuk." *TynB* 44 (1993) 33–53.
———. *Isaiah 40–66*. Epworth Commentaries. Peterborough, UK: Epworth, 2001.

Tiemeyer, Lena-Sofia. "To Read—Or Not to Read: Ezekiel as Christian Scripture." *ExpT* 121 (2009–10) 481–88.
Tilley, Terrence W. *The Evils of Theodicy*. Reprint. Eugene, OR: Wipf & Stock, 2000.
Trible, Phyllis. *Texts of Terror: Literary-Feminist Readings of Biblical Narratives*. London: SCM, 1992.
Villanueva, Federico G. *The "Uncertainty of a Hearing": A Study of the Sudden Change of Mood in the Psalms of Lament*. VTSup 121. Leiden: Brill, 2008.
Waters, Larry J. *The Contribution of the Speeches of Elihu to the Argument about Suffering in the Book of Job: A Study in Narrative Continuity*. Studies in Bible and Early Christianity, 67. Lewiston, NY: Mellen, 2009.
Watson, Francis. *Text, Church and World*. Edinburgh: T. & T. Clark, 1994.
Weiser, Artur. *The Psalms*. Translated by H. Hartwell. Old Testament Library. London: SCM, 1962.
Wenham, Gordon J. *Genesis 16–50*. Word Biblical Commentary 2. Nashville: Thomas Nelson, 1994.
Westermann, Claus. *Genesis 37–50: A Commentary*. Translated by John J. Scullion. Continental Commentary. London: SPCK, 1987.
———. *Joseph: Studies of the Joseph Stories in Genesis*. Translated by A. Kaste. Edinburgh: T. & T. Clark, 1996.
———. *The Living Psalms*. Translated by J. R. Porter. Edinburgh: T. & T. Clark, 1989.
———. *The Structure of the Book of Job: A Form-Critical Analysis*. Translated by C. A. Muenchow. Philadelphia: Fortress, 1981.
White, Norman. *Hopkins: A Literary Biography*. Oxford: Clarendon, 1992.
Whybray, R. Norman. *Ecclesiastes*. Old Testament Guides. Sheffield, UK: JSOT Press, 1989.
———. *Isaiah 40–66*. New Century Bible Commentary. London: Oliphants, 1975.
———. *Job*. Readings: A New Biblical Commentary. Sheffield, UK: Sheffield Academic, 1998.
———. "Qoheleth, Preacher of Joy." *JSOT* 23 (1982) 87–98.
———. *Thanksgiving for a Liberated Prophet: An Interpretation of Isaiah Chapter 53*. JSOTSup 4. Sheffield, UK: JSOT Press, 1978.
———. *The Second Isaiah*. Old Testament Guides. Sheffield, UK: JSOT Press, 1983.
———. *Two Jewish Theologies: Job and Ecclesiastes*. Hull: University of Hull, 1980.
Wiesel, Elie. *Night*. Translated by Marion Wiesel. London: Penguin, 2006.
———. *The Town Beyond the Wall*. Translated by S. Barker. New York: Avon, 1970.
Wildberger, Hans. *Isaiah 13–27*. Translated by Thomas H. Trapp. Continental Commentary. Minneapolis: Fortress, 1997.
Williams, Rowan. *Dostoevsky: Language, Faith and Fiction*. London: Continuum, 2008.
Williamson, Hugh G. M. *1 & 2 Chronicles*. New Century Bible Commentary. London: Marshall, Morgan and Scott, 1982.
Wilson, Gerald H. *Job*. New International Bible Commentary. Peabody, MA: Hendrickson, 2007.
Zobel, Hans-Jürgen. "ḥeseḏ." In *TDOT* 5: 44–64.

Index of Subjects

Abaddon, 136
Abel, 128
Abraham and Isaac, 149–50
Ashes. *See* Dust and ashes
Apocalyptic literature, 157–73
Ancient of Days, 165–67
Alexander the Great, 168
Antiochus IV Epiphanes, 158–59, 165–68
Atonement, 95–96

Belshazzar, 164–65
Behemoth, 146–47, 185–86
Bildad, 114–15, 121–22

Chaldeans, 64, 64 n.3
Conflict of religion and evil empire, 194
Covenant, 189–90
Cyrus the Persian, 86, 98, 168

Daniel, book of, 158–73, 188
Darius, 163
Deuteronomy, 8, 56
Deuteronomistic History, 8–11, 8 n.3, 11 n.6, 13, 56
Divine abandonment, *see* God, Abandonment by,
Dreams, 189
Dust and ashes, 113, 149

Ecclesiastes, 22–30, 190, 194
Elihu, 107, 115, 138–41, 153–54, 193
Eliphaz, 114–15, 118–21, 149–50, 153
Enoch, 83, 103
Evil in the world, 193, 195
   Problem of, *See* Theodicy
Exile, 10–11, 86, 97–99, 158

God
   Abandonment by, 34, 49, 51, 51 n.23
   Appearance of, 75, 142–45, 148, 179, 186
   Goodness of, 195
   Covenant relationship with, 103–4, 189–90
   Immanence and transcendence, 27–28, 34, 56–57, 132, 177–78, 189–94
   Mystery of, 136–37, 190
Guilt offering, 95–96

Habakkuk, 62–76
Holocaust/Shoah, 4, 4 n.8, 164, 178
Human
   Faithfulness, 71, 71 n.12
   Relationship with God, *See* God, Covenant relationship with
   Sinfulness, 143–45, 149

Isaiah, 14–16, 85–99

Index of Subjects

Jeremiah, 16, 35–57, 61
  "Confessions" of, 35–37, 115–16, 126, 177
  Jeremiah and Job, 55, 55 n.30
Jesus Christ, 94, 166, 188, 195
Job,
  Book of, 105–9, 194
  Intertextuality in book of, 115–16, 149, 149 n.73
  Job, the sufferer, 61, 113, 115–17, 150
  Job's "accuser," 125–26
  Job's "mediator," 129
  Job's "redeemer," 129–31
  Job's "witness," 128–29, 131–32, 144
  Job's "umpire," 126–27, 129, 132,
  Job's friends, 5, 114, 117–24, 127, 150, 153
  Job's wife, 113–14
  Zophar's "missing speech," 106, 117, 123
Joseph, 48, 76–80, 92, 194
Josiah, 9, 18–20
Justice, 2

Leviathan, 146–47, 185–86, 193
Life after death, 82–83, 94, 97, 103–4, 171–73, 187–88, 195
Lisbon earthquake, 4

Mishnah, 95 n.19
Moses, 48, 91–92, 174 n.1
Myth, 147, 147 n.68

Nebuchadnezzar, 161–62, 162 n.12, 164–65

Prosperity of the "wicked", 58–61

Qoheleth, See Ecclesiastes
Qumran, 73, 88 n.8, 97 n.22

Satan and "the satan," 111–12, 111 n.7
Scapegoat ritual, 95–96

Seleucid empire, 158–59, 164–65, 168
Shoah, See Holocaust
Sodom, 149
Son of Man, 166, 172–73
Song of Songs, 179 n.7
Suffering,
  and religion, 4 n.10
  and "enemies", 12 n.10, 39–40, 42–43, 47, 49, 52, 56, 178
  as punishment for human sinfulness ("deserved calamity"), 6–21, 54, 64, 66, 153
  for human discipline/education, 119–20, 138–41, 182–84, 193–94
  of God, 192–93
  of innocent people, 18–21
  human patience and trust in God, 40, 42, 47, 52–54, 59, 61–62, 74, 194
  and prayer, 40, 44–49, 54, 56–57, 96, 177
  strategies to deal with, 34, 57, 76, 113–14, 194
  suffering with a purpose, 94–97, 187–88, 194

Tamar, 149
Theodicy
  "Augustinian," 181–82
  Babylonian, 3
  Definition of, 3
  "Deserved calamity," 7–21, 61, 111, 118–24, 175, 193,
  "Divine discipline," 139–41, 186,
  "Irenaean," 182–84
  Limitations of "deserved calamity" theodicy, 150, 175–76, 181–82, 186, 190–93
  "Long term," 62–63, 70, 76, 79–80, 188–89
  and the Old Testament, 3–6
  "Vale of soul making," 183–84, 183 n.17, 193–94

Theodicy in
    Apocalyptic literature, 172–73, 194
    Babylonian literature, 3, 3 n.6
    Chronicles, 13, 175
    Daniel, 160, 162–64, 168, 172–73, 175, 194
    Deuteronomy, 8, 175
    Deuteronomistic History, 8–11, 61, 175
    Ecclesiastes (Qoheleth), 176, 190,
    Ezekiel, 16, 16 n.15
    Habakkuk, 62–76, 178–79
    Haggai, 17
    Isaiah, 14–16, 85–99
    Jeremiah, 175, 194
    Job, 109–10, 112, 123–24, 151–56, 175, 180–87
    "Joseph story" (Gen 37–50), 76–80, 179–80
    Lamentations, 11–12, 175
    New Testament, 192–93, 195
    Oracles against the nations, 63, 68
    Other religions, 3–4, 4 n.10, 112
    Proverbs, 14, 175
    Psalms of Lament, 12, 31–34, 36, 40, 51, 53–55, 66, 74, 126, 175
    Wisdom of Jesus Ben Sirach, 14
    Wisdom Psalms, 176
    Wisdom of Solomon, 182
Theophany, *See* God, Appearance of

Ugaritic texts, 101, 179

War, 174 n.1
"willing suspension of disbelief", 160–61, 160 n.9
Wisdom literature and thought, 136

Index of Authors

Achtemeier, Elizabeth, 65 n.4
Adams, Marilyn McCord, 182 n.11, 183 n.19, 189, 189 n.24, 192 n.33, 194, 195
Allen, Leslie C., 38 n.7
Amos, Clare, 76 n.19
Andersen, Francis I., 64 n.3, 65 n.4, 70 n.10
Anderson, Arnold A., 83 n.4
Astell, Ann W., 4 n.8
Augustine, Saint, 35, 181, 181 nn.9 and 10, 189, 189 n.23
Aulen, Gustaf, 195 n.36

Barton, George A., 190 n.27
Barton, John, 4–5, 5 n.11, 85 n.1, 170 n.23
Baumgartner, Walter, 46 n.20
Bellinger, William H., 86 n.6
Berggrav, Bishop, 57
Bernard of Chartres, 105 n.1
Blenkinsopp, Joseph, 88 n.8, 92 n.13, 93 n.14, 98 n.24, 171 n.29
Boethius, Anicius Manlius Torquatus Severinus, 3, 3 n.7
Bowker, John, 4 n.10, 175 n.2
Boys, Mary C., 4 n.8
Briggs, Charles A. and Emilie G., 31, 31 n.1
Broyles, Craig C., 31 n.2, 32 n.3

Brueggemann, Walter, 32 n.4, 38 nn.7 and 8, 52 nn.24 and 25, 55 n.30, 59 n.5, 169 n.22
Buber, Martin, 102 n.6
Burrell, David B., 176 n.3, 189, 190, 190 n.25, 191 n.29

Calvin, John, 79 n.20, 114 n.12
Camus, Albert, 7, 7 n.1, 14, 20–21, 21 n.23, 175, 182, 182 n.12, 191–92, 192 n.30
Carlyle, Thomas, 105–6, 106 n.2
Carroll, Robert P., 37, 37 n.5, 38 nn.8 and 9, 51 n.23
Casey, Maurice, 166 n.15
Chapman, John, 183 n.18
Childs, Brevard S., 171, 171 n.30
Clements, Ronald E., 170 nn.23 and 24, 171 n.26
Clines, David J. A., 101 n.4, 105 n.1, 113 n.10, 114 n.11, 117 n.17, 120 n.20, 124 n.26, 126 n.30, 129 n.35, 131, 131 n.38, 132, 132 n.43, 133 n.44, 134 n.46
Coats, George W., 76 n.19
Collins, Adela Y., 158 n.2
Crenshaw, James L., 8 n.4, 14 n.14, 20 n.21, 23, 23 nn.2 and 3, 27, 27 n.7, 30, 30 n.15, 42 n.15, 63 n.2, 94 n.17, 100, 100 nn.1 and 2, 106 n.3, 136, 136 n.50, 174 n.1

Index of Authors

Croft, Steven J. L., 32 n.5
Curtis, Adrian, 33 n.7, 52 n.26, 101, 101 n.3
Danby, Herbert, 95 n.19
Davidson, Robert, 34 n.9, 57, 57 n.31, 61 n.6, 81 n.1, 176, 176 n.4
Davies, Eryl W., 175 n.1
Davies, Philip R., 158 n.3, 159 nn.4 and 7, 168 n.19
Day, John, 31 n.2, 32 n.3, 59 n.4, 147 nn.65 and 67
Dell, Katharine, 14, 14 n.13, 58–59, 59 nn.3 and 4, 113 n.9
Dostoevsky, Fyodor, 1–2, 5

Eaton, John, 58 n.2
Eliot, George, 183 n.18
Emmerson, Grace I., 85 n.1
Fabry, Heinz-Josef, 81 n.2, 187 n.21

Farmer, William R., 86 n.6
Farrer, Austin, 182–83, 183 n.16, 196, 196 n.37
Ferguson, Duncan S., 195 n.35
Frazer, James G., 95 n.19
Freedman, David R., 58 n.1
Fretheim, Terence E., 192, 192 n.32
Frost, Stanley B., 19 n.19
Fyall, Robert S., 135 n.48, 147 n.65

Garrison, Roman, 4 n.10
Gaster, Theodor H., 96 n.20
Gese, Hartmut, 30 n.13
Gibson, Edgar C. S., 127 n.32
Gibson, Jeffrey B., 111 n.17
Gibson, John C. L., 107 n.4, 114 n.11, 120, 120 n.21, 121 n.22, 135, 135 n.49, 145 n.63, 147 n.67
Goldingay, John E., 86, 86 n.4, 87 n.7, 88 n.8, 89 n.9, 92 n.13, 93 n.14, 161, 161 n.10, 168 n.19, 169 n.22, 171 n.26
Gordis, Robert, 27, 27 n.6, 106 n.2, 133–34, 133 n.45, 155–56, 156 n.79
Gottwald, Norman K., 11 n.7

Gowan, Donald E., 70 n.10
Grabbe, Lester L. 159 n.6
Gunkel, Hermann, 31–32
Habel, Norman C., 116, 117 n.16, 127 n.31, 135 n.48, 139 n.53, 145, 145 n.62
Hayes, John H., 18 n.18
Hayward, C. T. Robert, 95 n.19
Heaton, Eric W., 168 n.19, 169, 169 n.21
Hebblethwaite, Brian, 4 n.10
Heiler, Friedrich, 33 n.6
Hick, John, 3, 3 n.5, 160 n.8, 181, 181 n.8, 182, 182 nn.13, 14, and 15, 183, 183 n.18, 190–91, 191 n.28, 194
Holladay, William L., 37–38, 38 nn.7 and 8
Hopkins, Gerard Manley, 42, 42 nn.16 and 17
Houtman, Cornelis, 8 n.2, 76 n.19, 79 n.21
Hügel, Friedrich von, 192 n.33
Humphries, W. Lee, 30, 30 n.14

Irenaeus, Saint, 182

Jagersma, H. A., 18 n.18, 159 n.6
Janowski, Bernd, 86 n.6
Janzen, J. Gerald, 133 n.45
Japhet, Sara, 13 n.12
Jeanrond, Werner G., 195 n.35
Job, John B., 38 n.7, 155 n.77
John of Salisbury, 105 n.1
Johns A. H., 176 n.3, 190 n.25, 191 n.29
Johnson, Bo, 2, n.3
Johnston, Philip S., 83 n.4, 103 n.8, 169 n.20, 171 n.28
Johnstone, William, 13 n.12
Jones, Douglas R., 39–40, 40 n.11
Jones, Edgar, 141, 141 n.58, 154, 154 n.75
Jones, Gwilym H., 13 n.12
Jones, Malcolm V., 1 n.1
Joyce, Paul M., 16 n.15, 192 n.31

Index of Authors

Keats, John, 183 n.17
Kellermann, Diether, 96 n.20
Kirkpatrick, A. F., 61 n.8
Klein, Ralph W., 11 n.6
Korpel, Marjo C. A., 175 n.1
Kraus, Hans-Joachim, 100 n.2

Laato, Antti, 4 n.10, 8 n.4, 11 n.6
Lambert, W. G., 3 n.6
Leibniz, Gottfried W. F., 3, 3 n.4
Lepinsky, E., 147 n.65
Levenson, Jon D., 193 n.34
Linafelt, Tod, 11 n.7
Lindström, Fredrik, 32 n.4, 59 n.5, 81 n.1, 100 n.2
Lundbom, J. R., 58 n.1
Luther, Martin, 61, 62, 194

MacLeish, A., 113 n.9
Martin-Achard, Robert, 169 n.20
Mays, James L., 82, 82 n.3
McKane, William, 37, 37 n.6, 38 nn.8 and 9, 39, 39 n.10, 41, 41 nn.13 and 14
McKay, John W., 139 n.53
McKeating, Henry, 43 n.18, 47 n.21
Melville, Herman, 176 n.4
Mettinger, Tryggve n.D., 116 n.14, 125 n.28
Miller, J. Maxwell, 18 n.18
Mills, Mary E., 42 n.15
Milton, John, 17 n.17
Moberly, R. Walter L., 174 n.1
Moltmann, Jürgen, 192 n.33
Moor, Johannes C. de, 4 n.10, 11 n.6
Morrow, William S., 34 n.8
Muddiman, John, 5 n.11
Munro, Jill M., 179 n.7
Murphy, Roland E, 28, 28 nn.9 and 10
Mursell, Gordon, 32 n.4

Newman, John Henry, 149, 149 n.72
Newsom, Carol A., 110 n.5
Newton, Isaac, 106 n.1
Nickelsburg, George W. E., 166 n.15

Nicholson, Ernest W., 140–41, 141 n.56, 183 n.19, 190 n.26
Niditch, Susan, 174 n.1
North, Christopher R., 86 nn.5 and 6, 92 n.13, 97 n.23, 98, 98 n.24

O'Connor, Kathleen M., 11 n.7, 36, 36 nn.2 and 3
Orlinsky, Harry M., 95 n.18
Otto, Rudolf, 143, 143 n.61

Parkinson, Michael, 160 n.9
Parry, Robin A., 11 n.7
Payne, David, 86, 86 n.4, 87 n.7, 88 n.8, 89 n.9, 92 n.13, 93 n.14
Peake, Arthur S., 122, 122 n.23, 129, 130 n.36, 131 n.41, 145, 145 n.64, 146
Perrin, Norman, 166 n.15
Phillips, Catherine, 42 n.17
Philo of Alexandria, 95 n.19
Pope, Marvin H., 139, 139 n.54
Porteous, Norman W., 162, 162 n.13, 167, 167 n.16, 168 n.19
Provan, Iain, 11 n.7

Rad, Gerhard von, 13, 13 n.11, 76 n.19
Reventlow, Henning G., 38 n.9
Roberts, J. J. M., 64 n.3, 65 n.4, 70 n.10, 73 n.15, 75 n.17
Robinson, H. Wheeler, 142 n.60
Rodd, Cyril S., 137 n.51
Rogerson, John W., 147 n.68
Römer, Thomas C., 8 n.3
Rowland, Christopher, 157, 157 n.1, 158 n.2
Rowley, Harold H., 130 n.36, 131, 131 n.38, 134 nn. 46 and 47, 135 n.48, 139, 139 n.55, 155, 155 n.78, 167, 167 n.17

Salters, Robert B., 11 n.7, 52 n.26
Sanders, E. P., 95 n.19
Schneiders, Sandra M., 195 n.35
Schoors, Antoon, 27 n.8, 30 n.15

Seibert, Eric A., 175 n.1
Senior, Donald, 166 n.15
Seybold, K., 23 n.3
Shakespeare, William, 176, 176 n.4
Silberman, L. H., 2 n.2
Skinner, John, 37, 37 n.4
Smith, Ralph L., 65 n.4
Smith-Christopher, Daniel L., 189 n.22
Soelle, Dorothee, 125 n.27, 182 n.11, 192 n.33
Soggin, J. Alberto, 76 n.19
Strahan, James, 4, 4 n.9, 149, 149 n.71
Stuhlmacher, Peter, 86 n.6
Surin, Kenneth, 184 n.19, 193 n.34
Sweeney, Marvin A., 4 n.8, 11 n.6, 19, 19 n.20, 164 n.14, 174 n.1

Tate, Marvin A., 102 n.5
Terrien, Samuel, 34 n.10, 103 n.9, 141, 141 n.58, 154, 154 n.76, 176, 176 n.4, 177, 177 n.5
Thiselton, Anthony C., 195 n.35
Thompson, Michael E. W., 33 n.6, 48 n.22, 53 n.28, 70 n.10, 76 n.18, 86 nn. 2 and 3, 88 n.8, 91 n.10, 96 n.21, 168 n.18

Tiemeyer, Lena-Sofia, 16 n.15
Trible, Phyllis, 175 n.1

Villanueva, Frederico G., 33 n.6, 53 n.28

Watson, Francis, 195 n.35
Wenham, Gordon J., 76 n.19
Westermann, Claus, 76 n.19, 100 n.2, 116 n.13
White, Norman, 42 n.16
Whybray, R. Norman, 23 n.1, 24, 24 n.4, 29, 29 nn.11 and 12, 85 n.1, 86 nn.2 and 5, 88 n.8, 94, 94 n.16, 111, 111 n.8, 118 n.18, 122, 122 n.23, 128, 128 n.33, 129, 129 n.34, 131, 131 nn.38 and 42, 133 n.45, 134 nn.46 and 47, 137, 137 n.51, 151, 151 n.74
Wiesel, Elie, 4 n.8, 178, 178 n.6
Wildberger, Hans, 170, 170 n.25, 171 n.26
Williams, Rowan, 1 n.1
Williamson, Hugh G. M., 13 n.12

Zobel, Hans-Jürgen, 33 n.7

Index of Biblical References

Old Testament/Hebrew Bible

Genesis
4:10	128
5:24	83, 103
12:1–3	77, 180
18:27	149
22	174 n.1
37–50	62, 76–80, 179–80
35:29	150
37:24–28	48
39:23	189
40:8–19	189
41:1–36	189
45:4–5	78
45:5	79 n.21, 92
45:8	78, 79 n.21
49:24	192
50:20	78, 79 n.21, 80

Exodus
19:16–25	142 n.59
22:15	51 n.23
23:5	65
31:18	70
32:11–14	48
32:30–34	48
32:11–13	96
32:31–32	91–92, 91 n.11, 96
34:6–7	17 n.16

Leviticus
7:1–10	96
16	95
25:25	131

Numbers
14:18	17 n.16
24:17	170

Deuteronomy
4:39	27
5:32–33	8
8:12–14	185
9:9	70
9:18–21	96
29:26–27	9–10

Judges
5:4–5	142 n.59
5:20	170

Ruth
4:1–12	131

1 Samuel
29:9	170

2 Samuel
13:19	149
14:17	170
14:20	170

Index of Biblical References

1 Kings

3:9	23
3:28	23
8	96
22:20–22	51 n.23, 111

2 Kings

2:1	187 n.21
2:11	187 n.21
2:9–11	83
17	10
17:7–9a	10
17:22–23	10
18:3	9
18:5–8	9
21:12	10
21:14–15	10
22–23	9
22:1	19
23:24–25	9
23:26–27	20
23:28–30	18, 61

2 Chronicles

15:2	13

Ezra

9:6–15	17 n.16

Nehemiah

9	11 n.5
9:6–37	17 n.16

Esther

1–10	175 n.1
4:3	149

Job

1:1—42:17	105–56
1:1—2:13	110–14, 152–53, 155, 180–81
1:5	113 n.10
2:7–8	131
2:7	113
2:8	113, 149
2:9–10	113–14, 113 n.10
3:1—42:6	115
3:1–26	101 n.4, 115–17, 180
3:8	146
3:26	54
4:1—5:27	118–21, 125, 139–40
5:17–18	140, 153, 183
6:1—7:21	124–25
6:14–20	45 n.19
7:7–18	116
8:1–22	121, 124
8:2–3	5
9:1—10:22	125–27
9:33	126–27, 129, 132, 139
11:1–20	122–23
12:1—14:22	127–28
13:3	144
15:1–35	120
16:1—17:16	128–30
16:11–13	151
16:19	127, 131, 132, 144
18:1–21	121
19:1–29	130–33
19:25	127, 129
19:26–27	144
20:1–29	123
21:1–34	133
21:13–16	5–6
22:1–30	120–21
23:1—24:25	133–34
24:18–25	134 nn.46 and 47
25:1–6	106, 121–22
26:1—27:6	134–35
27:7–23	106, 123
27:7–12	134 nn.46 and 47
27:13–23	134 nn.46 and 47
28	107, 115, 135–37, 153, 154, 184–85
29:1—31:40	137–38
30:19	149
32–37	107, 119, 138–41, 153–54, 182–84
33:23	129
38–41	137
38:1—40:2	75, 139, 142–43, 146, 154–55, 185

Index of Biblical References

Job (continued)
38:1	75, 138, 185
38:2	148 n.70
38:3	148 n.70
38:7	170
40:3–5	138, 143–45, 187
40:6—41:34	75, 145–48, 154–55, 185–86
40:6	75, 185
42:1–6	138, 148–49, 187
42:2	189
42:3b	189
42:5	189
42:3	196
42:5–6	155
42:7–17	149–51, 155
42:7–9	181, 186
42:7	153

Psalms
1	17 n.16
3–7	31
4	73
5:7	53
5:11–12	53
6	73
6:2	46
7	73
7:10–11	53
7:17	53
8	116
9–10	31
13	31–34
13:6	189
14:1–2	34, 189
15	17 n.16
17	31, 73
18:5	83
18:7–15	142 n.59
22	31
22:1	174
23	192
24:1	59
25–28	31
25	33, 53
29	142 n.59
30:3	83
31	31
31:17	83
35	31
37	58–61, 175, 194
37:39–40	189
38–40	31
38–39	33, 53
41:4	46
42–43	31
44:24	174
49	59, 81–84, 169, 175
49:15	82–83, 97, 103, 189
51–52	31
54–57	31
54–55	73
55:15	83
55:19b–21	53
55:22–23	53
57:5	53
57:7–11	53
59	31
59:10	53
59:16–17	53
61	31, 73
61:5	53
61:12	53
64	31
67	73
68:7–10	142 n.59
69	31
70(=40:13–17)	31
71	31
73	59, 100–104, 169, 175, 177
73:23–24	97
73:24	83
73:25–26	196
73:25	189
74:14	146–47
76	73
77	31
77:16	179
78:13	179

86	31, 73	3:12	29
86:12–13	53	3:14	28
86:15–17	53	3:16	25
88	32, 33, 53	3:22	29
90	73	4:1–3	25
93:2–4	179	5:2	27
94	32	5:6–7	28
94:12a	119	5:17–20	29
94:16–23	33	6:1–2	26
102	32, 73	7:13–14	26–27
102:12–22	53	7:15	26
102:25–28	53	7:18	28
104:26	146–47	8:12–13	28
106	17 n.16	8:15	29
107:23–32	73	8:17	28
107:25	75, 187 n.21	9:1	28
107:29	75, 187 n.21	9:7–10	29
109	32	11:6	28
109:20–21	53	11:9–10	29
109:30–31	53	12:1	29
120	32, 33, 53	12:9	25
130	32	12:13	28, 176
137	52		
140–43	32		
141	33		
142	33, 53, 73		
143	33, 53, 73		

Song of Songs

8:7	179 n.7

Proverbs

3:11a	119
4:7	136
11:6	13
13:21	14

Isaiah

1:1	70
1:7–9	15
2:1	69
5:1–7	14–15, 38 n.9
5:19	46
6:1–13	38 n.9
6:1	144
8:1–22	38 n.9
8:17	174
10:5–11	63
13:1	65 n.5
14:28	65 n.5
15:1	65 n.5
17:1	65 n.5
19:1	65 n.5
21:1	65 n.5
21:11	65 n.5
21:13	65 n.5

Ecclesiastes

1:1–3	22–23, 23 n.1
1:2	190
1:4–8	24
1:8–9	25
1:13	28
1:17–18	25
2:24	29
2:25–26	28
3:1–8	22
3:11	28

Index of Biblical References

Isaiah (*continued*)
22:1	65 n.5
22:25	65 n.5
23:1	65 n.5
24–27	158, 170, 173
26:7–21	170–71
26:19	170–71, 173, 188
27:1	146–47
28:14–22	67
29:6	187 n.21
30:6	65 n.5
34	158, 170
38:20	73
40–55	85–86, 187
40:1–2	16
40:6	38 n.9
40:24	187 n.21
41:14	131
41:16	187 n.21
42:1–6	87
42:1–4	85, 87, 99, 187
42:4	97
43:14	131
44:6	131
45:15	174
49:1–6	38 n.9, 85, 87, 99, 187
49:6	98
50:4–9	38 n.9, 85, 87, 99, 187
52:13—53:12	85–99, 187–89, 194
52:13–15	87–90
53:1–3	89–90
53:4–6	88 n.8, 90–92, 94–95
53:5	85
53:7–9	92–94, 94 n.17
53:10–12	83, 93–97, 187
53:14–15	88–89, 88 n.8
59:17–18	16
61:1–4	38 n.9

Jeremiah
1:1	55
1:4–19	38 n.9
1:9–10	35
2:1–37	16
2:8	47
4:11–18	63
6:3	47
10:21	47
11:18–23	36–40, 177
11:21–23	55
12:1–6	36, 41–43, 177
12:3	56
12:10	47
15:15–21	36, 43–45, 177
15:15	56
15:20–21	56, 162
16:18	171
17:14–18	36, 45–47, 177
17:18	56
17:21	65
17:27	65
18:19–23	36, 47–49, 177
18:21–23	56
20:2–3	55
20:7–18	36, 49–54, 177
20:11–13	56
20:11	189
20:12	178 n.6
20:13	57
20:14–18	116
23:19	187 n.21
30:23	187 n.21
37:15–16	55

Lamentations
1:5	12
1:8	12
1:14	12 n.8
1:18	12 n.8
1:20	12 n.8
1:22	12 n.8
2:4	12 n.8
2:11	12
3:1–20	12
3:22–66	12
4:2	12
4:6	12 n.8
4:13	12 n.8
4:22	12 n.8
5:7	12 n.8

5:16	12 n.8	11:36	165
5:22	12	12:1–3	83, 168–70
Ezekiel		12:1	166, 168
1	165	12:2	169 n.22, 171, 173, 188
1:1–7	38 n.9	12:7	168
1:27	38 n.9	12:11	159, 168
1:4	142, 187 n.21	12:12	168
5:2	16	**Hosea**	
5:13–17	16	1–3	38 n.9
7:5	16	5:1–15	191
13:11	187 n.21	11:1–9	191
13:13	187 n.21	**Joel**	
17:1–21	63	1–3	158
18:3	16 n.15	**Amos**	
33–37	192	1:1	69
Daniel		4:6–11	119, 140, 182
1–6	158, 159, 159 n.4, 160–64, 161 n.11, 172	5:7	2
1:1—2:4a	159 n.4	5:24	2
1:8	189	7:1—9:4	38 n.9
2:4b—7:28	159 n.4	7:1–6	96
2:20–22	162	**Jonah**	
3	161	3:6	149
3:25	162 n.12	**Micah**	
4:1–34	163	1:1	69
6	161	**Nahum**	
6:1–24	163–64	1:1	65 n.5
6:10	189	**Habakkuk**	
6:26b–27	163–64, 172	1–3	62–76, 178–79, 194
7–12	157–60, 159 n.4, 164–73	1:1	65, 69
7	164–67	1:2–4	38 n.9, 65–66
7:9–14	111, 165–66	1:5–11	66–67
7:16–28	166–67	1:12–17	67–68
7:25	168	2:1–5	38 n.9
8:1–27	166, 167–68	2:1	68–69, 189
8:10	170	2:2–5	69–71
9	11 n.5, 168 n.18	2:4	71 n.12, 72, 75
9:4–19	17 n.16	2:6–20	71–73
9:27	168	3	38 n.9, 73–76, 142 n.59
10–12	168–71		
10:5	166		
11:31	159		

Index of Biblical References

Haggai
1:5–11	17

Zechariah
9:1	65 n.5
9:14	142, 187 n.21
12–14	158
12:1	65 n.5

Malachi
1:1	65 n.5
2.17	2, 31
3:1	2

Apocrypha and Pseudepigrapha

Apocalypse of Baruch
29:4	147 n.66

Bel and the Dragon
1–42	159 n.4
14:3	65 n.6
14:34	65 n.6
14:35	65 n.6
14:37	65 n.6
14:39	65 n.6

1 Enoch
60:7–9	147 n.66
104	170

2 Esdras
1:40	65 n.6

4 Esdras
6:49–52	147 n.66

1 Maccabees
1:24	165
1:54	159 n.5
1:59	159 n.5
4:43–47	159 n.5

2 Maccabees
6:2	159 n.5
6:7	159 n.5

Song of the Three Children
	159 n.4

Susannah
1–64	159 n.4

Testament of Moses
10:9	170

Wisdom of Jesus Ben Sirach
1–51	14
2:10	14

Wisdom of Solomon
3:1–9	182

New Testament

Matthew
5:5	61

Mark
1:13	111
8:34	195

Luke
13:1–5	181

John
9:1–2	181

Acts
14:15	56

Romans
4:9	71 n.12

Galatians
3:19–20	127 n.32

Colossians
1:24   195

1 Timothy
2:5   127 n.32

Hebrews
5:7   57
8:6   127 n.32
9:15   127 n.32
12:24   127 n.32

James
5:7   56

Revelation
21:1   147 n.69

www.ingramcontent.com/pod-product-compliance
Lightning Source LLC
Chambersburg PA
CBHW062022220426
43662CB00010B/1434